WITHDRAWN

Twenty Years of Multiculturalism

D1739170

Twenty Years of Multiculturalism: Successes and Failures

Stella Hryniuk, Editor

ST. JOHN'S COLLEGE PRESS

Printed in Canada
Cover design: Norman Schmidt
Printed on recycled, acid-free paper

Cataloguing in Publication Data

Main entry under title:

Twenty years of multiculturalism

Proceedings of a conference held March 1991 at St.
John's College, University of Manitoba.

ISBN 0-920291-10-4

1. Multiculturalism - Canada.* I. Hryniuk, Stella M.,
1939-

FC104.T84 1992   305.8'00971   C93-098001-8
F1035.A1T84 1992

Contents

vii   Acknowledgements

3   Introduction

Part I: History and Workings of Canadian Social Policy
9   *Greg Gauld*
     Multiculturalism: The Real Thing?
17   *Kas Mazurek*
     Defusing a Radical Social Policy:
     The Undermining of Multiculturalism
29   *Marek Debicki*
     The Double Mythology of Multiculturalism in Canada

Part II: Multiculturalism: The Personal View
39   *Myrna Kostash*
     Eurocentricity: Notes on Metaphors of Place
45   *Richard Ogmundson*
     On the Right to be a Canadian

Contents

Part III: Francophones and Multiculturalism
59   Raymond Hébert
        Francophone Perspectives on Multiculturalism
73   Gisèle Lalande
        A Sceptical View of Multiculturalism
77   Cécyle Trépanier
        Ethnic Survival the American Way:
        The French Louisiana Case

Part IV: Ethnicity and the Arts
99   Fred Wah
        A Poetics of Ethnicity
111   Per Brask
        Toward a Theatre beyond Multiculturalism
119   Paul Matthew St. Pierre
        The Cult of Minorities in Recent Canadian Literature
133   Gerhard Stilz
        The Use of a "Mother" Tongue: German-Canadian
        Poetry in Multicultural Canada
149   Carole Carpenter
        Folklore as a Tool of Multiculturalism

Part V: Living Canada's Ethnic Diversity
163   Pamela White
        Challenges in Measuring Canada's Ethnic Diversity
183   John Berry
        Costs and Benefits of Multiculturalism:
        A Social-Psychological Analysis
201   Leo Driedger
        Eth-elders: Keepers of the Multicultural Core
221   Ralph Masi
        Multiculturalism in Health Care: Understanding and
        Implementation
233   Allan Smith
        First Nations, Race and the Idea of a Plural Community:
        Defining Canada in the Postmodern Age

255   Contributors

Acknowledgements

The publication of this book was financially assisted by the Multi-culturalism Directorate of the Department of Secretary of State, the Social Sciences and Humanities Research Council of Canada, and St. John's College, the University of Manitoba. I am grateful to Lynn Kopeschny for her assistance in preparing the manuscript, and to Barry Ferguson for his valuable advice and editorial comments at various stages of the publication process. Special thanks are due to Carol Dahlstrom for her expertise in the copy-editing of the book.

Twenty Years of Multiculturalism

Introduction

The policy of multiculturalism, proclaimed by the government of Canada in 1971, set into motion a variety of changes in Canadian society. In the political sphere, the "founding" peoples of the country viewed it with some suspicion. Francophones began to take a hostile view of the policy, especially when they were regarded as an ethnic group and not as a distinct people with "charter" privileges. Anglophone Canadians of British ancestry saw the policy as a sop to the ethnic groups, seeking their votes for the Liberal Party. Some ethnic groups were insulted that the policy made them appear to be outside the mainstream of Canadian life. Over the 20 years of its existence, Canadians in the media, the arts, academe and politics have periodically enunciated their positions on the value of multiculturalism. In the past years, when debates regarding Canadian unity have become increasingly vociferous, the federal multi-culturalism policy has come under attack by some while at the same time being credited with adding to Canadian society a uniqueness that would not have been possible without it. This volume contains a cross-section of the informed views of persons who have been actively engaged in discussions surrounding the implementation of the multiculturalism policy. The authors of the papers were participants in a conference entitled "Twenty Years of Multiculturalism: Successes and Failures" held at St. John's College, the University of Manitoba, in early 1991. The speakers were mainly university preofessors, but a number were not. The audience was drawn from a variety of constituencies – government, ethnic organizations, academics, students and members of the general public.

The topic of the conference generated a very broad range of feelings and perceptions, especially on the last afternoon, when in a open forum all participants were given an opportunity to speak extemporaneously. It would not be an exaggeration to say that as many new questions were raised at that forum as had been addressed by the conference speakers. Everyone on that occasion seemed to agree that the goal of the policy of multiculturalism – a tolerant, ethnically diverse but politically stable Canadian state – was clear, but that the means to attain that goal posed the greatest difficulties. While some papers had addressed economic and political constraints involved in the effective implementation of the policy, there was a sense that power relations in Canada and the relationship of multiculturalism to other broad social movements had not been explored. Several speakers thought that the rhetoric and the reality of multiculturalism and power sharing were vastly different. A palpable cynicism was evident in remarks of various speakers and members of the audience, typified perhaps by the person who was certain that multiculturalism was but a phase on the road to a melting pot.

One of the most memorable voices was that of Gerhard Stilz, from Germany, who complimented the conference participants on the depth and seriousness with which they had reviewed the theme of the conference. Coming from Europe where the term *multiculturalism* is practically a taboo, he offered the opinion that Europeans lived in a "state of multiculturality" but were not yet fully conscious of the implications of this fact. On the other hand, there were those who could see no common Canadian values being forged in the wake of the multiculturalism policy. Clearly the discussions raised issues worthy of conferences in themselves.

This volume offers a selection of the papers delivered at the conference. As is not uncommon in a book of conference proceedings, the papers reflect their authors' conceptualizations of their topics. They are uneven in length and in the ways the subjects are approached. Nevertheless, they are important, informative, occasionally polemical, and exciting. They are here presented as a contribution to an ongoing dialogue – one that is of great significance in the development of our society.

A number of authors express criticism of the multiculturalism policy and claim that its effects were generally divisive of Canadian society and detrimental to the creation of a unified Canadian polity. Myrna Kostash,

Richard Ogmundson and Marek Debicki, although writing from very different perspectives, decried the faulty notions of identity imposed upon Canadians by a process generated in the aftermath of the multi-culturalism policy. Kas Mazurek went so far as to claim that the failure of the policy was inevitable because it was a threat to the status quo. Social institutions that were entrusted with its implementation had, and continue to have, a vested interest in maintaining the status quo, and have turned multiculturalism into an ineffective tool for resolving questions of Canada's cultural diversity. Less pessimistic but neverthe-less disappointed with spin-offs of the policy were Carole Carpenter and Per Brask. They contrasted the weak and contradictory outcomes in their fields to the promise held out by the policy. Alternate models for con-structing a Canadian identity were offered by Fred Wah and Paul Matthew St. Pierre. On the basis of their different literary experiences, they argued that writers of various ethnic and other backgrounds speak from an "unacknowledged world" as they seek their place in Canadian writing discourses, and that their experiences and insights are valuable to society at large as it works out the issues of differentness in Canada's population. The papers of Greg Gauld and John Berry outline the structural and psychological underpinnings of multiculturalism policy in the past and present. They come closest of all the participants to saying that there have been measurable successes as a result of the policy in that Canadian society is now more attuned to its realities concerning race and ethnicity. Allan Smith, in contrasting the American and Cana-dian experiences, shows that over time the symbols and rituals of Canada have been adapted to the fact of multiple ethnically based cultures. Leo Driedger and Ralph Masi point out some practical implications that arise from the lack of awareness and sensitivity of health and other care-givers of racial and ethnic diversity. Pamela White describes the trials of creating census questions that would reflect the population mix of our country. Cécyle Trépanier, Gisèle Lalande and Raymond Hébert present insights based on studies of the attitudes of Canadian and American Francophone populations in the era of multiculturalism.

Nation-building is a long and arduous process, no matter where and when it is attempted. This volume presents some of the particularly and peculiarly Canadian ingredients in this process – elements that are seen as obstacles by some, and as essential parts of Canadian reality and indeed as uniquely defining assets by others. The fact that people of many origins form the population of Canada is certain to continue for the foreseeable future. It is certain, too, that Canadians will continue, as Andrew H. Malcolm, an American writer, has put it, to be "notorious for their seemingly endless struggle to define the character of the improbable nation that somehow has come to occupy the northern half of North America in defiance of the apparent logic of history, geography, language, economics and weather." And, one might perhaps add, the policy of multiculturalism.

Part I

History and Workings of Canadian Social Policy

Multiculturalism:
The Real Thing?

GREG GAULD

The title of my paper in a way sums up a lot of the frustrations many of us directly involved in multiculturalism in recent years have been feeling: while there are lots of perceptions and misperceptions of multi-culturalism and lots of debate about it, much of this is off-base and has little to do with the real policy today and the real work going on. You can understand why I have been looking forward with some enthusiasm to the chance to speak at the beginning of this conference. I propose to cover three points that I hope will be helpful in your review of successes and failures: first, a somewhat simplified review of the evolution of the federal policy and its supporting programs; then, an insider's view of the intent and content of the multiculturalism policy of Canada today; and finally, some thoughts on the successes, and the challenges, to be met. You don't really expect me to talk about failures, do you?

EVOLUTION OF MULTICULTURALISM POLICY

To get to the origins of the policy and the programs, it is necessary to go back before 1971. During the war years, the government became concerned about hastening the integration of immigrants, and with relations between groups. A citizenship branch was organized in the Department of Immigration and Citizenship. In the mid-sixties, the Citizenship Branch moved to the Department of Secretary of State and continued to support these immigrant integration objectives. But, with international human rights developments following the war, and the awakening during the sixties to the aspirations of "the other" cultural communities, Canada became concerned as well with the protection of cultural rights, and the recognition of ethnocultural minorities. After the declaration of the first multiculturalism policy in 1971, the government began to support activities of ethnocultural communities – not just first-generation Canadians. The newly established multiculturalism directorate took over responsibility for the earlier programming, which was restructured, but which retained elements relating to long-term integration. While the policy did not close the door to equality issues, new programming concentrated on the cultural-retention concerns of communities and on cultural sharing. It dealt with cultural and integration needs as they were defined by ethnocultural communities themselves, but it was left largely to the communities to take the initiative. At the provincial level, at least in central Canada and the West, we began to see parallel policy developments, with an emphasis on cultural programming.

Even in the early stages, though, there was a realization among some federal officials, and some ministers, that a cultural focus was not enough. By the late seventies, the non-discriminatory immigration policy introduced in the late sixties had begun to change the face of Canada. The voices of visible-minority communities were beginning to be heard. During this same period, an international consensus on standards of fairness and justice in dealing with diversity, and with minorities, was growing. In the seventies, Canada ratified three important United Nations conventions: on the elimination of racial discrimination; on civil and political rights; and, on social, economic and cultural rights. The commitments we subscribed to in these were to be reflected in subsequent Canadian legislation, policies and programs, including those dealing with multiculturalism. Government began to give more attention to equality issues. The Canadian Human Rights Act of 1977 gave Canadians legal protection from, and recourse against, individual discrimination.

In the early eighties, multiculturalism programming began to extend into race relations. The Charter of Rights and Freedoms in the 1982 constitution recognized multiculturalism for the first time in federal legislation, calling for the whole charter to be interpreted in a way that "preserves and enhances the multicultural heritage of Canada." It also guaranteed equal protection and equal benefit of the law, free from discrimination on the basis of race, national or ethnic origin, colour and religion. Beyond this, it allowed for positive measures to ameliorate the conditions of disadvantage experienced by individuals or groups. In 1985, following the Equality Now! Report and the Abella Report on employment equity, federal employment-equity legislation and programs were introduced, targeting visible minorities and Aboriginal Canadians, as well as women and disabled persons. The same year, multiculturalism took on new status within the federal bureaucracy, when the Multiculturalism Directorate became a full sector within the Department of Secretary of State, equivalent to the official languages or citizenship sectors. A standing committee of the House of Commons was also established for the first time to review the implementation of multiculturalism policy across the government.

During the eighties, new considerations emerged: (1) that equality issues facing communities were in many cases systemic and beyond the capability of the community to resolve, requiring the cooperation and active involvement of government, and of Canadian institutions; (2) that there existed the need for positive measures such as employment equity, and for building a certain degree of acceptance for them; (3) that, within more and more established communities, it was becoming an issue that they be recognized as a part of the Canadian mainstream, not something apart from it. People were saying, "Let's get this straight. We are the mainstream. Multiculturalism is the mainstream." These led to the new multiculturalism policy of Canada, set out in the Canadian Multiculturalism Act of 1988.

MULTICULTURALISM POLICY TODAY

How is this policy different from what we started with? First, it is based on an important premise, which is clearly stated in the Act itself. It "recognizes the diversity of Canadians as regards to race, national or ethnic origin, colour and religion as a fundamental characteristic of Canadian society." This means that the policy starts from a view that the multicultural reality of Canada is a permanent and central reality – not a transient one or something outside the mainstream. I will spare you the demographics that support this. That is a whole other presentation. Second, the policy is much more than a cultural policy, or a cultural integration policy. This is clear in the nutshell definition embedded in the Act: "A policy . . . designed to preserve and enhance the multicultural heritage of Canadians while working to achieve the equality of all Canadians in the economic, social, cultural and political life of Canada."

11

Third, the policy is addressed to all of Canadian society, not just to ethnocultural minority communities. It takes the position that societal change is a responsibility of the entire society, including major institutions and government itself.

All the stakeholders are now involved in the policy implementation. Government institutions have a responsibility to implement the multiculturalism policy. Other institutions are encouraged to adopt it; and program assistance is available not only to ethnocultural communities, but to Canadian institutions and others. There are other differences. Multiculturalism policy, for instance, is no longer positioned "within a bilingual framework." Both policies now have their own legislative and constitutional bases, and are complementary. One of the more exciting aspects of multiculturalism, in fact, is the development of its *visage français*, with the growing diversity of Francophone Canada.

POLICY IMPLEMENTATION

So, you must be asking, Where is the beef? What is going on beyond the fine words and intentions? To implement the new policy, multiculturalism programs were re-oriented to focus on policy objectives. The four new program areas were announced in 1988: race relations and cross-cultural understanding, through which activities to combat racism and systemic discrimination were supported; community support and participation, in which minority communities and immigrant-generation Canadians were encouraged to play an active role in Canadian society; heritage cultures and languages, in which Canadians were encouraged to preserve, enhance and share their cultural heritages. The fourth area is not a financial assistance program. It consists of a multiculturalism secretariat set up to advance the commitment to have all federal departments and agencies implement the policy.

I will give you just a few examples of recent multi-initiatives:

1. The National Public Education Campaign each year leading up to 21 March, the International Day for the Elimination of Racial Discrimination. You may have seen our transit ads, billboards, public-service announcements, information kits, or signs of activities by the scores of community, institutional and municipal partners across the country. This is just one element of our national strategy to eliminate racial discrimination in Canada, announced in 1988.

2. Two federal bills that will further strengthen the national infrastructure to advance multiculturalism. They will create two new national resources, at arm's length from government. They are the Canadian Heritage Languages Institute, and the Canadian Race Relations Foundation.

3. A Canadian police-minority resource centre, which is part of a national action plan on police-minority relations.

4. A comprehensive race-relations strategy in the Halifax area school system.

5. A package of heritage-culture initiatives announced in the fall of 1990 including: an apprenticeship in the arts program; a summer institute to train young folkloric performing artists; a folk-arts source book; seed funding for "inside stories," prime-time television plays that bring the multicultural reality to life; Gemini and Gémeaux awards for excellence in television portrayal of multicultural Canada; two new university chairs of study in ethnicity and pluralism (which makes a total of 19 ethnic-studies chairs created, including three here in Manitoba).

And what is coming out of other federal departments and agencies? Here are a few examples:

1. A new broadcasting act that explicitly requires Canada's broadcasting systems to reflect in their programming and in their operations the multicultural character of Canada;

2. A review by the law-reform commission, now in progress (at the request of the Minister of Justice), of the sensitivity of the Criminal Code and related statutes to the multicultural nature of Canada;

3. A joint, state-of-the-art review of research related to nation-building in Canada's multicultural society (with the Social Sciences and Humanities Research Council);

4. Work by the Federal Business Development Bank, International Trade, and other agencies to recognize the economic potential of multiculturalism;

5. A new federal immigrant-integration strategy, involving several departments, with $200 million more over the next five years for language training and for settlement and integration programs. For more details, I commend to you the annual reports to Parliament on the operation of the Canadian Multiculturalism Act. The second report,

covering the first full year of the Act, 1989-90, should be tabled tomorrow [1 March 1991].

SIGNS OF SUCCESS

How do you judge the success of the policy? Are we on the right track? I leave it to this conference to look in detail at this. I will only throw out a few indirect indicators, to start the discussion. One usual indicator of the success of an approach is the extent to which it is emulated by others. For example, by the end of 1990, nine of the ten provinces had adopted formal multiculturalism policies that reflected the broader approach to multiculturalism taken at the federal level. We are receiving an increasing number of foreign government delegations and enquiries, particularly from western and eastern European countries faced with European unification and with changing populations.

As another indicator, the Economic Council of Canada released a report last week called "New Faces in the Crowd," following a two-year study of the economic and social benefits of immigration. They looked at some length at multiculturalism, and concluded that, as an approach for managing ethnic differences, as an integration rather than assimilation approach, "it fits the best theory." They found that the multiculturalism strategy has "already registered some modest success in reducing the amount of intolerance in Canadian society." Or you can look at the national recognition of work that was assisted at some point by multiculturalism programs. I am thinking, for instance, of the Governor-General's Awards for Canadian Literature earned by Joseph Skvorecky and by Nino Ricci.

Perhaps one of the most significant signs of societal change is that tough issues critical to a truly multicultural society are regularly getting on to the national agenda and are being seriously debated. Such issues include: hate propaganda and freedom of expression; voices for minority writers in Canadian literature; constitutional recognition of the multicultural character of Canada; domestic effects of foreign policy in our multicultural society, for example, our role in the Gulf War.

WHAT DOES THE FUTURE HOLD?

It is obvious to all Canadians that we are at a critical point in nation-building. The prime minister spoke earlier this month of "a renewed

Canada – one that is proud of its diversity and stronger in its unity." What is coming more clearly into focus is the role of multiculturalism in nation-building, in contributing to an inclusive sense of common citizenship – one that all Canadians can buy into, as equals. The new Department of Multiculturalism and Citizenship will emphasize inclusive and active citizenship, and shared Canadian values such as those enshrined in the Charter. Citizenship, like multiculturalism, is a two-way street. On one side are the rights and freedoms that we all enjoy; on the other side are our responsibilities to be active citizens, and commitments to basic values like democracy, equality, mutual respect and understanding. Multiculturalism, and other policies for the management and accommodation of Canadian diversity, will, more than ever, need to be forces for inclusiveness, to create a compelling Canadian citizenship. They are not ends in themselves. In the words of my minister, Gerry Weiner, "Multiculturalism is a way to tear down the barriers that have divided Canadians and left too many out of the mainstream." Or, in the words of a young Canadian of French and Haitian descent, in a discussion group I was at last night in Montreal, "Am I a Canadian when I feel Canadian – or when others say I am Canadian?"

CONCLUSION

After two decades of multiculturalism (going on five), we are seeing a shift from developments contributing to multiculturalism policy to those flowing from it. This trend is likely to continue in the years to come, as more and more Canadians, and Canadian institutions, become involved in making multiculturalism work. Perhaps our greatest failure has been our inability to communicate this growth in the policy to the Canadian public. It has not been an easy task to try to turn that around. One of the reasons is that much of what we do is achieved indirectly and invisibly, through the work of community, institutional and individual partners whom we support. But the process has begun, and I hope this conference will be part of it. For those of you who would like to keep close tabs on federal multiculturalism policy, I suggest you get on the free subscription list for our quarterly newsletter, *Together / Ensemble*, a 32-page compendium of real-world multiculturalism initiatives across Canada. My colleagues have also asked me to put in a plug for our publication's display here at the conference. And as compensation for listening so attentively, I have brought along for everyone free copies of our just-released *Guide to the Canadian Multiculturalism Act*.

Defusing a Radical Social Policy:
The Undermining of Multiculturalism

KAS MAZUREK

It is my opinion that the inauguration of multiculturalism as official state policy in 1971 represents one of the most elevating and enlightened moments in Canadian history. Canadians should be proud that, while today much of the rest of the globe is caught up in ethnic and racial conflicts, we have nurtured and allowed to evolve over two decades a formal social policy that actively promotes intercultural harmony and ethnic/racial equality. The result is that, in the international community, Canada is looked to as a model nation of tolerance and respect for minority groups.

Such recognition is well-deserved. For example, the Charter of Rights and Freedoms explicitly forbids discrimination on the basis of ethnicity or race. Canada is also the first nation in the world to pass a multicultural act, which further reinforces legal support of multiculturalism; and human rights commissions possessing real authority have been created across the nation. Furthermore, ethnic and racial relations are assured of receiving the highest government attention through the federal cabinet office of the Ministry of Citizenship and Multiculturalism; and at the federal, provincial and even municipal levels multicultural policies have been drafted and endorsed, and enabling agencies have been created.

Working in a faculty of education, my special interest is, naturally, the manifestation of multicultural ideals in the sphere of public schooling. There, results are equally dramatic. Depending upon the jurisdiction, we may find heritage language instruction, and even the establishment of bilingual ethnic language schools, within the public school system. Many school boards and schools have developed their own multicultural policy statements and plans for implementation, curricula now have a multicultural focus, and teachers in training at universities have opportunities to be exposed to multicultural materials and pedagogical practices.

Thus, it would seem that both the ideal and the reality of multiculturalism are firmly established in Canadian society, and the policy of Multiculturalism within a Bilingual Framework, launched two decades ago, can be deemed a resounding success. In some fundamental and important senses, that is correct. However, it is equally valid to caution that in other and equally fundamental ways Canadian multiculturalism has been frustrated in realizing the full scope of its original and laudable mandate.

Indeed, multiculturalism today is coming under open attack. Whereas a decade ago multiculturalism was almost never publicly assailed, now it is being undermined and questioned from many quarters. It is even a target of ridicule. I was struck by a recent newspaper cartoon that showed five faces in a row. The first announces, "I am Québécois"; the second, "I am a Native Indian"; the third, "I am a Multi-Ethnic-Multi-Cultural-Multi-Racial-Multi-Hyphenated-Canadian." Because the fourth hapless figure can only add, "I'm just a Canadian," this evokes the response (from a caricature of the prime minister) of, "Must you always be so negative?"[1] While the significance of this cartoon is certainly debatable, it does illustrate an important point, that is, it is difficult to imagine such a cartoon appearing a decade ago. At that time the concept of multiculturalism was almost a sacred cornerstone of Canadian social ideology. It was not to be mocked. Today, multiculturalism is open to question and criticism.

The challenges to multiculturalism come from a variety of sources. For example, a recent survey by the *Toronto Globe and Mail* and "CBC News" is said to have reported that "nearly half of Canadians believe the country accepts too many immigrants, including too many refugees who abuse tax laws."[2] In a speech in my home province the chairperson of the Alberta Human Rights Commission reportedly cautioned his audience that there is a growing negative public perception about multiculturalism. That perception is that multiculturalism, "far from uniting us in our diversity, is divisive. It creates ethnic ghettoes that are out of phase with the kind of Canada the policy describes. Multiculturalism is seen as a policy for ethnic minorities that has little to do with so-called mainstream Canadians."[3] Even established Canadian academics have begun to question the degree to which multiculturalism has eroded national and communal social goals and values,[4] a new and sizeable political party has appeared, which has the elimination of multiculturalism as one of its main political platforms, and respected media analysts ask pointed questions:

> Spending $276 million a year to preserve Canada's multicultural heritage may improve the government's electoral prospects in ethnic ridings. But there is little evidence that it helps immigrants adjust to Canadian life, promotes racial harmony or makes native-born Canadians more sensitive to the needs of newcomers. There may have been a time when Canada needed to break out of its White Anglo-Saxon mold. But now, with citizens of British origin making up less than 40 per cent of the population of Metropolitan Toronto, it is surely time to move beyond handout-inspired pluralism.[5]

My view is that the current questioning of multiculturalism is but the tip of the iceberg. Increasingly critical examinations of multiculturalism will appear, and the next decade will witness a fundamental re-definition of what multiculturalism is and a re-thinking of its role as a social policy and as an element of the national Canadian vision. The halcyon days are behind us; multiculturalism may well celebrate the close of its third decade as a subdued, emasculated and comparatively minor force in Canadian society.

Some of the obvious reasons making the above a plausible conclusion would have to include the following: First, the continuing so-called constitutional crisis has polarized discussion on the "Quebec-Canada" debate. *Multi*culturalism has taken a back seat to resolving what is perceived as a *bi*cultural conflict tearing apart this nation. Second, there is a growing perception in significant and influential sectors of Canadian society that multiculturalism has somehow got out of hand. At the very least, it is believed to have produced some disconcerting negative, divisive, effects. Third, this perception is likely to grow as the demographic fact of a rapidly aging population forces Canada to accept as immigrants more and more people of diverse races, religions and cultures. Disturbing and sometimes ugly incidents such as confrontations over racism in the workplace and in the enforcement of the law, the rights of minority cultural groups to modify the dress and grooming regulations of public agencies to reflect their religions and cultures, the ghettoization of some minority groups and race and culture-related violence in our schools and on our streets will unfortunately continue and likely escalate. Fourth, the economic realities of today can only exacerbate the already evident erosion of funding for Canada's cultural groups.

These are but some of the factors that clearly portend hard times for multiculturalism as we have come to know it in Canada. However, in attempting to understand the current crisis in and troubled future of multiculturalism, I believe it is misleading to concentrate upon the above factors. They imply a misleading causal relation. That is, in my view, we must not be misled into thinking that because multiculturalism is under attack today for reasons such as the above we can therefore "fix" the problem by addressing each line of attack. In other words, we would be in error if we concluded that, if the constitutional debate were to be resolved tomorrow and if the economy improved drastically thereby making more funds available for multiculturalism and if we hired more policemen, firemen, teachers and others from minority cultures and races, the current questioning and sometimes outright criticisms of multiculturalism would stop. They would not.

The above are not the fundamental, underlying causes of the current crisis multiculturalism faces. They are merely manifestations of deeper problems. Until these underlying problems are addressed, we will be treating only the symptoms, not the disease. The essence of that disease is that the social policy of multiculturalism has endemic structural contradictions that require tremendous political and social will to remedy. Unfortunately, I do not believe that such fortitude will be forthcoming and the crisis in and criticisms of multiculturalism will continue into the foreseeable future.

The heart of the matter is that multiculturalism – as articulated at its formal inception as state policy in 1971 – was a genuinely radical social vision that was soon seen to constitute a threat to the hierarchical status quo in Canada. In consequence, to preserve the status quo, the policy had to be subtly transformed and its radical potential neutralized. Multiculturalism has, in the above sense, become "de-fused" over the last two decades. In consequence, as a result of this mutation, it has manifested the contradictions and negative elements that make it so vulnerable to criticism today.

Canada's policy of Multiculturalism within a Bilingual Framework was born into and nurtured by the ideology of the Just Society. Accordingly, at its inception, the policy did, indeed, offer real hope for an

20

amelioration of the inequalities of condition and opportunity that many of Canada's ethnic groups endure. The policy was to be broadly based, involving the participation and cooperation of diverse and powerful social sectors such as federal and provincial legislatures, ministries, councils and agencies, the judiciary, crown corporations, cultural and artistic organizations, the media and all levels of public schooling. The policy was also focused. It set for itself the goals of first, materially improving the socio-economic conditions of disadvantaged ethnic groups, second, increasing equality of opportunity for ethnic groups in areas such as schooling and employment, and, finally, the nurturing, perpetuation and social acceptance of diverse cultures.

It is this broadly based social, political, economic and cultural original mandate of Canada's multicultural policy that is now downplayed. Today, it is the nurturing, perpetuation and social acceptance of cultural diversity that is associated in the public mind with multiculturalism. What is less often discussed is the fact that the original policy was every bit as much a policy directed toward the amelioration of material economic, political and other social disadvantages suffered by minority ethnic groups as it was a policy aimed at the acceptance of cultural pluralism.

In other words, to use an illustration from my academic area, it is only partly the case that children in schools should be educated to understand, accept and celebrate each others' racial, cultural, linguistic, religious and other differences. That is certainly a desirable and humane schooling objective. However, schools must also move beyond acceptance and understanding to provide real equality of educational opportunity and, by extension, the increased equality of employment opportunity this hopefully would ultimately provide. Thus schools retain their merit-ocratic imperative: they have to be "fair" to all students, and that means removing ethnocentric biases from curriculum and pedagogy. This idea of "fairness" goes well beyond the cultural objective of embracing plural-ism. It also clearly includes the political/economic objective of providing equality of educational opportunity for Canada's disadvantaged ethnic groups.

The inevitable result is obvious. Once schools provide a more level playing field for all students, then the cultural capital that some students (those from dominant groups) bring with them and that once automati-cally advantaged them no longer provides an advantage. A "multicultu-ral" school system is, in other words, much more than a school system

21

characterized by cultural pluralism. It is also a school system that is characterized by increased equality of educational opportunity because such areas as curriculum and testing are now more "culturally fair."

The same reasoning holds true in other significant areas such as employment. As a result, it is not difficult to see how such a re-structuring of the rules of the game, if you will, leads to the recognition that those who benefited disproportionately under the old rules will lose their unearned advantage. Thus, multiculturalism became a threat to the status quo, not because majority-group Canadians now understood that prejudice based on such characteristics as colour and dress is morally and socially wrong, but because jobs, housing, entrance to professional faculties in universities – in other words concrete socio-economic rewards and privileges – were now seen to be in jeopardy.

That multiculturalism is such a threat should have been obvious from the very inception of the policy. It must be remembered, as Professor Kallen succinctly put it, that "the impetus for Canada's multicultural policy lay in the negative response of immigrant ethnic minorities to the mandate of the Royal Commission on Bilingualism and Biculturalism in the 1960s. Reacting against a policy that would relegate non-English and non-French Canadians to the status of second-class citizens, spokespersons for the . . . immigrant ethnic collectives demanded equal treatment."[6]

Demanded is certainly the correct term. As it held its hearings, the Bilingualism and Biculturalism Commission was confronted by well-organized ethnic groups who insisted that their needs be addressed while virtually ignoring the central issue before the committee – the issue of Anglo-French cultural and linguistic relations. At the national level, prominent ethnic leaders made their voices heard, and the "third force" in Canadian politics proclaimed by Senator Yuzyk appeared to be a distinct possibility. His vision was of a "coalition of all non-English and non-French ethnic collectives in Canada . . . [representing] almost one-third of the Canadian population and as a united organizational force they could hold the balance of power between the French and the English."[7] The cold realities of power politics guaranteed that government would respond. That response was the policy of Multiculturalism within a Bilingual Framework.

Understandably, some leaders in Quebec were outraged that a Royal Commission that was supposed to articulate and alleviate their concerns had somehow given rise to what they perceived to be a policy of

22

preferential treatment to Canada's ethnics (that is, non-Anglos and non-French). That preferential treatment was seen to be at Quebec's expense and to diminish the status and privileges of one of the so-called founding races of Canada. Accordingly, as Professor Wilson notes, "Opinion in Quebec, both official and unofficial, has been hostile to the federal policy of multiculturalism from its inception."[8]

However, the suspicion that Canada's heretofore disadvantaged ethnic groups were gaining something at another group's expense is not limited to Francophone militants in Quebec alone. Certainly it would be the Anglophone community that would "lose" the most if Canada's ethnic groups secured a greater portion of Canada's finite socio-economic-political resources. If this is indeed a concern, it then becomes an acute ideological dilemma for politicians and policy makers who cannot ignore this large power base. However, if the government were to back away from the policy of multiculturalism, it would be perceived to be turning its back on its own past rhetoric and stated commitment to liberal pluralism. This, obviously, would invite public and political condemnation. However, to continue with the original mandate of the policy would be to risk the consequence of disrupting the always-delicate balance of power constituted by the competing interests reified in the status quo.

The solution lay in finding avenues by which the policy could be rendered impotent as a tool for social transformation, yet would be *perceived* to be vibrant and working toward its stated aims. That is precisely the thesis of some scholars who argue that "multicultural *policy* . . . constitutes a *political* program, with clearly designed political means and ends, rather than a serious attempt to implement the mosaic ideology" (emphases in original).[9]

Some scholars have stated and defended the above thesis very bluntly:

Multiculturalism . . . was originally intended to buy off the compliance of a potential Third Force of immigrants, while bilingualism was intended to appease a revitalized Quebec and to contain its claims to political power. As a whole, . . . the policy served as a technique of domination which legitimated the entrenched powers of the ruling Anglo elite when its super-ordinate national position was threatened by Quebec's claim to political power, on the one hand, and by the growing numerical and economic strength and increasing cultural vitality of immigrant ethnic collectives, on the other hand.[10]

The process of such "domination" of ethnic groups – from this theoretical perspective – is seen to be managed through the control of funding for multiculturalism. This analytical interpretation places great emphasis upon the fact that

... the dominant fund-giving agency sets the terms (conditions) under which funds are allotted, selects the recipients, and oversees and regulates the process through which the funds are distributed and expended. Government funding of minority ethnic organizations thus allows (indeed facilitates) government (and, indirectly, dominant) intervention in minority affairs. Through this subtle and sometimes not-so-subtle process the ethnic minority is kept in a dependent position, and minority protest is contained and defused.[11]

Thus, the dominant group is able politically to control the ethnic community through the skillful puppetry of pulling financial strings via a plethora of granting agencies. Credence for such a scenario of cultural hegemony can be found in information from varied and reputable quarters. For example, the Canadian Education Association reports an astounding address to its national convention by Keith Spicer:

In a blunt no-nonsense style, he told the audience that multiculturalism as we know it was originally considered to be a short-term sentimental transitional phase to calm down the insecurities of ethnic groups in the early 1970s and to show them that they were respected at a time when Francophones were demanding a greater voice in government. Multiculturalism is now in danger of becoming an institutionalized business that will affect Canada's development towards nationhood.[12]

If some, indeed, view multiculturalism as a "short-term sentimental transition phase," that would certainly explain the frustrations of Laureano Leone. As president of the Council of National Ethnocultural Organizations of Canada he is reported as saying that "the Canadian[s] accepted the idea of multiculturalism 'as long as we were singing and dancing.' Today, the establishment is worried about the political strength of minorities, . . . when minorities started to unite and to seek a greater role in the political process, 'a strong backlash developed.'"[13]

If one interprets multiculturalism from a conflict-theory perspective, then certainly the above throws light on further structural contradictions in the policy. I believe there clearly is considerable merit in such an interpretation and have argued so, in extended form, elsewhere.[14] However, there is not necessarily a suggestion here of conscious conspiracy by dominant groups against ethnic minorities. Such structural contradictions can be (and hopefully are) the unhappy manifestations of a hastily constructed social policy that tried to be all things to all people. In the process it was jerry-built, and only now are the structural flaws becoming fully manifest.

We must remember that the policy of Multiculturalism within a Bilingual Framework was the result of a royal commission that tried simultaneously to solve the enormous problems of re-affirming the dual Anglo-Francophone Canadian state, to do so while appeasing both dominant groups, and to ensure the cultural, political and economic amelioration of Canada's other ethnic groups. These tasks, in retrospect, may have been impossible. Certainly Quebec was and is not placated; "English" and "French" Canada today are more suspicious of each other than they were two decades ago; ethnic, racial and cultural tensions continue today as fiercely as ever.

With the balance already so delicate, it is understandable that, as Canada's newly empowered ethnic groups began to make their political weight felt, succeeded in working toward greater social and economic equality, and articulated their unconditional demands from increasingly prominent national platforms, this would be interpreted as a major social disruption and direct challenge to an already precarious status quo. As a result – whether advertently or inadvertently, whether through conscious manipulation or through genuinely free and conscious choice by all parties concerned – a change in the primary foci of the policy began to occur. Both the broad social base of the policy and its most potentially radical objectives – those of immediate material improvement and long-term enhancement of equality of opportunity for ethnic groups – were transferred to respected but ultimately conservative and ineffective institutions and forums.

One such institution is the public school. Nowhere in Canada is the policy of multiculturalism as ubiquitous and fervently embraced as within our public schools. For example, the Ontario Ministry of Education directs:

The province of Ontario has a tradition of providing opportunities for people of various cultural, linguistic, racial, and religious origins to build a life together as Canadians. The policy of multiculturalism officially adopted by the Government of Ontario accepts this diversity as a unique characteristic of Canadian identity and requires the schools to help prepare all students to live in our multicultural society and in an increasingly interdependent world. It is essential that every individual, of whatever color, race, religion, age, or sex, have the right to be treated with respect.

25

The philosophy of multiculturalism, then, should permeate the school's curriculum policies, teaching methods and materials, courses of study, and assessment and testing procedures, as well as the attitudes and expectations of its staff and all of its interactions with students, parents, and the community. Programs, policies, and services that will contribute to a harmonious, positive relationship among all members of a school community must be established for resident Canadians as well as newcomers to Canada. Teachers should be encouraged to develop courses that are consistent with the educational goals of multiculturalism and that reflect fairly and accurately the reality of Canada's multicultural society. Principals should ensure that, where possible, core units are incorporated into compulsory subjects so that elements of multiculturalism will become part of every student's program.[15]

Certainly Ontario schools have to be complimented on their hard work and sincere efforts in ensuring that "multiculturalism will become part of every student's program." Indeed, most of Canada's school jurisdictions have a laudable record in this regard and their sincerity is beyond question. However, even if schools can make students more tolerant of cultural differences (and it must be stressed that there is little empirical evidence that this is being accomplished), why is it assumed that this will then somehow automatically result in equality of educational opportunity or an amelioration of socio-economic-political inequalities for disadvantaged ethnic groups?

Such a leap of faith is unwarranted, and I have for years consistently carried the message that schools as they exist in Canada today, for a variety of reasons, neither do nor can accomplish this. The sad reality is that the sociology of education has dramatically documented that, "despite its claims for 'democracy,' 'objectivity' and 'equality of opportunity,' schooling has continued to reinforce a social structure which is highly stratified along class, gender and racial lines."[16]

Similarly, other social arenas where multiculturalism is most embraced and given the highest profile – such as media, the arts, ethnic festivals, and ethnic community, club and recreation groups – fulfill the cultural mandate and spirit of the policy of Multiculturalism within a Bilingual Framework. However, as in the case of multiculturalism in public schools, it is not at all clear that the mandates of facilitating socio-political-economic amelioration and equality of opportunity are being served.

It is these latter mandates of the policy of Multiculturalism within a Bilingual Framework that are the most difficult to fulfill. Pursuing them results, and increasingly will continue to result, in the "strong backlash"

Laureano Leone brought to our attention, and the questioning of multiculturalism that I alluded to earlier. The gains made over the last two decades by Canada's disadvantaged ethnic minorities in cultural arenas such as the funding of ethnic artistic and community celebrations, eliciting a favourable portrayal of ethnic groups through the media and through the celebration of pluralism in school curricula and activities are dramatic and have been relatively easily secured. They have also been largely symbolic.

On the other hand, the gains made through court actions, through the securing of advantageous legislation (such as the Multiculturalism Act), through confrontations in the workplace, with public bureaucracies and in the streets, and through working with human-rights commissions have been hard-won victories. It is these latter gains that are not symbolic – they are material, concrete, socio-economic-political advances that have evoked the "backlash" against multiculturalism. They have genuinely disrupted the status quo, have realized tangible progress in the amelioration of material inequalities, and have polarized the politics of dominant-minority-group relations in our country. It is for these reasons that the next decade of multiculturalism in Canada will be a contentious one; indeed, the battle has just begun.

Of course, it is possible that Canada's ethnic groups may decide to be content with and further secure the progress they have seen in the "cultural" spheres of Canadian society – the pluralism in the schools, the funding of ethnic communities and activities – and to give up the difficult battles that await them in the public, judicial, enforcement and legislative arenas. Certainly, the temptation will be great. As those who have experienced the frightening flare-ups of racial tensions in major Canadian cities or have endured the delays and frustrations of seeking redress and justice for discriminatory treatment through the courts and human rights commissions can attest, the terrains are difficult and the battles fierce. Yet, it is in those arenas that the full scope of the promise of Multiculturalism within a Bilingual Framework will be realized. If we do not go beyond the "cultural" mandate of the policy of multiculturalism, that policy will continue to become subtly transformed from the genuinely radical social policy with great potential for social amelioration, to a placebo that reiterates but does not fulfill the ideological promises of a meritocratic liberal democracy.

KAS MAZUREK

NOTES

1 *Lethbridge Herald* (8 October 1991), p. A4. Source credit is given to the *Vancouver Sun* and Peterson.
2 *Ibid.* (5 November 1991), p. A3.
3 *Alberta Report* (9 April 1990), p. 8.
4 R.W. Bibby, *Mosaic Madness* (Toronto: Stoddart, 1990).
5 Carol Goar, "Ottawa's Pockets are our Pockets," *Lethbridge Herald* (6 October 1989), p. A6.
6 E. Kallen, *Ethnicity and Human Rights in Canada* (Toronto: Gage, 1982), p. 165.
7 *Ibid.*, "Multiculturalism: Ideology, Policy and Reality," *Journal of Canadian Studies* 17, 1 (1982), p. 57.
8 J.D. Wilson, "Multicultural Programmes in Canadian Education," in R.J. Samuda, J.W. Berry and M. LaFerriere, eds. *Multiculturalism in Canada: Social and Educational Perspectives* (Toronto: Allyn and Bacon Inc., 1984), p. 70.
9 Kallen, "Multiculturalism," p. 62. Professor Kallen is summarizing the arguments of others.
10 *Ibid.*, p. 55. It is to be stressed that Professor Kallen is not necessarily expressing her own views here; she is only summarizing the argument put forth by Karl Peter. Professor Kallen's references to Peter are: K. Peter, "Multicultural Politics, Money and the Conduct of Canadian Ethnic Studies," *Canadian Ethnic Studies Association Bulletin* 5 (1978), pp. 2-3; and K. Peter, "The Myth of Multiculturalism and Other Political Fables," paper presented at the Canadian Ethnic Studies Conference, Vancouver, B.C., 11-13 October 1979.
11 *Ibid.*, p. 59.
12 *Canadian Education Association Newsletter* (October 1986), p. 1.
13 *Globe and Mail* (11 June 1984), p. M5.
14 K. Mazurek and N. Kach, "Culture and Power: Educational Ideologies in Multicultural Canada," in N. Kach, et al., *Essays on Canadian Education* (Calgary: Detselig, 1986); K. Mazurek and N. Kach, "Multiculturalism, Society and Education," in E.B. Titley, ed., *Canadian Education: Historical Themes and Contemporary Issues* (Calgary: Detselig, 1990).
15 Government of Ontario, Ontario Schools, Intermediate and Senior Divisions (Grades 7-12/OACS) *Program and Diploma Requirements,* Section 2.8 (1984), as cited in S. Davies, "Multiculturalism in Canada," *The B.C. Music Educator* 29, 3 (1986), pp. 25-26.
16 T. Wotherspoon, "Introduction: Conflict and Crisis in Canadian Education," in *The Political Economy of Canadian Schooling,* edited by T. Wotherspoon (Toronto: Methuen, 1987), p. 1.

The Double Mythology of Multiculturalism in Canada

MAREK DEBICKI

In little over a decade the word *multiculturalism* made a remarkable career in the legal and political language of Canada.[1] The term acquired prominence with the publication of the fourth volume of the Royal Commission on Bilingualism and Biculturalism (B and B Commission),[2] and ultimately achieved the high status of a constitutional norm.

An increasing number of jurisdictions have either statutory instruments or written policies on multiculturalism.[3] Thus in a relatively short time multiculturalism acquired a high legitimacy similar to that assigned to such lofty concepts as *democracy* or *equality*.

Given the short history of the concept and the manner in which it was introduced to the top of the hierarchy of legal norms, it is surprising that it lacks definition or even established usage. The B and B Commission did not develop a definition of multiculturalism, nor can one find one in any of the statutory or other policy instruments.

Section 27 of the Constitution Act of 1982 is perhaps the best illustration of this point. Its function within the Charter is that of an interpretative rule, which deems that it is a norm through which other parts (sections) of the Charter are to be interpreted.

Potentially one can argue that this is the most powerful amongst interpretative constitutional norms contained in the Charter. Unlike other interpretative rules, section 27 has two functions. In the first place it is there to "preserve" and thus prohibit interpretation of the Charter, which would "abrogate" or "derogate" the "multicultural heritage of Canadians." Second but equal in priority, section 27 shall cause interpre-

29

tation of the Charter "enhancing" that heritage. That construct calls for a dynamic interpretation creating positive legal duties.

Leaving aside the problem of a dynamic interpretative rule, the major problem with this section is a total absence of content. As Howard Brotz accurately points out, this section requires a coherent statement (or understanding) of the term *culture* as well as a model of cultural interaction.[4] In the absence of such definitions we have an interpretative rule that requires interpretation before it can perform its constitutional function. That definitional vacuum creates a situation in which section 27 might become nothing more than a mirror with interest groups, experts and politicians pushing and shoving for space, allowing them to see their own reflection.

This weakness of section 27 leads many constitutional experts either to simple dismissal or to expression of great doubt as to its utility. Thus the leading constitutional authority Peter Hogg states that section 27 is nothing more than a "rhetorical flourish."[5] Abe Arnold sees it as a "semantic inflation leading to greater misunderstanding and more superficiality."[6]

Even those who do not share these views are far from optimistic as to the future of section 27. They generally point to some promising judicial decisions with respect to individual rights but at the same time note that "the collective rights system has been marked by tragic disappointments throughout Canadian constitutional history."[7] In order to understand the concept of multiculturalism in Canadian law and public policy beyond advocacy by those "who see it as a path to employment, status, power or privilege,"[8] we should first examine the context leading to formation of such norms.

Not unlike the push to accept the metaphor (or historiography) of the "two founding nations," multiculturalism has its own view of the formation of modern Canada. The Manitoba 1990 policy on multiculturalism is a good illustration of this point: "We have been from our inception a multicultural society."[9]

Another typical account of the past is the well-known statement by the (then) Minister of Employment and Immigration, Ron Atkey: "Except for our native peoples, we are all immigrants or the descendants of immigrants."[10] This view came to be seen as one of the major distinctions between Canada and the United States. According to it, the U.S.A. was a "melting pot," whereas Canada accepted the model of the cultural mosaic. The history of immigration policies gives an entirely different perspective from that presented by the "multiculturalists." The government immigration pamphlet of 1907, for example, stated that "Canada is situated in the North Temperate Zone. . . . The climate is particularly suited to the white race. It is the new homeland of the British people. British people soon find themselves at home in Canada. It is a British country, with British customs and ideals."[11] The Immigration Act of 1910 translated such sentiments into a norm, allowing the government to "prohibit for a stated period or permanently, the landing in Canada . . . of immigrants belonging to any race not suited to the climate or requirements of Canada."[12] Perhaps Stephen Leacock's statement on immigration is a good illustration of both the wishes and the attitudes of the elites and the government when he wrote in 1930:

Canada, especially in its northwest provinces, is badly damaged (as a result of foreign immigration) before the war. From the point of view of the Russians and Galicians, etc., this meant improvement of the northwest. Not so from ours. Learning English and living under the British flag may make a British subject in the legal sense, but not in the real sense in the light of national history and continuity. . . . A little dose of them may even by variation do good, like a minute dose of poison in medicine. . . . I am not saying that we should absolutely shut out and debar the European foreigner, as we should and do shut out the oriental. But we should in no way facilitate his coming. He is lucky if he is let in on his own."[13]

The two major forces driving the immigration policy between 1867 and 1949 were the preference for British people and the demand for labour. It was only the unavailability of sufficient numbers of immigrants from the United Kingdom (and the United States) that forced Canada to turn to Continental Europe as an alternate source of "lower grades of labour" and "stalwart peasants."

Thus the history of racism, discrimination, contempt for immigrants from other than British cultures combined with differential legal treatment, including the denial or removal of the right to vote, has been transformed into a multicultural mythology of the contribution of the waves of immigrants to the development of Canadian values, institutions and policies.

There are other areas of enquiry into the Canadian polity which give little or no support to the mythology of the cultural mosaic. Studies of Canadian political elites, interest groups or political parties rarely (if ever) show a significant participation of Canadians of other than the "two founding races."[14] What is even more interesting is that most of such work does not test the "melting pot" versus "cultural mosaic" hypothesis. Another area is that of public policy, both in academic work as well as in policy formation. Very rarely studied are the continental European, Asian or African experiences, raising further doubt as to the contribution of "other" cultures to the development of Canada.[15]

Ironically, in drawing up the "parentage" of section 27 of the Charter, the often-cited International System for the Protection of Minorities might be a misapplication in the case of Canada. That system was introduced at the conclusion of World War I and was based on the 1919 peace treaties, which responded to the redrawing of the political map of Europe and dealt with indigenous populations rather than with immigrants.

Perhaps a better explanation for the alleged differences between Canada and the United States can be found in looking at the fact that the United States demanded undivided loyalty to the new society, whereas Canada and Canadians had two masters. Thus, both structurally and attitudinally, Canada was in a more complex situation. That situation required loyalty to the British Empire and to Canada, with the latter having a constitution similar in principle to that of the United Kingdom.

The second general theme in multicultural policies is that of anti-discrimination. We find this principle in the 1971 federal multicultural policy,[16] the 1988 federal legislation,[17] Manitoba's 1990 policy.[18] Joseph Magnet sees this principle of freedom from discrimination as an "important element which ultimately led to entrenchment of section 27."[19] Similarly, Joy Cohnstedt states that "proponents of multiculturalism point to racial and ethnic inequalities in job status."[20]

Given that the arsenal of anti-discrimination weapons contains section 15 of the Charter, the Federal Human Rights Act, and provincial human rights acts or codes, these statutory or policy norms and statements are redundant and from the perspective of potential litigants of very limited utility. What such norms do is contribute to the lack of clarity as to the meaning of multiculturalism. This notion is based on a doubtful proposition that the concept of culture (in one of its important facets) is based on performance of negative duties on the part of others (that is, I have a right to rent accommodation, and others have a duty not to discriminate against me in that respect on the basis of my ethnic origin, colour, nationality, etcetera).

Inclusion of such norms in the multicultural legislation and policies can also lead to possible misuse or misinterpretation of data derived from application of anti-discrimination law *sensu stricto*. Thus reduction of discrimination can be interpreted as increase of multiculturalism!

The third component of multiculturalism is perhaps the best indication of the unresolved tension within the system that is still very much in the process of nation building – tension between the need for integration and the preservation of the cultures that the immigrants brought with them from the countries of their origin, which makes an operation of multicultural policies on other-than-symbolic levels very problematic and ridden with contradictions. The Manitoba policy provides the following ideal model:

The Government of Manitoba believes that a multicultural society is not a collection of many separate societies, divided by language and culture. Rather, Manitoba is a single society – united by shared laws, aspirations and responsibilities – with persons of various backgrounds; the freedom and opportunity to express and foster their cultural heritage; and the freedom and opportunity to participate in the broader life of society; and the responsibility to abide by and contribute to the laws and aspirations that unite society.[21]

Most policies of this kind contain a variety of tools that have to be viewed as means of adaptation and assimilation. Typical examples of this function of multiculturalism are government programs of assistance in the acquisition of the language of the dominant group, literacy and skills "in order to become successful members of our society."[22] It is self-evident that people should learn the national languages, acquire marketable skills, etcetera. What is confusing is the proposition that the traditional tools of assimilation become one of the objectives of multiculturalism. It is likely that such statements express irrational fear on the part of the policy maker that without such objectives the process of assimilation and integration will stop or, even worse, suffer reversals. Such components of multicultural policies put in doubt commitment to cultural pluralism. This gives credence to those who argue that it is a device for political control.

This view was perhaps most brutally expressed by Larry Zolf:

In fact, multiculturalism was and is a Trudeau boondoggle to get the ethnics to stay grateful and vote Liberal. Multiculturalism, which was supposedly out to make Diefenbaker and me the racial equals of Walter Gordon and Pierre Trudeau, was a bastard child of political patronage, born in the Neanderthal ooze

33

and slime of ethnicking. Multiculturalism encourages double loyalties, ghetto political machines that would shame a Tammany Hall, and daily gives the fledgling Canadian Identity, already frail and wan, near fatal kicks in its most sensitive organs.[23]

Finally, multicultural policies deal with matters that properly fall within any concept of culture. There are two types of policy objectives in this area. The first deals with the usage of languages (other than English and French). The second is that of the preservation and enhancement of the cultures of immigrants, or at least some important aspects of both material and intellectual heritage. The importance of language for culture and ethnicity cannot be overemphasized. Language is the medium through which people interact within their world as well as the mechanism that in turn shapes them as individuals and as part of a larger group.[24]

It is disappointing that the multicultural policies seem to be totally insensitive to the complexities of language retention, usage and learning in the Canadian context. It seems that multicultural policies benefited very little from the extensive research conducted and reported by the B and B Commission.

Any serious treatment of linguistic pluralism in Canada would at least have to deal with the extensive research on the relationship between languages and power,[25] status and self-esteem. Instead we are given a diet of "encouragement to retain languages" and/or "facilitation of the acquisition, retention and use of all languages that contribute to the multicultural heritage of Canada." Such "powerful" policies will assure that linguistically in a relatively short time most of the linguistic groups in Canada will become the symbolic "white niggers" of America.

There is also commitment without creating legal duties to a variety of programs assisting a wide range of organizations and groups involved in preserving, promoting and enhancing multiculturalism and/or cultures other than those of dominant groups. The range of groups and programs is so wide that any attempt at generalization given the absence of comprehensive descriptive data does not seem possible.

The mythology of the multicultural past perhaps has potential for increasing self-esteem of those Canadians who are of neither British nor French origin. With time it could become a national myth of the golden age.

The second myth is that we are moving to a future that symbolically could be viewed as a new social contract between all the groups constituting the Canadian mosaic. That myth is based on policies that are partly symbolic, partly irrelevant and at best having extremely limited capacity for change. Perhaps the only certainty about these policies is that they have no capacity for the radical transformation of a society.

NOTES

1 Search of standard texts on Canadian government, Canadian constitutional law and civil rights published prior to the Royal Commission on Bilingualism and Biculturalism failed to produce any instances of the usage of that word.

2 Report of the Royal Commission on Bilingualism and Biculturalism, Book 4, Ottawa, Queen's Printer, 1970.

3 See, for example: The 1971 Policy on Multiculturalism; The Saskatchewan Multicultural Act, 1973; An Act for the Preservation and Enforcement of Multiculturalism in Canada, 1988; Manitoba's Policy for a Multicultural Society, 1990.

4 H. Brotz, "Multiculturalism in Canada: A Model," *Canadian Public Policy* vol. 6 (1980), p. 41.

5 P.W. Hogg, *Constitutional Law of Canada* (Toronto: Carswell, 1982), p. 72.

6 A.J. Arnold, in *Handbook of Intercultural Training*, D. Landis and R.W. Brislin, eds. (Toronto: Pergamon Press, 1983), p. 265.

7 J.E. Magnet, in *Multiculturalism and the Charter* (Toronto: Carswell 1987), at 61.

8 E.Y. Smith, *Canadian Multiculturalism: The Solution or the Problem* (New York: Pergamon Press, 1983), p. 26.

9 A Statement of Government Policy for a Multicultural Society, Manitoba, 15 May 1990, p. 8.

10 R. Atkey, Submission to the Canadian Consultative Council on Multiculturalism, Ottawa, 1979, at p. 7.

11 In Helen Potrebenko, *No Streets of Gold* (Vancouver: 1977), at p. 23.

12 Immigration Act, 1910, SC1910 C27 S38.

13 Cited in John Porter, *The Vertical Mosaic* (Toronto: University of Toronto Press, 1965), p. 67.

14 See, for example: Porter, *Vertical Mosaic*; Harold D. Clarke, C. Campbell, F.Q. Que and A. Goddard, eds., *Parliament, Policy and Representation* (Toronto: Methuen, 1983): H.G. Thorburn, ed., *Party Politics in Canada,* 5th ed. (Scarborough: Prentice-Hall, 1985); A.P. Pross, ed., *Pressure Group Behaviour in Canadian Politics* (Scarborough: McGraw-Hill Ryerson, 1975); R.J. Jackson, D. Jackson, N. Baxter Moor, *Politics in Canada,* 2nd ed. (Scarborough: Prentice-Hall, 1989), and the literature cited in that book.

15 See, for example, R.F. Adie and P.J. Thomas, *Canadian Public Administration,* 2nd ed. (Scarborough: Prentice-Hall 1989), and the literature cited in this book.

16 House of Commons *Debates,* 8 October 1971.

17 Sec. 3, An Act for the Preservation and Enforcement of Multiculturalism in Canada, Chapter 27, 1988.

18 Manitoba Policy for a Multicultural Society (Winnipeg: Queen's Printer, 1990), p. 6.

19 J.E. Magnet, in *Canadian Charter of Rights and Freedoms,* G. Beaudoin and E. Ratushny, eds., 2nd ed. (Toronto: Carswell, 1988), p. 744.

20 A Brief to the House of Commons Legislative Committee on Bill C-53, 12 April 1988.

21 Manitoba Policy for a Multicultural Society, 1990, p. 4.

22 Ibid.; see also, An Act for . . . Multiculturalism in Canada, sec. 3, I and J.

23 L. Zolf, "Mulling Over Multiculturalism," *Macleans,* 14 April 1980, p. 93.

24 J. Zerezan, "Language: Origin and Meaning," *Ethnicity and Culture* 46 (Fall 1989).

25 See, C. Krameree, M. Schultz and W.M. O'Barr, eds., *Language and Power* (Boston: Sage Publications, 1984).

Part II

Multiculturalism: The Personal View

Eurocentricity:
Notes on Metaphors of Place

MYRNA KOSTASH

WHERE DOES EUROPE END? WARSAW

The historian and I emerge from the alleyways of the old city onto the ramparts of the Barbican and we turn together to face the Vistula River. We are looking eastward, to the suburb of Praha. Here the Red Army crouched long, indolent weeks while the Nazis, death already rattling in their throats, mopped up the partisans of the Warsaw Uprising before retreating to Berlin. The historian draws my attention to the domes of the Russian Orthodox church in Praha. "There," he says, "is the frontier of Europe. There is where Asia begins." I do not say anything, but I am thinking, There, at the end of your finger, in "Asia," is where I come from. "There" is the village of Tulova, and it too has a church with onion domes. Just like that I have been expelled from Europe.

A couple of weeks ago, I heard a panel discussion on CBC Radio about multiculturalism and writing in Canada. One of the panelists was Maxine Tynes, a Black poet in Halifax. She said, among other things, that it was important that she identify herself in her writing as a Black person (I am paraphrasing her here) and to express pride in that Blackness as a kind of corrective to the overwhelming "Eurocentricity" (her word) of Canadian letters.

Eurocentricity. The condition of being centred in Europeanness. Of placing Europe at the centre of our concerns. Of monopolizing debate about writing by hijacking the agenda and imposing European questions; about greatness and genius and individualism and inspiration. And,

39

more broadly, the questions of freedom of expression, human rights, tolerance of opinion, the rule of law; in short, all those achievements of the European bourgeoisie – its state, its intelligentsia – which we are pleased to call Western culture and by which we distinguish ourselves from the non-Europeans, notably Asians and Arabs.

Eurocentricity. Also the condition of being White, of "coming from" Europe, of having homeland, "motherland," elsewhere. It is the condition of one who is non-indigenous to Canada, whose "centre" is displaced to "over there."

"Over there," of course, because it is inhabited by the rich and powerful, which is to say Europeans, becomes the centre; and the here, the Canada underfoot, becomes the margin.

This is a bizarre condition for all concerned. Writers whose traditions are non-European, whose very language may be non-European, are right to challenge this pre-eminence of the European in the New World and to seek to redraw the geography of our society like those cartographers who give us maps of the world in which the North Pole, say, or Madagascar are the "centre," the rest of the planet arranging itself concentrically around this arbitrary *omphalos,* so that Europeans suddenly see themselves as inhabiting the edge of the known world. Such challenges, such maps, are another way of imagining the "here" and the "there."

It is even salutary, I suppose, that multiculturalism be reframed as a doctrine concerning *origins* (race, traditions, homelands) rather than as a notion referring to a dynamic process toward a hoped-for future. It reminds us second- and third-generation White ethnics who are assimilating into the Eurocentric cultural mainstream that there are some things that are unassimilable.

WHERE DOES EUROPE END? BELGRADE/ZEMUN

Here at the confluence of the Danube and Sava rivers the "east" hardly brushed the Serbs living on the western banks. On their side, in Zemun, the Habsburgs had pushed the line of Europe against the Turks who would get no further west than the abortive siege of Vienna. But on the other side, on the eastern bank, the citizens of Belgrade sat three hundred years within the Ottoman house. "They're not at all like us," say the people of Zemun. Gina lives in a capacious turn-of-the-century flat in Zemun. It has parquet floors and a large number of stately, ceramic-tiled stoves in all the rooms. I look at two portraits on the soiled walls,

Gina's great-grandparents. I guess that the woman is a Viennese matron, the man a post-office official, and I am right, except that they lived in Zemun, not in Vienna. Never mind. At least it was in Europe.

Eurocentricity. Thus the charge against me from a Black writer in Canada. It has the effect, though, of flinging me, granddaughter of Ukrainian immigrants, centripetally into the centre of considerations. This is a very odd sensation. Ukrainians have never imagined themselves at the centre of anything. To the contrary, they have seen themselves as the despised inhabitants of coveted borderlands ("krainy"), whose only relationship to the centre is to have been summarily attached to it, usually through violence. The centre is the zone from which all misfortune issues – laws and punishments, decrees, purges, plans – and which whirls one rather like the hapless partner (and here comes another metaphor) in a frantic dance, let us say a polka, not of our devising.

Suddenly, because Ukrainians are Europeans (to the Black poet if not to the Polish historian), I am at the very centre of the drama, as seen by someone watching from the orchestra pit. I am the drama. This will take some getting used to.

WHERE DOES EUROPE END? ZAGREB

Viera's husband's family lives in a spacious Habsburgian flat downtown, where, alongside the Swedish dining-room fixtures and the American bath towels (their brand-name labels faced outwards for the appreciation of the discerning house guest), one may admire the chandelier saved from the old summer house on the Dalmatian coast. Viera and her detested husband work for the media. The newer intelligentsia – those who are the children and grandchildren of peasants – live in horrid phalanxes of featureless apartment blocks in the "new town." The new town lies on the other bank of the Sava, eastward. It is said to be located "outside Europe."

I may be European, but what kind of European? Ukrainians, I would argue, are not European Europeans. We have never had a Renaissance, Reformation or Industrial Revolution. We never spoke French. We didn't live in cities. (The Jews and the Poles were the Europeans in our midst.) The ideas of Enlightenment, Revolution and National Liberation were a kind of *dementia praecox* afflicting our housebound intelligentsia.

So, if you are going to accuse me of Eurocentricity, you'd better be specific.

41

The centre of *which* Europe, exactly? Are serfdom, famine and pogroms in Europe? Are the death camps? The gulag? How about the illiteracy of my grandparents, the chattel that were their grandparents, the scattered bones of Galician peasants dead in Bosnia in service to the Viennese emperors? Are all these "European"? Are they a problem for you, too?

Where does Europe end? Just east of here. Look, just over there: on the other riverbank. Look who's huddled there. Hordes. Teeming. Asiatic. Their backs to the east, they face the coveted hinterlands of the capital cities of the west. As long as *they* are east of me – the Huns, the Mongols, the Tatars, the Pechenegs, the Ottomans – I know that I am still in Europe. Barely. But still on *this* side of "otherness."

The frontier of Europe is porous – it lets all these Asiatic hordes through and back out and through again – and it is unstable, shifting in a slithery line from Constantinople all the way west to Prague and Vienna and east again indecisively to Moscow.

(Are the Russians in Europe? Or have they succumbed to the dumb Asiatic brute at their gates, kidnapped by un-Europe's paganism, sadism and inscrutability?)

For more than a thousand years, this slithering, undulating frontier has bent itself to, bent itself around, the force of the eastern tribes and their dazzling sorties into our European fields. It was a very close encounter, this irresistible arrival of the barbarian – the Asian, the not-I or we, the other – and for the European on the edge of Europe, the Other was always very close at hand.

The Turkish bey in the Bosnian town on the Drina. The imam in the mosque on the Danube. The Tatars waving their sabres uselessly at the miraculous image of Our Lady at Czestochowa. The Turks rounding up Ukrainian peasants for the slave markets in the Crimea. *Cossack* is a Turkish word. So is *haiduk* and *haidamak* – the brigands in Serbia and the Ukrainian steppelands, respectively. Because the Other was among us, we discovered who we were. Freedom fighters. Highwaymen. Booty.

WHERE DOES EUROPE END? TULOVA

"And how did Tulova get its name?" I asked second-cousin Hryhoriy as we made the rounds of the village from which the Kostashchuks had emigrated in 1901. I knew there would be an interesting, if fanciful, derivation, for I'd already learned that in the important Bukovynian town of Kitsman a man had been drowned, head down in a barrel of sauerkraut, while yelling out the name of his intended victim, "Kitsya!" and a curse: "Ahman! Ahman!" . . . "Tulova," replied Hryhoriy, "comes from the word *tulub* (meaning "trunk of the body"). The Tatars would raid our village and take away our heads as trophies, leaving the rest behind." We both stood silent so I could contemplate this scene of my ancestors making their anonymous contribution to the defence of Europe while the *real* Europeans, in Florence and Paris and Berlin, could get on with their minuet.

An edge, a frontier, a margin becomes so because of its relationship to what comes next. Europe ends so that the "other" may begin. This is the service the margin provides the non-European; in my ambiguousness is the eruption of your subjectivity. And its service to the centre: my copulations with the "other" leave you unmolested at the heart of the known world.

In the New World, when I begin to tell my story, the Other is already present. We are caught together in the same condition; you could say we are Euro-ec-centrics. We are wrestling on the border.

On the Right to be a Canadian

RICHARD OGMUNDSON

The theme of this conference is "Twenty Years of Multiculturalism: Successes and Failures." As one might anticipate from the title of my talk – "On the Right to be a Canadian" – it is my plan to focus on some of the shortcomings of multiculturalism as a policy. The talk will be divided into two parts – a personal, visceral, *cri de coeur* concerning the topic, to be followed by a more philosophical critique.

MY STORY

To begin with, my personal background is "third ethnic" – Icelandic in this case. My grandparents arrived in the Canadian prairies in the great wave of settlement in the two decades before the First World War. My parents were born in Manitoba, as I was, although I've spent most of my life in British Columbia. I might be viewed then as a third-generation, third-ethnic, western Canadian.

OUR SOCIAL CONTRACT

The Canadian "social contract" that my parents and grandparents, cousins and relatives, understood to exist was very clear. A first part of the contract was that the "old country" was to be left behind. Any identification or concern with Iceland was to be secondary and peripheral. It was the kind of trivia to be used as filler at dull cocktail parties. A second part of the contract was that one's cultural identification was to be with Canada – first, last and always. A third part of the contract was that those of us who were born in Canada would have full rights as Canadians. It was understood that the first generation couldn't expect it to be easy, but it was also understood that anybody born in Canada was a Canadian who was as good as any other Canadian, regardless of heritage. This belief was reinforced by the participation of a number of my uncles in the Second World War. Our understanding was that the implicit contract had been sealed in blood.

A fourth part of the understanding was that the Canadian world and Canadian culture was to be a distinct New World creation, which would leave the Old World behind. It was to be a new fusion that was different from, and better than, that of the United States. Most emphatically, it was not to be an Old World remnant – it was understood not to be British or French or anything else. In particular, it was understood that, although the English language and British political institutions were to be utilized as a matter of convenience, the content of the culture was in no way supposed to be primarily British or "Anglo." Rather, the content of the culture was supposed to be something distinctively new and North American. In a word, it was supposed to be Canadian. When the English language was adopted and used, this was not understood to be "Anglo-conformity." Indeed, few people were resented more keenly than the uppity Anglo who refused to lose his or her accent, and who otherwise attempted to trade on the declining prestige of the empire.

So this, then, was and is part of my cultural heritage. Sadly enough, perhaps, I took my identity as a Canadian very seriously. It had a central influence on my life and career. So much so, in my own case, that when I graduated with a Ph.D. from a leading American university, I applied only to Canadian universities for jobs. I deliberately studied Canadian topics, and, after publishing in a couple of leading American journals just to prove that I could, I made a point of publishing in Canadian journals. My belief, pathetic and naive as it seems now, was that I would be contributing to the development of my country.

THE NEW SOCIAL CONTRACT OF MULTICULTURALISM

However, times have changed and we have moved on, apparently in the most accidental fashion, to a new social policy called multiculturalism. My visceral understanding of this is that the old social contract, upon which I based my life, has been terminated. It has apparently been replaced with a new social contract that emphasizes "Old World" cultural identifications. It would appear that the *cultural ideal* has become that of a hyphenated Canadian. Apparently, one is now supposed to identify primarily as Aboriginal French, British, Italian, Sikh or whatever, and only secondarily as Canadian. In this view, it would appear that there is no cultural space available for someone, like myself, who wants to be a Canadian. At best, this category is considered secondary, residual or anomalous. At worst, someone who wishes to identify as a Canadian is likely to be considered chauvinist, reactionary, racist and bigoted.

My visceral reaction to this sequence of events is that I've been deprived of my primary cultural identification by the well-intentioned opportunists who run this country. In a way, one might consider the multiculturalism program to be a form of cultural genocide aimed at the destruction of a pan-Canadian identity.

I feel an acute sense of betrayal. I feel a sense of demotion. I feel that I have been told that, by virtue of my ethnic heritage, I'm not good enough to be a full-fledged member of Canadian society. I've been told to return to an ethnic ghetto; to go back to the back of the bus. I suddenly feel a sense of identification with other British and American colonials – let's say like Ghurkas in India or the Chinese in Hong Kong or the Catholic Chinese Vietnamese in Saigon – who have been tricked, betrayed and abandoned when they no longer serve the needs of the empire.

I find suggestions that I should be happy to be an "ethnic"; that I should study Icelandic Canadians as a topic area; and I should set out, like so many others, to be a happy and prosperous "professional ethnic"; to be demeaning and offensive in the extreme. I view such thoughts as racist and bigoted.

I wonder where dispossessed, marginal people like me are supposed to go. Where do you go and what do you do if you just want to be a Canadian?

BACK TO ACADEMIA

That ends the explicitly personal, or visceral, part of my talk. Now I'd like to turn to the question of assessment, response to likely criticisms, and analysis.

RICHARD OGMUNDSON

ASSESSMENT OF MY OWN VIEWPOINT

While it would be interesting to know how widely shared my visceral reactions are, it would be very difficult to measure this in an unbiased way. Most survey researchers will be people who have a pronounced pro-multiculturalism position, and it would be difficult for them to avoid biasing the responses. Similarly, most members of the general public understand in a crude way that the elites of the country have signalled that any sign of Canadian patriotism is out of fashion. This would influence their responses in a predictable way.

Nonetheless, I did my own unsystematic "mini-survey" of friends and acquaintances in preparation for this talk. I found that "third ethnic," second- or third-generation, western Canadians over the age of 40 understood exactly what I was talking about. Indeed, the mere mention of the topic was often enough to set them off on their own tirades. Younger Canadians, raised on multicultural propaganda, viewed multiculturalism as sacrosanct, and a Canadian identification as an embarrassment except when being anti-American. Somewhat to my dismay, people of British ancestry had no idea whatsoever what I was talking about. Their sense of identification was not the least bit threatened. They felt totally secure. To them, *multiculturalism* meant entertainment in the form of ethnic restaurants, summer festivals and exotic down-town areas that could be visited when one felt the need for diversion.

If the results of my mini-survey were found to apply to the country as a whole, it would follow that my position, like my cultural identification, is a minority viewpoint that is destined to quite literally die off in another generation. It is encouraging to note, however, that Porter (1979, 158) reports that a full 86 percent of the respondents in a 1972 national survey "chose Canadian as the cultural group to which they now felt they belonged," and that Pamela White (1991) of Statistics Canada notes that increasing proportions of census respondents insist on identifying themselves as Canadians.

It is my argument that the moral claim of people like myself is every bit as legitimate as that of other groups. Surely our value judgement is just as good as that of others. Surely our cultural identification is as meaningful as any other.

Indeed, an argument can be made that the moral claim of the third-generation, third-ethnic Canadian deserves some priority over those who have arrived more recently in the country. Aboriginal Cana-

48

dians have a claim because they were here first. Québécois have a claim because they were here second. By the commonly accepted logic of chronological priority, the sociological category that arrived about 1900 should have a claim superior to that of those who have arrived subsequently.

However, notwithstanding the foregoing, it would also seem clear that those who came to this country since 1970 with a different set of understandings also have a legitimate moral claim. My concern is that all these claims are very probably incompatible. In the end, it will not be a matter of justice but rather of pure power politics as to which view will prevail.

Many listeners or readers of this paper will probably consider my position racist or bigoted. I consider the truth to be precisely the opposite. It is my culture and identification that is being destroyed. People like me are the victims. People like me have been dispossessed, in a cultural sense, of their birthright. All I am trying to do is to defend the right to be a Canadian in Canada.

Not coincidentally, the position I express is uncommon, in part, precisely because Canadians who want to be Canadian are subjected to intense psychological abuse whenever they speak up. There is also enormous career discrimination against anyone who espouses views that counter those of intellectual and bureaucratic establishments. To be a Canadian is to be a nigger in one's own country.[1] Moving from the realm of value judgements and political interests to the realm of scholarly understanding, it is important to emphasize once more that my understanding of Anglophone Canadian culture before multiculturalism was that it was, and was becoming ever more so, distinctively Canadian, but emphatically not British. I reject the common assertion of academics in this area that "Anglo-conformity" in the sense of absorption into a British way of life was taking place. Indeed, western Canadian culture was notable for its explicit rejection of many central elements of British culture.[2] If my understanding of reality were the same as that propounded in much of the academic literature on ethnicity in Canada, I would certainly have rejected an Anglo-conformist, imitation English model of cultural identity. One important basis of disagreement between myself and the proponents of multiculturalism would have to do with the nature of cultural reality in the Canadian West during the twentieth century. It would take more than one dissertation to unravel this issue to the satisfaction of unbiased academic minds.

Moving farther into the realm of "social science": another major basis of misunderstanding between people like myself and the proponents of multicultualism has to do with understandings of the nature of ethnic stratification in Canada. People who have been nurtured in a tradition running from *The Vertical Mosaic* of Porter to *The Canadian Corporate Elite* of Clement to *Racial Oppression in Canada* by Bolaria and Li quite naturally believe that the situation in Canada is outrageously unjust and view multiculturalism as one small step that might help to remedy the situation. If I personally believed in the verisimilitude of this tradition, I would no doubt also support multiculturalism as a policy. However, it is my view as an academic sociologist that this tradition of thought is fundamentally mistaken. Serious and competent work has shown that ethnic stratification is minimal (ethnicity explains only two percent of the variance in socio-economic status), is declining, and looks good in an international perspective. Universalism, as a cultural ideal, was working remarkably well. According to the work I respect, there are only two groups born in Canada who are getting an especially raw deal – these are Aboriginal peoples and Blacks, especially those born in Nova Scotia. I would wholeheartedly support efforts to help them. A second grievance would be that Anglo-American immigrants sometimes get treated better than Canadians born in Canada. I would be all in favour of doing something about that.[3] Perhaps there is some hope here. Social-scientific disputes about reality can normally be resolved if enough effort is put into the enterprise. One's policy recommendations quite naturally flow from one's understanding of reality. If we can reach consensus on the nature of reality, we might be closer to reaching consensus on policy.

To move, then, from social science to policy, it is important to distinguish intentions from consequences. The intentions of most people who support multiculturalism are laudable. However, the history of social policy is clogged with instances of the unintended negative consequence of benevolent intentions (for example, Boudon 1982; Sieber 1981). In the end, it is results, not motives, that matter.

It is my contention, of course, that multiculturalism, and the "affirmation action / reverse discrimination" that seems to go along with it, may have all kinds of unintended negative consequences. In Sri Lanka, for example, it seems to have been a direct cause of civil war (Sowell 1990).

PHILOSOPHICAL CRITICISM OF MULTICULTURALISM
FROM A NATIONALIST PERSPECTIVE

Moving on from customary concerns to do with values, scholarship, social science and policy, I should like to conclude my remarks with some criticism of multiculturalism as policy. These criticisms are based upon nationalist values and collectivist analysis of a type not commonplace in Anglophone Canada. (For some elaboration, see Grant 1965; Hardin 1974; and Horowitz 1985a, b, c.)

My position is that the whole idea of encouraging multiculturalism has been a grave error from the point of view of the Canadian community as a whole. It is a mistake based on a misunderstanding of Canadian reality, which is in turn based on excessive foreign influence over our thoughts.

The basic error is one of mistaken identity. Our American and English professors, and those taught by them both here and abroad, tend to *assume* that Canada is a nation-state like the United States, the United Kingdom or France. Then we and they make the mistake of recommending policies that might be appropriate for those countries, but which are inappropriate in the Canadian case.

The problem here lies in the fact that Canada differs from these models of the standard nation-state in that it has a weak military, a colonial history, a dependent resource-based economy, a balkanized culture and a paucity of nationalism. Though some of Canada's "ascribed" characteristics are traditionally associated with power and prestige (Western, Anglo-Franco, Christian, Caucasian, etcetera), the fact of the matter is that Canada is a weak, vulnerable, quasi Third World country with an artificially inflated standard of living. Our economic situation is not at all dissimilar to that of rich Third World countries like Saudi Arabia. We enjoy temporary wealth as we sell off a variety of natural resources. Our sociological situation is characterized by a divided culture not that different from places like Northern Ireland, Belgium, Switzerland, Yugoslavia, Cyprus and Lebanon. Like those countries, we are constantly threatened by the possibility of disintegration. In a geopolitical sense, we are not unlike places like Poland, Belgium and Korea, whose unhappy fate it is to lie between two super powers.

In a case such as ours, the federal government should be doing everything it can to foster a strong Canadian identity. This would help us to protect our economic interests, preserve our internal stability, and maintain an independent existence. The policy of multiculturalism, by contrast, seems designed to maximize internal divisions, encourage foreign exploitation, and facilitate eventual disintegration and foreign absorption.

There are many who, in reaction to the American or German example, are fundamentally opposed to nationalism of any kind. Nonetheless, it must be obvious that there is a major difference between the nationalism of the imperialist empire (the nationalism of the strong) and the nationalism of those who are attempting to defend themselves from the empire (the nationalism of the weak) (see Horowitz 1985c).

In our case, the choice to be made is not between too much nationalism and a moderate amount. Rather, the choice is between a minimal nationalism that is just barely sufficient to keep the country together and the multiple nationalisms that would be a consequence of the disintegration of the country.

Even without the actual disintegration of the country, the pursuit of multiculturalism is a policy that is fraught with peril. As people are driven into ethnic ghettos of one kind or another, life chances will depend increasingly on the power of one's ethnic category. Therefore, individual self-interest will be directed at increasing the wealth and power of one's group at the expense of others. Racial and ethnic antagonisms will multiply and intensify. After some period of struggle a very clear hierarchy will emerge. Life chances will again be a direct consequence of ethnic background. There will inevitably be those who end up at the bottom, and one can predict with confidence who these will be. Another predictable consequence in the fullness of time would be some kind of holocaust, very likely directed at traditional scapegoats.[4] Thus will be the consequences of emphasizing racial and ethnic divisions.

At an even more fundamental level, multiculturalism as a policy reflects the belief, rooted in American-style liberal ideology, that all behaviour is a consequence of socialization, and that we can do anything we want if only we advertise and educate enough. The total failure of the state socialist countries in this respect should give one pause. Similarly, multiculturalism is rooted in the liberal belief that desirable resources are more-or-less infinite, and that with sufficient good will we can always create a "win-win" situation. In the case of culture, the corollary would be that we can be fully Canadian and fully hyphenated at the same time. In my view, this is a dubious doctrine.[5]

REFERENCES

Berton, P. 1990. *The Promised Land: Settling the West, 1896-1914.* Markham, Ontario: Penguin.

Boudon, R. 1982. *The Unintended Consequences of Social Action.* London: Macmillan.

Boyd, M., et al., eds. 1985. *Ascription and Achievement.* Ottawa: Carleton University Press.

Brym, R., with B. Fox. 1989. *From Culture to Power.* Toronto: Oxford University Press.

Darroch, G. 1979. "Another Look at Ethnicity, Stratification and Social Mobility in Canada." *Canadian Journal of Sociology* 4(1):1-25.

Glaser, K., and S.T. Possony. 1979. *Victims of Politics.* New York: Columbia University Press.

Grant, G. 1965. *Lament for a Nation.* Toronto: McClelland and Stewart.

Hardin, H. 1974. *A Nation Unaware: The Canadian Economic Culture.* Vancouver: J.J. Douglas.

Herberg, E. 1990. "The Ethno-Racial Socioeconomic Hierarchy in Canada: Theory and Analysis of the New Vertical Mosaic." Paper presented at CSAA Meetings, Victoria, B.C.

Horowitz, G. 1985a. "Tories, Socialists and the Demise of Canada." In *Canadian Political Thought,* edited by H.D. Forbes, 352-358. Toronto: Oxford University Press.

_____. 1985b. "Mosaics and Identity." In *Canadian Political Thought,* edited by H.D. Forbes, 359-363. Toronto: Oxford University Press.

_____. 1985c. "On the Fear of Nationalism." In *Canadian Political Thought,* edited by H.D. Forbes, 364-368. Toronto: Oxford University Press.

Kuper, L. 1981. *Genocide.* New Haven: Yale University Press.

Lambert, M., M. Ledoux, and R. Pendakur. 1989. *Visible Minorities in Canada, 1986: A Graphic Overview.* Ottawa: Multiculturalism and Citizenship Directorate.

Ogmundson, R. 1980. "Towards Study of the Endangered Species Known as the Anglophone Canadian." *Canadian Journal of Sociology* 5.

_____. 1990. "Perspectives on the Class and Ethnic Origins of Canadian Elites . . ." *Canadian Journal of Sociology* 15(2):165-178.

Pineo, P. 1976. "Social Mobility in Canada: The Current Picture." *Sociological Focus* 9(2):109-23.

Pineo, P., and J. Porter. 1985. "Ethnic Origin and Occupational Attainment." In *Ascription and Achievement,* edited by M. Boyd, et al., 357-392. Ottawa: Carleton University Press.

Porter, J. 1979. "Melting Pot or Mosaic: Revolution or Reversion?" Chapter 6 in J. Porter *The Measure of Canadian Society.* Toronto: Gage.

Rose, R., and D. Urwin. 1971. "Social Cohesion, Parties and Strains in Regimes." In *European Politics: A Reader,* edited by M. Dogan and R. Rose, 217-236. Boston: Little, Brown.

Rummel, R.J. 1990. *Lethal Politics: Genocide and Mass Murder since 1917.* New Brunswick, N.J.: Transaction.

Sieber, S. 1981. *Fatal Remedies: The Ironies of Social Intervention.* London: Plenum.

Sowell, T. 1990. *Preferential Policies: An International Perspective.* New York: Morrow.

Vallières, Pierre (translated by Joan Pinkham). 1971. *White Niggers of America.* Toronto: McClelland and Stewart.

White, P. 1991. "Problems in Measuring Canadian Ethnic Diversity." Paper presented at conference, "Twenty Years of Multiculturalsim: Success and Failure." St. John's College, University of Manitoba.

Winn, C. 1985. "Affirmative Action and Visible Minorities: Eight Premises in Search of Evidence." *Canadian Public Policy* 9(4):684-700.

_____. 1988. "The Socio-Economic Attainment of Visible Minorities: Facts and Policy Implications." In *Social Inequality in Canada,* edited by J. Curtis, et al., 195-213. Scarborough: Prentice-Hall.

NOTES

1 To use the word in this sense is obviously to imitate Pierre Vallière's *White Niggers of America* (1971). The argument is that Canadians generally, not just French Canadians, are in a subordinate position. (See also Ogmundson 1980). A student, Gordon Behie, tells me that it is now common for working-class British Columbians to make a statement something like this: "Niggers come in all colours nowadays." Sayings such as this indicate a clear understanding of the Canadian reality.

2 For example, the popular historian Pierre Berton (1990, 190) reports that "the words 'No Englishman Need Apply' attached to newspaper advertisements became a kind of slogan in the West." His account (1990, 188-229) of the low esteem in which the English were held in Western Canada corresponds well with my own impression.

3 For the two-percent figure, see Pineo 1976. For the conclusion regarding Aboriginals and Nova Scotian Blacks, see Winn 1985; 1988. Other key works include Darroch 1979, and Boyd, et al. 1985. In Boyd, et al., especially chapters 10 and 11. For a recent summation at the mass level, see Brym and Fox 1989, chp. 4, and Herberg 1990. On visible minorities, see Lambert, et al. 1989. For a recent summation at the elite level, see Ogmundson 1990. Finally, please note especially the last word of Porter himself: "Our final table shows that after controls are in place only two ethnic groups in contemporary Canada show evidence of their ethnicity having directly handicapped their occupational achievements. These two groups are: the French and the English. While the magnitude of the effect is too small for serious consideration its existence reminds one that any lingering privileges of the charter groups are being effectively challenged in contemporary Canada" (Pineo and Porter 1985, 391).

4 Although we do our best to repress consciousness of it, genocides (physical, not cultural) are quite common. (See Glaser and Possony 1979; Kuper 1981; Rummel 1990). There have been a number in this century alone comparable to, or worse than, the well-known case of Nazi Germany. More than one has been directly associated with the Marxist-Leninist ideology currently in favour among Canadian sociologists and political scientists. Given that genocides are common and recurrent, it is not unreasonable to suggest that Canada could experience such if a series of poor decisions are made. My experience

with students at the University of Victoria leads me to believe that the brutal insensitivity to human life necessary for such policies is extremely common among the next generation of Canadian decision makers – especially those on the Left.

5. At a conceptual level, my implicit assumption is that cultural space is, by its very nature, limited, or "zero-sum." It follows, therefore, that the growth of hyphenated Canadianism can take place only at the expense of those who prefer a Canadian identity. While the topic could be discussed endlessly, I see no reason to question this premise. As Rose and Urwin (1971, 235) note in a similar context, "a flag cannot be British on one side and Irish on the other."

Part III

Francophones and Multiculturalism

Francophone Perspectives on Multiculturalism

RAYMOND HEBERT

My purpose in presenting this paper is twofold: first, to provide a Francophone perspective on multiculturalism in the Manitoba context; second, to draw on the limited empirical data that exist in this area to describe Francophone attitudes in Canada generally toward multiculturalism. I will conclude with a few theoretical considerations.

FRANCOPHONE ATTITUDES TOWARD MULTICULTURALISM IN MANITOBA

Any serious consideration of multiculturalism in Manitoba must begin with a brief delineation of two complex, yet fundamental, sets of realities: first, the realities of Manitoba's historical and constitutional development; and, second, demographic realities in the province today. We neglect either of those realities at our peril.

HISTORY

Manitoba's history is, of course, partly related to Canadian history and partly unique. Its prehistory is instructive: both English and French can trace their roots in this province back to the seventeenth century. It is in the nineteenth century that its links with Canada become more intense, first through the evolution of the North-West Company and gradually intensifying economic and social relations, and, starting in the mid-1800s, with increasing waves of immigrants from Ontario. These economic and social upheavals led directly to the Riel Rebellion in 1869, which attempted to ensure for the Métis and Francophones a basic recognition of their linguistic and religious rights. These rights were enshrined in sections 22 and 23 of the Manitoba Act and recognized in various other ways, such as the creation of an upper house, in which Anglophones and Francophones would be equally represented.

By 1890, all these safeguards, without exception, had been abolished; in that year, the Official Languages Act made English the only official language of Manitoba, whereas, up until that point, French had shared that status with English. This act was subsequently found *ultra vires* of the provincial legislature by the courts on several occasions, but successive governments simply ignored these rulings. The Public Schools Act abolished the dual school system, Catholic and Protestant, as well as public funding of denominational schools.

The schools question in particular generated tremendous controversy, not only in Manitoba, but also far beyond, including the Canadian Parliament and ultimately the British Parliament. In 1897, the Laurier-Greenway compromise allowed for religious instruction after school hours and, more important perhaps, it allowed any language group to provide instruction in its own language as well as English, provided ten parents or more requested it. This was perhaps the "golden age" of bilingualism and multiculturalism in Manitoba!

Unfortunately, this policy was all too successful for the Anglo-Saxon majority of the province at that time and, in 1916, all instruction in languages other than English was outlawed, as was all religious instruction. Whereas ethnic groups, particularly the French, the Ukrainians, the Poles and the Irish in Manitoba had, from 1890 to 1916, actively cooperated through their churches in ensuring the survival of their schools and hence of their cultural identities, links between them weakened significantly in the years following adoption of this legislation by the Norris government.

Neil MacDonald, formerly of the Faculty of Education at the University of Manitoba and co-founder of the Manitoba Association for the Promotion of Ancestral Languages, has described these events and their consequences in the following terms:

When the Liberal Greenway government of 1890 passed the Official Languages Act of Manitoba making English the sole official language of this province, a gross miscarriage of justice was perpetrated on all citizens of this province. The first affected were of course the French residents of Manitoba who had believed in the written constitutional guarantees of their government and who discovered all of a sudden that their language had in fact become illegal in government. The second group affected were the English-speaking people of this province; three generations were raised in the mistaken concept that English was the sole government language of Manitoba and that any recognition of the French fact in this province was either a privilege accorded by a majority or a courtesy accorded by the government. Finally all other ethno-cultural groups were negatively affected by the 1890 decisions and even more so by the 1916 Education Act revision which made English the sole official language of instruction in Manitoba.[1]

A former president of the Société Franco-Manitobaine, Gilberte Proteau, has accurately summarized the reaction of the Francophone community to these events, particularly to the 1916 legislation. In a speech she made in 1984, she said:

Between 1890 and 1916, the French-Canadians had worked in close cooperation with other language groups in their struggle to preserve their language and their institutions, and to try to regain what they knew to be their basic constitutional rights. Now, ironically, their alliance had backfired on them. The proliferation of multilingual schools had resulted in complete abolishment of all languages of instruction other than English. . . .

Thus died the strategy of cooperation between various ethnic groups and the Franco-Manitobans. . . . Both World Wars, massive immigration and government insensitivity to encourage cultural diversity caused both groups to go their way. The Franco-Manitobans . . . lost all interest in the ethno-cultural cause, preferring to struggle internally in order to preserve their language and religion. In some instances, Franco-Manitobans blamed ethnic groups for having been the reason that the provincial government abolished the rights of the Franco-Manitobans.[2]

DEMOGRAPHY

Riel and his Métis and French-Canadian followers had guessed right: within a very few years they went from being a majority in their land, in 1870, to being a small minority, about six percent, at the turn of the century. First came the Anglo-Saxons, and a not inconsiderable number of Orangemen from Ontario who attempted to impart their own particular brand of democracy, and their own identity, upon a land that the Métis and the Francophones saw, quite properly, as being theirs. Next came waves of immigrants, many from eastern Europe, who were necessary to fuel the tremendous economic boom that was generated in the West in the late nineteenth and early twentieth century.

MacDonald points out that "in the late 1800s and the early 1900s, the evidence shows that Canadians had a certain vision of its immigrants. They were seen by many as 'drawers of water and hewers of wood.' From these earlier times too, there grew up the notion that the most favoured immigrants were those who were most easily assimilated into the Anglo-Celtic mainstream. The unassimilated, it was argued, were a threat to national unity."[3] Raymond Breton of the University of Toronto describes the process in these words: "Historically, nation-building in its symbolic-cultural dimension was oriented toward the construction of a British-type society in Canada.... The prevailing normative model called for the coincidence of nation and state. It was unitarian and oriented toward cultural homogeneity. The attempts by other groups such as the Ukrainians and the French to maintain their own language and culture and to build their own sub-societies seemed to threaten the British model of cultural unity sought for in this country."[4]

Through the late-nineteenth and most of the twentieth centuries, Manitoba became home for immigrants by the hundreds of thousands; starting in 1919, the overwhelming majority of them were taught that Manitoba was an "English-only" province, and one can therefore imagine their bewilderment when Georges Forest won his case in the Supreme Court in 1979 and the English-as-official-language act was struck down.[5] Yet Manitoba in the late 1980s is made up of a clear majority of ethnic groups – over 50 of them; the British today constitute only 37 percent of the province's population. Most members of most ethnic groups believe in what has been called the "prairie compact," which, according to William Thorsell, is "best summed up as multiculturalism under an English umbrella."[6] Thorsell adds that "Mr. Trudeau redefined the linguistic umbrella to include French as well as English, a process immediately perceived in the West as the unfair elevation of one cultural minority above the rest."[7]

CONSTITUTIONAL AND LEGISLATIVE CONSIDERATIONS

Constitutional realities in the area of language in Canada and in Manitoba are based upon historical realities. These constitutional realities are section 133 of the Constitution Act, 1867; sub-section 16-23 of the Charter of Rights and Freedoms, 1982; section 23 of the Manitoba Act, 1870; and related jurisprudence. Legislation, also founded upon, and emerging from, historical realities, includes the federal Official Languages Act, 1969, and the provincial Public Schools Act, 1980, which allows instruction in French in Manitoba schools. Certain provisions of the Meech Lake Accord of 1987 also had implications for official-language minorities.

FRANCO-MANITOBAN POSITIONS ON MULTICULTURALISM

Though Franco-Manitobans turned inward for a good part of the twentieth century and devoted their energies toward survival, they came to realize in the early 1980s that not only were relations with other ethnic groups helpful politically and otherwise, but that indeed they were essential if Manitoba society in the late-twentieth century were to be re-defined in ways that allowed Francophones and all Manitobans to develop their full potential. Two recent presidents of the Société Franco-Manitobaine took clear, unambiguous positions on the question of multiculturalism. Léo Robert, in the heat of the language controversy in Manitoba, affirmed the following position in his brief to the legislative committee that examined the language proposals:

I wish to state, clearly and unequivocally, that the SFM fully supports the right of all ethnic minorities to develop their own cultural institutions within the context of official bilingualism in Canada and Manitoba. Further, we shall continue to support them in the future in promoting their own programs, should they meet with intolerant or unsympathetic attitudes at any level of government.[8]

A year later, in a speech given at UBC, Léo Robert's successor, Gilberte Proteau, said: "If . . . we truly believe in equality, justice, freedom and harmony, we must support and encourage both official bilingualism and multiculturalism in Canada, as they represent the very fibre of the Canadian fabric."[9] In concluding her talk, she added, more candidly perhaps:

We have learned that we, Francophones, need to understand multiculturalism in depth; we need to give ourselves a chance to look at it, feel it, experience it. We need to ask you to be patient with us – to give us time to feel that official bilingualism is secure in Canada, in our provinces, so that we may also feel secure with multiculturalism. We ask of you, as well, to think very positively about official bilingualism – to try it on for size, perhaps, to encourage it in any way you can, to support it openly.[10]

RAYMOND HEBERT

FRANCOPHONE ATTITUDES TOWARD MULTICULTURALISM IN CANADA

Since the adoption of the Official Languages Act in 1969 and the multiculturalism policy in 1971, much has been said and written by Francophones about both policies. I believe it is fair to say that most of what has been written by Francophones, mainly Quebecers, about multiculturalism is hesitant at best and overtly hostile at worst. An example, taken at random, by Guy Rocher, a well-known professor of sociology in Quebec, is typical of much that was written in the mid-seventies:

I have already had occasion . . . to express four reservations regarding multi-culturalism. I feel it would be useful to repeat them here. First, . . . this new concept of Canadian society seriously jeopardizes the future of bilingualism. . . . The second reason is one of practicality. Thirty percent of the population of Canada is French-speaking. . . . These Canadians, wherever they live, must be able to deal with their government in their own language. . . . My third reservation has to do with multiculturalism itself. I do not believe that nation-hood can be founded on multiculturalism. Canada, as the Trudeau government defines it, no longer has a clearly identifiable cultural nucleus. It is a kind of Grand Central Station for all the nations of the world, and regardless of their numerical importance they are all entitled to the recognition and financial support of the Canadian government. . . . My fourth and last reservation is that the new multicultural policy represents a retrograde step, as far as French-Ca-nadians are concerned, although they have not yet realized it. . . . By separating bilingualism from biculturalism, the Trudeau government is betraying all the hopes French-Canadians might have placed in bilingualism, as they conceived it – that is, clearly tied to its symbol and essential condition, biculturalism (emphasis in original).[11]

This attitude toward multiculturalism, expressed by a well-known and respected *Québécois* academic, leads us to ask whether these attitudes toward multiculturalism are generalized among French-speaking Quebecers (and French-speaking Canadians generally), and whether there are differences in attitudes held toward multiculturalism between French-speaking and English-speaking Canadians. Unfortu-nately, there is little empirical documentation on this topic, but data that do exist indicate that there are, indeed, significant differences between the attitudes of French- and English-speaking Canadians toward multi-culturalism.

64

ATTITUDES TOWARD MULTICULTURALISM IN QUEBEC

A major survey (a one-hour interview administered to over 2,600 Canadians, including 488 in Quebec) conducted in the mid-1970s on attitudes toward multiculturalism found that Quebecers had the least favourable perception of the consequences of immigration and were more likely to hold discriminatory attitudes toward immigrants themselves than Canadians generally. Within the Quebec sample, French-Canadians were the most likely to fear the consequences of immigration, and were most preoccupied by issues related to unemployment and to the maintenance of "racial purity"; they were also most likely to harbour discriminatory attitudes. Similar attitudes were found among French-Canadians living elsewhere in Canada.[12]

Regarding multiculturalism policy as such, attitudes in Canada generally toward the policy were mainly positive, despite lack of specific information regarding the policy; the least favourable attitudes toward multiculturalism were again found among French-Canadians living in Quebec. Again, similar attitudes were found among Francophones living outside Quebec. Berry et al. concluded that French-Canadians

... appear more authoritarian and ethnocentric and less favourable to immigration and multiculturalism; they appear more positive regarding their own group, and less [positive] toward other ethnic groups than respondents in other ethnic categories. This does not mean that all French-Canadians, or even most of them, are ethnocentric. This means only that French-Canadians are more ethnocentric than members of the other large ethnic groups in Canada.[13]

The attitudes of French-Canadians outside Quebec closely resembled those of Francophone Quebecers, while those of English-Quebecers closely resembled those of Anglophones outside Quebec. The authors attribute these attitudes to the "siege mentality" that evolved in Quebec over two centuries and to its relative isolation from the rest of the country over most of its history:

"The essential goal of French-Canadians was to preserve their way of life. They succeeded in part by isolating themselves from the surrounding English culture. Psychologically, this position of retrenchment gave birth to ethnocentric attitudes."[14]

The Tremblay Commission report in 1966 described the phenomenon in similar terms, adding an economic dimension: "The long continued isolation of French Canadians, the defence reflexes arising from their minority situation in Canada as a whole and their economic inferiority in Quebec have without doubt poorly prepared them to extend a generous welcome to new citizens whose ways of life and whose mentality differ from their own."[15]

Over time, as Richard Wardaugh and others have pointed out, Quebec moved progressively from pan-Canadian bilingualism as a solution toward an inward-looking unilingualism, mainly because of the increasingly massive assimilation of Francophones outside Quebec and of traumatic events such as the Manitoba language crisis of 1983-84, which demonstrated again, in the view of Francophone Quebecers, the fundamental intolerance and lack of sensitivity of the English-language majority outside its borders. This move had major implications for ethnocultural groups within Quebec; increasingly, Quebec adopted the same assimilationist policies toward them that the Anglo-Saxons had used so effectively for over a century in Ontario and across the West. In recent years, Quebec sovereignists have generally agreed that there could be no other language policy in Quebec; in their view, the survival of the French language in Quebec requires such policies.

Wardaugh rightly points out, however:

Much as Bill 101 is an attempt to bring immigrants within the fold of French society, at the same time that society has little understanding of what is involved in the task. To newcomers to the province Quebec's policy appears to be one of assimilation, and not even the Italians, the immigrant group generally acknowledged to be "closest" to the French in Quebec, willingly accept assimilation. While English society outside Quebec has increasingly become pluralistic, French society within Quebec is almost as monolithic as it ever was. It is not even particularly sympathetic to certain francophone immigrants, as many Haitians have discovered.[16]

The Quebec Francophone leadership would indeed appear to be in a bind. On one hand, it feels it must adopt rigorous measures aimed at integrating non-Francophone immigrants into its ranks; on the other hand, the only major groups among which Francophone immigrants can be recruited are non-Caucasian;[17] these are the very groups that are likely to have the lowest social standing in the eyes of Quebec and Canadian society.[18] Quebec policy makers, in other words, are setting the stage for major social problems if they do not come to acknowledge rapidly that they cannot at the same time work toward the massive assimilation of non-French ethnic groups without bringing about major change in the attitudes of Quebecers to other ethnic groups. Paradoxically, this may bring them back to a belated realization of the benefits of multiculturalism. Certainly, given the real possibility of Quebec acquiring some form of sovereignty in the future, non-Francophone ethnic groups in Quebec will surely not give up their hard-won recognition under federal multiculturalism policy, limited though it may be, without a fight.

QUEBECOIS AND FRANCOPHONES OUTSIDE QUEBEC: SIMILARITIES AND DIFFERENCES

While Francophone Quebec elites have generally been hardening in their resolve to use state means to assimilate non-Francophone ethnic groups, Francophones elsewhere in Canada, and particularly in the West, have slowly come to the realization that they are not "islands unto themselves," and that in many ways other ethnic groups share exactly the same aspirations as they do. One Ukrainian-Canadian analyst, Manoly Lupul, put it this way:

Ever since October 1971, when the policy of "multiculturalism within a bilingual framework" was announced in Ottawa, there has been more unhappiness than joy among politicians of language and culture in Canada. The Ukrainians have been unhappy with official bilingualism, and the French, especially in Quebec, have been unhappy with multiculturalism. Why is this so? The main reason is that in matters of language, culture, identity and education, the French and Ukrainian positions in Canada have always been identical. To the French, there is an indispensable link between language, culture and identity, and it is the school's purpose to forge that link. . . . Thus, the outcome of good French schooling is the bicultural individual who is also bilingual in French and English. The outcome of good schooling for the Ukrainian . . . is identical – only it is to develop a bicultural individual who is also bilingual in Ukrainian and English.[19]

The similarities, of course, throw the fear of God into most Francophones, both inside and outside Quebec, and provoke two contradictory responses. The first is that other ethnic groups are really not serious about maintaining their language and culture. They have largely, and happily, assimilated into the dominant English culture and merely want to maintain folkloric remnants of their ancient past. If this is the aim of multiculturalism policy, then it cannot be taken seriously and is a waste of scarce resources, resources that would be better spent on ensuring the survival of at least one ethnic group on the prairies – the French. An Acadian leader, Father Léger Comeau, took this position in his remarks to the Second National Multiculturalism Conference in 1976: "In the vast majority of cases, Canadian multicultural manifestations and activities take place in English only. Multiculturalism too often means English unilingualism. The tendency to equate the French-language group in Canada with multicultural minorities can only be a process of Anglicization and thus of loss of identity."[20]

The second response says that if ethnic groups are really serious about maintaining their languages and cultures, and that multiculturalism policy is there to foster this objective, then multiculturalism is intolerable because it means the destruction of Canada as a state founded on dualism, on two founding nations. Construction of a national identity centring on two national ethnic and linguistic groups is difficult enough without complicating the picture by responding to the cultural and linguistic claims of a vast number of other ethnic groups. An Acadian lawyer, Michel Bastarache, described the "dangers" of such a policy in a talk he gave in 1987. Distinguishing between "symbolic" (or individual) ethnicity and "structural" ethnicity, Bastarache warned of the dangers of the second type:

Structural ethnicity refers to the possibility for a cultural group to maintain itself, to resist assimilation and to develop by participating fully in the activities of the State as a group. . . . Cultural pluralism, which would translate into collective rights granted to ethnocultural groups constitutes a denial of the principle of socio-cultural duality. How could one then justify the promotion of the Francophone cultural group or of the French fact in the name of dual official languages?[21]

THE PRODUCTION AND ALLOCATION OF SYMBOLIC RESOURCES

One of the most interesting and provocative analyses published on the problem we are discussing today is Raymond Breton's article entitled "The Production and Allocation of Symbolic Resources: An Analysis of the Linguistic and Ethnocultural Fields in Canada." Breton argues that, as Canada evolved toward nationhood,

. . . the process of construction and imposition of a British model of identity and a symbolic system was fairly successful in most parts of Canada. . . . The success was . . . evident in the process of acculturation. The children and grandchildren of immigrants were being progressively incorporated into a collective identity and an institutional system whose symbolic character was fundamentally

British, but regarded as Canadian. Thus, "being Canadian" was in the process of being defined as speaking English within a British-type institutional system. The legitimacy of this symbolic order was becoming established in most segments of the population.[22]

In the 1960s,

. . . with the growing awareness of their own collective identity, Québec franco-phones began to express the fact that they did not recognize themselves in the central politicial institutions, and indeed in the evolving symbolic order of the entire society. Their intense feeling was that Canadian society was not their society, its institutions not their institutions, its meanings and symbols not their meanings and symbols. They felt alien or strangers, and in increasing numbers, they wanted out. Thus, a profound crisis of legitimacy emerged for society's institutions, especially for the state institutions. One of the ways in which institutional elites reacted to this crisis was to attempt to change the symbolic character of the institutions so that the French segment of the population could identify with them.[23]

However, problems have emerged in the new "symbolic order": some, perhaps, mainly in the West,

. . . have expressed negative reactions ranging from annoyance, resistance, all the way to outright opposition. In these cases, the interventions have been perceived and/or experienced as disruptions of their symbolic universe. They could not identify as easily as they used to with the new system of symbols; they did not feel at ease with the new culture of the public institutions; the new symbolic order was unfamiliar and a source of anxiety.[24]

Breton added that, "at the more extreme pole, we find those who saw the changes as an assault on their own identity, institutions, language, and way of life." He identified three specific sources of conflict: First,

. . . for some, these changes no doubt presented a disruption of their career chances or a decreased access to governmental channels. I would argue, however, that most Canadians have remained unaffected in their material interests. For them the disruption was symbolic. . . . Second, it represented a transformation of the symbolic universe such that many could not recognize themselves in the societal institutions any more. . . . Finally, even among the sympathetic and responsive elements of the population, it generated some uncertainty and therefore cultural anxiety.[25]

69

A major problem, however, with the new "institutional symbolic order," as Breton points out, is that these

... institutional interventions also had consequences for the distribution of social status or honour among social groups. . . . Individuals seek a favourable self-image. This self-image is tied to their social identity. . . . Moreover, the process whereby individuals seek a positive social identity is (according to Turner) "inextricably a matter of mutual comparisons between groups."[26]

Breton wrote his paper in 1983, and it was published in 1984. In late 1987, the German-Canadian Congress appeared before the Etats-Généraux de la Francophonie Manitobaine, and, in an unusually honest and straightforward brief, had this (among other things) to say about Francophones in Manitoba: "Your identity is seen as high profile, high status, influence, access to power and money. You occupy many positions of power in cultural, linguistic and political areas."[27]

By contrast, German-Canadian identity "is best described as low profile, unknown status. We exercise some political influence but not nearly in proportion to our numbers. Looking at boards and commissions and the general government bureaucracy, one encounters few German-Canadians." Elsewhere in the brief, the Congress stated that

... German speaking people have been in Canada since the 17th century and in Manitoba since the early 19th, and yet their contribution to building Canada is not generally known. . . . With this, I have at the outset identified one of the concerns of the German-Canadian community – a selective memory on the part of the Canadian historians and lack of recognition within the Canadian society. We, as Canadians, are proud of our heritage and our identity and we feel badly if we are not recognized.[28]

These comments are as clear an illustration as one can find of Breton's underlying thesis, which is that Canada as a nation is facing a major problem in terms of its institutional symbols and its perceived, if not real, status allocation process. Unfortunately, Breton did not shed much light as to possible solutions. If Rocher is right, and that a nation cannot be founded on a notion as vague as multiculturalism, then the answer to the dilemma is clear: let Quebec separate and define its own institutions and symbols based upon one language and one culture, and let the rest of Canada do the same. Unfortunately, perhaps for the ethnic groups in the rest of Canada, the one language would be English, and the symbolic manipulation which has gone on in Canada since the 1960s would cease to attempt to accommodate a second language and culture, much less others.

In conclusion, I would like to say that the only concern of Francophones in Manitoba, as it has always been since the nineteenth century, is the survival of their language and culture. It is certainly not to raise themselves somehow "above" other groups, it is not to create jobs for themselves, though this may be the net effect of the bilingualism policy. Our challenge, then, as a province and a country, is to devise ways in which everyone, every member of every ethnic group, will not only be equal to all others in every way, but will also *feel* equal to everyone else, feel that his or her contribution is every bit as important as everyone else's. Yet who can give us this feeling? Politicians? Bureaucrats? The media? Ourselves?

Nation-building may yet turn out to be a much more complex endeavour than anyone had imagined in 1867.

NOTES

1 *Debates and Proceedings of the Legislative Assembly of Manitoba*, Second Session, 32nd Legislature, Standing Committee on Privileges and Elections, 31, 52, 3 October 1983, p. 1,064.

2 G. Proteau, "Official Bilingualism and Multiculturalism," speech given at the Twenty-Fifth Annual Congress of the Union of Ukrainian-Canadian Students, University of British Columbia, Vancouver, 23-25 August 1984, pp. 7-8.

3 *Debates and Proceedings*, 31, 52, p. 1,064.

4 R. Breton, "The Production and Allocation of Symbolic Resources: An Analysis of the Linguistic and Ethnocultural Fields in Canada," *Canadian Review of Sociology and Anthropology* 21, 2 (1984):127-8.

5 In 1976, Georges Forest received a parking ticket in English only; he went to court arguing that the ticket and the City of Winnipeg Act were unconstitutional, having been drafted in English only, contrary to section 23 of the 1870 Manitoba Act, which stated explicitly that all Manitoba laws and regulations had to be drafted in both French and English. This part of the Act had been ignored after the adoption, in 1890, of the Official Language Act which stated that henceforth Manitoba laws could be adopted in English only. The Supreme Court found in favour of Forest.

6 W. Thorsell, "Has the West been won?" *Language and Society* 16 (September 1985):21.

7 *Ibid.*

8 Debates and Proceedings, 41, p. 792.

9 Proteau, "Official Bilingualism and Multiculturalism," p. 2.

10 *Ibid.*, pp. 15-16.

11 G. Rocher, "Multiculturalism: The Doubts of a Francophone," *Proceedings, Second Canadian Conference on Multiculturalism,* Ottawa, 1976, pp. 47-53.

12 J.W. Berry, R. Kalin and D.M. Taylor, "Attitudes envers le multiculturalisme et les groupes ethniques au Canada," *Proceedings, Second Canadian Conference on Multiculturalism,* pp. 163-184.

13 *Ibid.*, p. 181 (translated from the French).

14 *Ibid.*

15 Quoted in R. Wardaugh, *Language and Nationhood: The Canadian Experience* (Vancouver: New Star Books, 1983), p. 90.

RAYMOND HEBERT

16 *Ibid.,* p. 100.
17 According to Wardaugh, "the numbers of Haitians, French North Africans, and Vietnamese admitted to Quebec have helped turn the tide toward French and away from English" (Wardaugh, *Language and Nationhood,* p. 99).
18 See T.J. Samuel, "Third World Immigration and Multiculturalism," in S.S. Halli, F. Trovato and L. Driedger, eds., *Ethnic Demography: Canadian Immigrant, Racial and Cultural Variations* (Ottawa: Carleton University Press, 1990), pp. 387-388.
19 M.R. Lupul, "Official Bilingualism and Multiculturalism," remarks made at the Twenty-Fifth Annual Congress of the Union of Ukrainian-Canadian Students, p. 1.
20 L. Comeau, "Le multiculturalisme vu par la population canadienne-française," in *Proceedings, Second Canadian Conference on Multiculturalism,* p. 32.
21 Translated from M. Bastarache, "Dualité et multiculturalisme: Deux notions en conflit?" notes for a speech given to University of Moncton law students, 6 November 1987.
22 Breton, "The Production and Allocation of Symbolic Resources," p. 128. The changes mentioned by Breton include adoption of the Canadian flag; the renaming of Trans-Canada Airlines to Air Canada, and of the Dominion Bureau of Statistics to Statistics Canada.
23 *Ibid.,* p. 129.
24 *Ibid.,* pp. 129-130.
25 *Ibid.,* p. 130.
26 *Ibid.,* p. 131.
27 German-Canadian Congress, brief presented by Dr. Arno Jansen to Les Etats-Généraux de la Francophonie Manitobaine, 12 November 1987, pp. 3-4.
28 *Ibid.,* pp. 1-2.

A Sceptical View of Multiculturalism

GISELE LALANDE

As a broadcaster I am used to asking questions. I came here with a lot of questions about multiculturalism, hoping to find some answers, but at the end of this conference I found myself with very few answers and many more questions. Maybe this was inevitable.

My first question was a very simple one: What exactly is multiculturalism? I have no clear answer. At the beginning of the conference, Greg Gauld of Multiculturalism Canada gave us an answer with his paper entitled "Multiculturalism: The Real Thing." He gave us an update to that policy, explaining that multiculturalism is not only a policy to maintain and enhance the heritage, language and culture of the newcomers, that this policy is not only for the "ethnics" but is for all Canadians, that it is now part of the Canadian identity, part of the nation-building process. No ethnic should feel out of the mainstream, because multiculturalism is the mainstream.

But, if multiculturalism is supposed to be for all, why did we spend the next two days asking if the heritage language program was good enough to protect their language and their literature? How come we never talked about the changes that multiculturalism brought to the "real" Canadian culture? At this conference, all the participants were well aware of the pluralistic meaning of multiculturalism, all the participants knew very well that the worst thing for a person of "another ethnic background" is to be considered an "ethnic." In spite of that, I had the feeling during these three days that the "other ethnic groups" were the object of the study. I had the feeling that we were unable to go beyond the old distinction between "ourselves and themselves" (and at this point, as a French Canadian, I don't even know if I am part of "ourselves" or "themselves").

It was interesting to note that the harsher and the most emotive critics of the multiculturalism policy were people of "other ethnic background." For example, Richard Ogmundson asked for the right to be a Canadian, nothing more but nothing less. Mr. Ogmundson said that sometimes he has the feeling that multiculturalism was designed for the "real Canadians" so they can benefit from the dances, the restaurants or the songs of the "other ethnic groups." As a third-generation Icelander, he would like to be considered a real Canadian, not an hyphenated Canadian, not an "ethnic." So what exactly is multiculturalism? Is it part of the nation-building process of a pluralistic nation, or is it a way to be sure that some Canadians remain hyphenated Canadian, second-class citizens? I got no clear answer.

Another important concern that I had before this conference was about ethics and values: We cannot live in a society without an ethical foundation. What are the values that we want to safeguard and promote as a society or, dare I say it, as a nation? There were a few questions on that matter, but my feeling was that no one wanted to answer those questions, as if everyone was afraid to be considered imperialist. But can we avoid this debate forever? In the classrooms of hundreds of schools in this country, especially in Montreal, Toronto and Vancouver, the teachers have to face questions such as these: Are they supposed to be silent when they notice that a child has suffered physical punishments from his parents? How are they supposed to react when a 14-year-old girl tells them that she won't be in school the next day because she is going to be married? These are not rhetorical problems, they are part of the day-to-day lives of hundreds of teachers. In 1971, when the multiculturalism policy was announced, Canada was predominantly a White-Christian-European society. With the new non-discriminatory immigration policy, this is going to be less true. If, in the past, we – as a society – had difficulties accepting the little difference between the WASP and the European immigrants, we can easily figure out that the coming of new immigrants of completely different backgrounds will probably generate tensions. How are we going to handle those tensions? Nobody has answered that question at this conference.

But my main concern at the beginning of this conference was about the building of the "new *Québécois* identity." As all of you know, Quebec has now entered a new phase of its history, and the *Québécois* have started their own nation-building process. Here, I would like to refute part of what Raymond Hébert says in his presentation. In my view, his vision of the *Québécois* society is not completely accurate. It may be true that some *Québécois* are unable or unwilling to go beyond a narrow ethnocentric definition of themselves, but it is also true that a lot of *Québécois* are now trying to find a more pluralistic definition of what is a *Québécois*. In Quebec, we had in the last few months a commission *sur l'avenir politique et constitutionnelle du Québec*. During the public hearings of that commission the question "who is *Québécois*" was raised in many presentations. Most of them – I must admit – were by groups belonging to the Anglo community, or the "other ethnic groups," but not exclusively by them. This question was also at the centre of the government white paper on immigration published in December 1990: "Au Québec pour bâtir ensemble." Many *Québécois* know very well that the old identity of the French Canadians based on their language, their religion and their identification with the first settlers of the country is no longer accurate. More than 20 years after the Biligualism and Biculturalism Commission, Quebec is now trying to imagine a new symbolic order; instead of being a bilingual and multicultural society, it may be a unilingual and intercultural society. But at the end, the goal is more or less the same: it is to find the way to create a society in which all individuals could feel fully accepted and fully respected. I had hoped that with 20 years of multiculturalism behind them, Canadians could have provided some clues on the best way to achieve this difficult goal. But at the end of this conference, I have more questions than answers.

As long as we are unable to overcome the old conflict between the "two founding peoples," there will be no place for the "other ethnic groups." Maybe, paradoxically, by putting an end to this old conflict, the separation of Quebec may help both societies, the Canadian and the *Québécois*, to achieve this goal. Or maybe, it is exactly the contrary, and, as long as we will be unable to accept living in a dualistic society, it is unrealistic to talk about a pluralistic society.

NOTE

Gisele Lalande was the designated commentator on the Conference.

Ethnic Survival the American Way: The French Louisiana Case

CECYLE TREPANIER

FRENCH LOUISIANA: A CULTURE REGION ON THE VERGE OF EXTINCTION

French Louisiana is a unique place in North America, and this uniqueness alone would make the area worth studying. However, in the late 1970s many voiced their belief that the culture was on the verge of extinction.[1] Doubt about the persistence of French Louisiana, one of the oldest and most remarkable subcultures in the United States, inevitably raises the broader issue of ethnic survival in the United States. Can one realistically expect a non-Anglo culture to retain its identity inside the larger American culture that has traditionally employed the power of its technology and political institutions to assimilate significant ethnic diversity? In what form and under what circumstances can French Louisiana survive? In what ways has the culture of French Louisiana changed in the recent past, and in what ways is it changing now? Do those changes point toward continuation of the old ethnic identity, toward extinction, or toward some new form of ethnicity?

To find answers to these questions required making very basic inquiries about the territory, its people and cultural change. To this end, extensive fieldwork was conducted in southern Louisiana and surrounding areas. More than 200 interviews with local residents were realized. Thirty-five main study communities (big dots on Figure 1) were selected from a map over which a 48-by-48 kilometre grid had been placed. In each one the postmaster, the priest, a Protestant minister when possible,

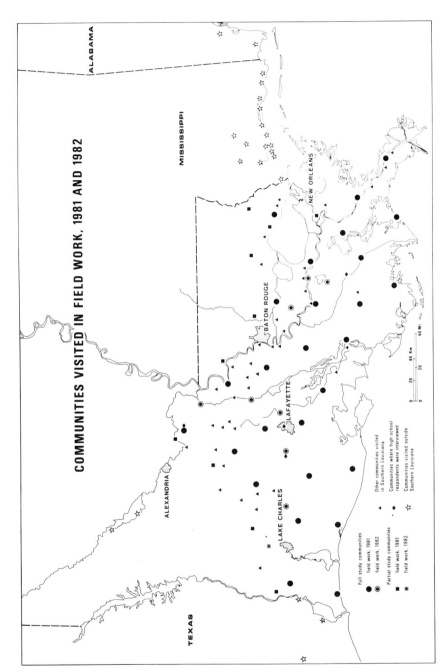

COMMUNITIES VISITED IN FIELD WORK, 1981 AND 1982

Full study communities
● field work, 1981
◉ field work, 1982

Partial study communities
■ field work, 1981
▨ field work, 1982

▲ Other communities visited in Southern Louisiana

◆ Communities where high school respondents were interviewed

☆ Communities visited outside Southern Louisiana

TEXAS

ALEXANDRIA

LAKE CHARLES

LAFAYETTE

BATON ROUGE

NEW ORLEANS

MISSISSIPPI

ALABAMA

0 20 40 Km
0   20   40 Mi.

Figure 1

and three senior respondents were formally interviewed.[2] Many other communities within or near the limits of the culture region were visited briefly either to verify their ethnic character or to determine the culture region's boundary. The results were clear: French Louisiana has become a truly American region.

TERRITORY

As defined by its residents and those of adjacent areas,[3] French Louisiana is expanding on its western side and contracting in the east (Figure 2). Expansion is linked to the population overflow from an adjoining well-established area of settlement. The contraction is the result of Anglo invasion drawn by petro-chemical industries in Plaquemines Parish.

Within French Louisiana, different areas are undergoing cultural change at varying rates. Anglos have entered the area from numerous directions and at diverse times; the level of competition between Anglos and French had varied regionally; and the recent Anglo influx has affected certain areas more than others. The outcome has been geographical differences in the degree of Frenchness across the territory. Four zones were distinguished inside the culture region (Figure 3):[4] (1) a *core* – the cultural focus and centre of the whole culture region; (2) a *domain* – a zone of strong French ethnic assertion, where respondents voiced no doubt about the French character of their communities, either numerically or culturally; (3) a *primary sphere* – where the French perceived themselves to be numerically dominant, but where respondents stressed the erosion of the culture in their communities; and (4) a *secondary sphere* – areas where the Louisiana French reside as a minority.

This regionalization of French Louisiana emphasizes two important aspects of the changing geography of the area: the emergence of a core, and cultural erosion within the territory. In the last 20 years, Lafayette, as the political centre of the French revival movement, the focus of French power, and the symbol of cultural vitality, despite being an important centre of Anglo penetration, has promoted itself as the hub of the culture region, and is generally recognized as such. This helped its new political institution, the Council for the Development of French in Louisiana (CODOFIL), assume the leading role in the redefinition of French Louisiana.

The emergence of the core coincides with the realization on the western prairies and Gulf Coast that persistent contact with Anglo-

FRENCH LOUISIANA:
TERRITORIAL CHANGE BETWEEN 1939 AND 1982

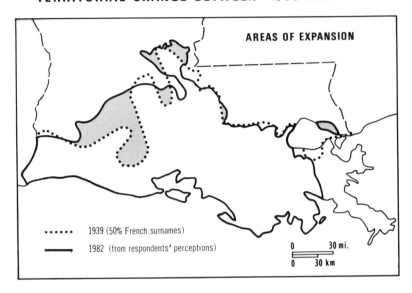

AREAS OF EXPANSION

•••••• 1939 (50% French surnames)

—— 1982 (from respondents' perceptions)

0   30 mi.
0   30 km

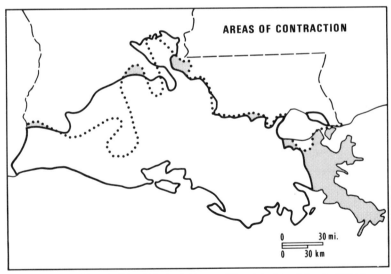

AREAS OF CONTRACTION

0   30 mi.
0   30 km

Sources: Peveril Meigs, "An Ethno-Telephonic Survey of French Louisiana" Annals, AAG 31
(December 1941): 249; field work 1981 and 1982

Figure 2

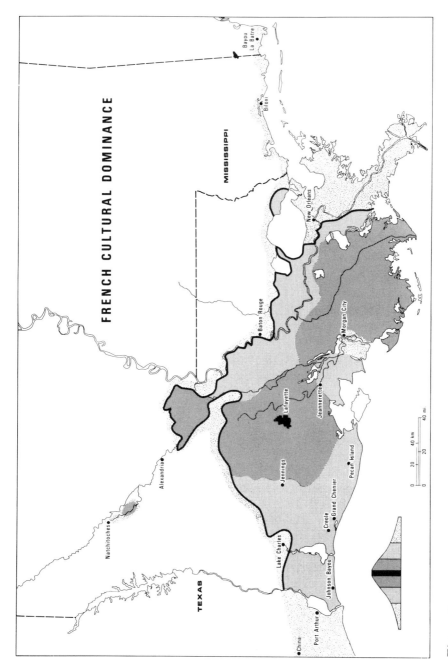

Figure 3

Americans has led to cultural attrition. In the Mississippi River region, heavy doses of industrialization and Anglo penetration have also taken their toll. The cultural fragility of these primary sphere areas has been countered by policy emerging from the core, notably the establishment of an official ethnic territory, Acadiana. For those living in the sphere, where French Louisiana culture is no longer dominant, the territorial base gives the reassurance that they may still belong to French Louisiana despite marked cultural differences with respect to the domain. Even the domain has not escaped the forces of modernism and industrialization. The resulting changes are not readily perceptible by residents, perhaps because of the absence of a large influx of outsiders and the more gradual alteration of the culture. However, when residents discuss changes in terms of language, religion and food, their answers reveal that cultural change is region-wide, even though it varies in intensity by zone.

CULTURAL CHANGE

The French language is no longer at the heart of the French Louisiana culture.[5] This change is the result of a systematic erosion of French language ability all over southern Louisiana (Figure 4). My fieldwork indicates that while only eight percent of my senior repondents speak only English, 36 percent of their children and 91 percent of their grandchildren do (Table 1). Within the bilingual families the willingness to speak French is also decreasing. The switch in the language spoken at home followed changes brought in the schools in the 1920s and in the churches in the 1930s. Nevertheless, present-day bilingualism does have important geographical dimensions. Bilingual senior respondents can be found throughout the culture region; those with bilingual children can be found in three main areas: southwest Louisiana east of Lake Charles, in small communities on the eastern edge of the Atchafalaya Basin, and in most of the southeastern part of the culture region. The latter two zones are relatively isolated. Along the eastern edge of the culture region, where the forces of modern urbanism have been the most aggressive, bilingualism is fading the fastest. It is no wonder that respondents begin to divorce their ethnic identity from the French language.

French Louisiana is still a Catholic island (Figure 5) in the Protestant South, and the Louisiana French use Catholicism as a means to distinguish themselves from outsiders. Yet the Catholic Church in Louisiana does not act as an ethnic institution. The twentieth-century Church has

Table 1
Language ability of senior respondents and their descendants
in southern Louisiana

	French Unilingual		Bilingual		Passive Bilingual		English Unilingual		Total
	N	%	N	%	N	%	N	%	N
Respondent	3	3	94	90	–	–	8	8	105
Children	–	–	224	50	64	14	160	36	448
Grandchildren	–	–	93	7	29	2	1,255	91	1,377

become Americanized.[6] Until the beginning of the century, Blacks and Whites worshipped together in Latin and French, led by a European and French-speaking clergy. By 1918, separate churches based on race had been accepted and had gradually become commonplace throughout the region.[7] Even today, the encouragment to integrate varies greatly from diocese to diocese. By 1945, 68 percent of the study communities no longer offered mass in French; in 1982 only one study community offered a French church service on Sunday (Table 2). Nor are the Louisiana French earnest Catholics. In a Louisiana seminary, Louisiana French religious practice is described as "hatch, patch, match, dispatch": people go to church for life's rites of passage, notably baptisms, confirmations, marriages and funerals, but as seldom as possible in between. In more than half of the study communities, priests evaluated Sunday mass attendance at 60 percent or less (Table 3). Given their parishioners' indifference to Catholic religious practice, priests are surprised by lay resistance to Protestant efforts in proselytization. Nevertheless, interfaith marriages performed in Catholic churches reach 25 percent or more within two old zones of Anglo intrusion (Figure 6).

French Louisiana cuisine is national news.[8] Also, food has become the most unifying cultural factor for the Louisiana French. Its appeal unites the generations and the French subcultures. Of course, it has always been important in the region, perceived as something to distinguish French Louisiana from the rest of the South.[9] But food, especially Cajun food, was also a cause for shame among the rural population of French

83

Table 2
French church services in study communities

	N	%
Never had French services or discontinued them in the late 19th century or early 20th century	12	34
Discontinued in 1921-1944	12	34
Discontinued in 1945-1964	7	20
Discontinued in 1965-1980	3	9
French services continuing in 1981-1982	1	3
Total	35	100

Louisiana. "Crawfish" were not always fashionable – one did not proclaim that he or she ate them. The food was not only distinctive, it also served as an effective ethnic boundary. Food is suddenly a positive reflection of the French Louisiana identity, more in tune with American tastes and tolerance. Of the three ethnic markers studied here, the only one that is thriving does so through American approval.

IDENTITY

The re-definition of the territory, which began with the emergence of a core, parallels a kind of ethnic unification. The French Louisiana population is diverse in both origin and experience. At least four subgroups can be identified: a Creole group claiming White, European ancestry; a Creole group of mixed racial ancestry that are referred to as the Black Creoles; the French-speaking Indians; and the Cajuns, descendants of Acadian refugees and of people of diverse origins who were absorbed into Cajun culture. The term *Cajun* is probably derived from the word *Acadian*. It was once used by Creoles and "Americans" alike to designate a backward, rural people with little education and limited knowledge of

Table 3
Priests' evaluations of Sunday mass attendance in their churches

		Churches	
		N	%
Less than	50%	5	15
	50%	6	18
Between	51-60%	7	21
	61-70%	10	30
	71-80%	3	9
	81-90%	1	3
More than	90%	1	3

Note: The total number of churches in this table is 33 instead of 35 since there are no data for two churches.

English. Even for Cajuns, the name became associated with a way of life looked down upon by others. They resented the word and preferred to call themselves French or Creoles, but they knew that for Creoles, Black or White, they were Cajuns.[10]

Yet nearly all French Louisiana today labels itself "Cajun." French Louisiana has been Cajunized, in name at least. The process began with the beautification of the word *Cajun* by CODOFIL. Trying to make the identity respectable, CODOFIL stressed the original genealogical definition of Cajun, that is, its Acadian character. The terms *Cajun* and *Acadian* became synonymous, but it was the latter that was promoted, hence the name *Acadiana* for the official French Louisiana designated in 1971 by the state legislature (Figure 7).

The second step in the Cajunization of French Louisiana came with the gubernatorial campaigns of Edwin Edwards in the 1970s. Edwards ran for governor while identifying himself as Cajun. By doing so he helped to destigmatize the word *Cajun*. He also enlarged its ethnic meaning by using it to address not only Acadians, but also everyone else of French culture or heritage in Louisiana. Within Louisiana,

LANGUAGE ABILITY OF SENIOR RESPONDENTS
AND THEIR DESCENDANTS

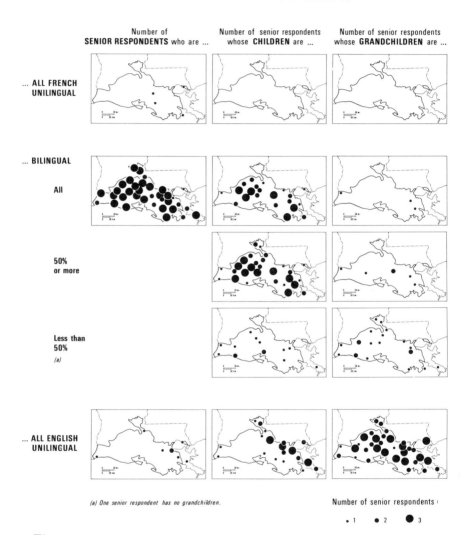

Number of
SENIOR RESPONDENTS who are ...

Number of senior respondents
whose **CHILDREN** are ...

Number of senior respondents
whose **GRANDCHILDREN** are ...

... ALL FRENCH
UNILINGUAL

... BILINGUAL

All

50%
or more

Less than
50%
(a)

... ALL ENGLISH
UNILINGUAL

(a) One senior respondent has no grandchildren.

Number of senior respondents :

• 1   ● 2   ● 3

Figure 4

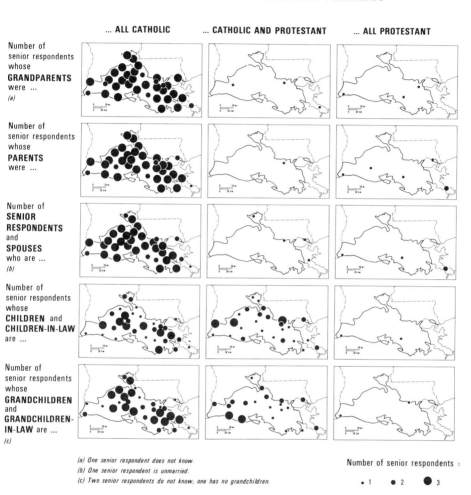

RELIGIOUS AFFILIATION IN DIFFERENT GENERATIONS
OF SENIOR RESPONDENT FAMILIES

... ALL CATHOLIC   ... CATHOLIC AND PROTESTANT   ... ALL PROTESTANT

Number of senior respondents whose **GRANDPARENTS** were ... *(a)*

Number of senior respondents whose **PARENTS** were ...

Number of **SENIOR RESPONDENTS** and **SPOUSES** who are ... *(b)*

Number of senior respondents whose **CHILDREN** and **CHILDREN-IN-LAW** are ...

Number of senior respondents whose **GRANDCHILDREN** and **GRANDCHILDREN-IN-LAW** are ... *(c)*

(a) One senior respondent does not know.
(b) One senior respondent is unmarried.
(c) Two senior respondents do not know; one has no grandchildren.

Number of senior respondents :
• 1   ● 2   ⬤ 3

Figure 5

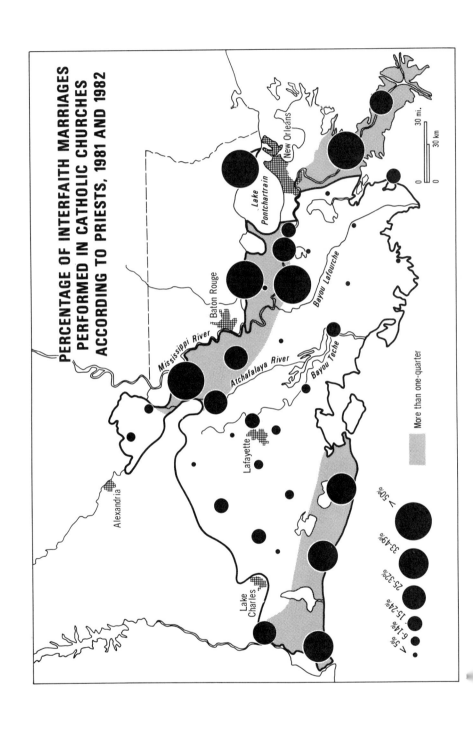

PERCENTAGE OF INTERFAITH MARRIAGES
PERFORMED IN CATHOLIC CHURCHES
ACCORDING TO PRIESTS, 1981 AND 1982

Alexandria

Lake
Charles

Lafayette

Baton Rouge

Mississippi River

Atchafalaya River

Bayou Teche

Bayou Lafourche

Lake
Pontchartrain

New Orleans

30 mi.

30 km

More than one-quarter

< 5%   6-14%   15-24%   25-32%   33-49%   > 50%

ACADIANA: OFFICIAL FRENCH LOUISIANA, 1971

Figure 7

CODOFIL's and Edwards's propaganda re-defined the Cajun identity. For my respondents, a Cajun was no longer rural, backward, uneducated. He or she could no longer be characterized by a single way of life or behaviour. Instead, Cajuns were, most of all, people who had some French roots (Table 4).[11] In the end, two types of Cajun have come to be recognized: the "real" or "pure" Cajun – of Acadian descent; and the "new" Cajun – any Louisiana native of French culture who is White. Cajuns define themselves as White persons and are also perceived as such by Black Creoles and French-speaking Indians. Thus the ethnic unification started by Edwards is incomplete. French-speaking Indians preserve their Indian identities in their home communities, while Black Creoles readily identify themselves as Creoles.[12]

Despite incomplete ethnic consolidation, Cajunization is important in White French Louisiana because in some measure it unifies the culture region, the territory. Cajunization, then, operates in the spatial realm as well. As a result, the old definitions of "Cajun country" as the bayous[13] or as the area west of the Atchafalaya are being replaced.[14] Instead, the whole of Acadiana, the official French Louisiana, is promoted as "Cajun Country,"[15] and people accept this re-definition across most of French Louisiana, even in areas where the White population was Creole.

ETHNIC SURVIVAL THE AMERICAN WAY

French Louisiana has become a truly American region. Its means are not ethnic confrontation but ethnic politics, a very American tool. Although it is shrinking, French Louisiana has received an "official territory" by the will of its politicians. Long fragmented and uncentred, a capital has also been created for it. Ethnically divided before, and still divided under its veneer of unification, a new regional ethnic identity has begun to emerge under the Cajun label. This identity, once associated with rural backwardness, refers now to a particular set of perceived cultural roots.

While ethnic politics are used to consolidate the old, poorly defined and crumbling French Louisiana, the culture itself has been newly repackaged to fit American norms of acceptable ethnicity. Religion, not taken too seriously, is used as a way to assert the area's distinct character. The French language revival is creating a cultural language that is ceremonial, but not used in everyday life. French Louisiana is concentrating on its food, a national fad. It increasingly uses outside approval of ethnicity to maintain itself.

The fate of rural Louisiana French at the threshold of the twenty-first century bears a resemblance to that of the New Orleans Creoles a century earlier. The latter may still eat their food and share it with outsiders in their excellent restaurants; they may also take pride in their Mardi-Gras celebrations. Nonetheless, New Orleans no longer has a living French culture.

ANY LESSONS TO BE DRAWN FOR CANADA?

It has been customary in this country to use the United States as a yardstick to evaluate Canadian successes and failures. Land of ice and rocks by its physical geography, Canada likes to portray itself as a much more humane place than the United States in terms of its values. In the ethnic arena, the image projected by each country is diametrically opposed.[16] Who has not heard of Canada's cultural mosaic and of the United States's melting pot? Canada's image is mostly rooted in the official policy of multiculturalism adopted by the federal government in 1971. However, if, as the sociologist Raymond Breton suggests,[17] cultural change is similar on both sides of the forty-ninth parallel, despite the Canadian policy of multiculturalism, one must question its efficacy.

Symbolically and psychologically, of course, the policy can be seen as a plus by all those who desire that Canada be a pluralistic society. It officially expresses the good will of the federal government, an act appreciated by the ethnic groups themselves. Since no society, at the present time, likes to be perceived as intransigent toward its minorities, Canada's policy gives it good press outside the country. It also strengthens the "Canadian" identity in the Anglo North American context in insisting on a difference in values between Canada and the United States.

The main problem with the policy is that it is not only a policy of multiculturalism but also one of a "bilingualism and multiculturalism." It is very hard to evaluate one part of the policy without touching the other. The general belief in Canada is that the French outside Quebec are the prime benificiaries of this policy. At first glance, this might appear true. This group has the advantage of having its language promoted at the national scale. However, what the French are realizing is that there is a difference between language and culture.[18] Even though more and more Anglophones in Canada are learning to speak French, the Francophone communities outside Quebec are shrinking. In the context of

Table 4
"What is a Cajun?"
Responses in 35 French Louisiana communities, 1981-1982

	Group of Respondents											
	PM[a]		GM		P		M		SR		Total	
Definition	N[b]	%	N	%	N	%	N	%	N	%	N	%
Genealogical	21	75	4	47	33	97	16	73	79	77	153	79
Uniquely genealogical	12	43	2	29	6	18	1	5	37	36	58	30
Not uniquely genealogical	9	32	2	29	27	79	15	68	42	41	95	49
Some Acadian origin	11	39	1	14	25	74	5	23	40	39	82	42
Some French origin	10	36	2	29	5	15	10	45	28	27	55	28
Other origin	–	–	1	14	3	9	1	5	11	11	16	8
Behavioural	12	43	3	43	18	53	17	77	39	38	89	46
Uniquely language	2	7	–	–	–	–	1	5	10	10	13	7
Not uniquely language	2	7	3	43	3	9	4	18	20	19	32	16
Uniquely other behavior	3	11	–	–	1	3	3	14	1	1	8	4
Not uniquely other behavior	7	25	–	–	16	47	12	55	11	11	46	24

Table 4 continued

Territorial	6	21	3	43	14	41	7	32	34	33	64	33
Uniquely territorial	1	4	1	14	–	–	–	–	3	3	5	3
Not Uniquely territorial	5	18	2	29	14	41	7	32	31	30	59	30
Louisiana	–	–	–	–	6	18	1	5	9	9	16	8
Southern Louisiana	1	4	2	29	4	12	4	18	5	5	16	8
Specific places	1	4	–	–	1	3	–	–	1	1	3	2
In the country	–	–	–	–	–	–	–	–	2	2	2	1
On the bayous	–	–	1	14	1	3	1	5	5	5	8	4
Here	4	14	–	–	2	6	1	5	12	12	19	10
Derogatory[c]	–	–	–	–	–	–	–	–	10	10	10	5
Hesitation	–	–	–	–	–	–	–	–	2	2	2	1
Total of respondents	28		7		34		22		103		194	

[a] PM–postmaster; GM–grocery manager; P–priest; M–minister; and SR–senior respondent.
[b] The subtotals do not necessarily add up since a respondent can give many elements in his or her answer.
[c] A Cajun was characterized as a stupid person, a country person, poor, low class or a person who speaks French badly. The word "coonass" is not included.

bilingualism, the ethnic groups in Canada have more of an opportunity to learn French than they do their own native languages. As a result, multiculturalism promotes cultures, but without these cultures' languages . . .

It is somewhat ironic that in Canada, outside Quebec, if things continue as they are, we are going to have French speakers without French culture and ethnic groups who will have retained only the ethnic markers that are not threatening to the present order, but not the language. Hence, I suppose the policy is very good for building a "new" Canadian who would master French and English and who would retain some mild public ethnic behaviours or strong private ones. If this situation is satisfying to most ethnic groups, fine. If not, a new orientation must be given to the multiculturalism policy. In my opinion, for this reorientation to be effective, and to touch the ethnic groups in a more profound way, it must be rooted in the geographical dimension of ethnicity in the country. Western Canada is basically multicultural in its ethnic reality. Eastern Canada is basically bicultural in its ethnic reality. How can we expect a policy that ignores this basic geographical reality to be effective?

French Louisiana has provided incentive for Quebec to assume greater control of the linguistic situation within its territory.[19] Let's hope now that it may inspire Canada to challenge profoundly, not only superficially, the United States's approach to ethnicity.

NOTES

1 Eric Waddell, *French Louisiana: An Outpost of "l'Amérique Française," or Another Country and Another Culture?* (Québec: Document de travail No. 4 du "Projet Louisiane," Département de géographie, Université Laval, 1979), 6-9, 21-22. Also, Terry G. Jordan and Lester Rowntree, *The Human Mosaic: A Thematic Introduction to Cultural Geography* (New York: Harper and Row, Publishers, 1979), 299.

2 The senior respondents were recommended most often by the postmaster or grocery manager (63 percent) and by the priest (37 percent). They had to be long-time residents who were especially knowledgeable about the community. Preferably, these older people were at least 65 years old, so they had been in or had finished with school when French was banished from the public schools in 1922. Preferably, they were married, with children and grandchildren, so that cultural changes from their grandparents' through their grandchildren's generations could be evaluated. Hence, the period of time covered by field research reached back to the last quarter of the nineteenth century. Note that four communities were visited for high-school respondent interviews.

3 The present cultural boundaries of French Louisiana presented here have been determined by asking respondents of the studied and visited communities the following question: Do you consider (name of the place) a Cajun (French, Creole) community?

4 The geographical conceptualization presented here is an adaptation of Donald Meinig, "The Mormon Culture Region: Strategies and Patterns in the Geography of the American West: 1847-1964," *Annals, AAG* 55, 2 (June 1965):191-200; and *Imperial Texas: An Interpretative Essay in Cultural Geography* (Austin and London: University of Texas Press, 1969). For a detailed discussion of these concepts and their pertinence to the Louisiana situation, see Cécyle Trépanier, "French Louisiana at the Threshold of the 21st Century," unpublished dissertation, Department of Geography, The Pennsylvania State University, 1988, 92-94.

5 William F. Rushton writes, "The heart of the Cajun culture is its language" (*The Cajuns: From Acadia to Louisiana* [New York: Farrar, Straus, Giroux, 1979], 289)."

6 A "European institution out of gear with American ideas." Such was the old American Catholic view of the Church in Louisiana through the nineteenth century. See, the Archdiocese of New Orleans, "Archbishop Blenk Made New Orleans American Diocese," *Catholic Action of the South, Archdiocese of New Orleans Centennial Supplement, 1850-1950* 18, 44 (5 October 1950): 56.

7 Dolores E. Labbé, *Jim Crow Comes to Church: The Establishment of Segregated Catholic Parishes in South Louisiana* (Lafayette: University of Southwestern Louisiana, 1971), 68.

8 For example, see: Mary Augusta Rodgers, "Louisiana's Acadia Country," *Gourmet* (October 1976):45-48, 86-90; Marjorie R. Esman, "The Breaux Bridge Crawfish Festival," *Natural History* (April 1984):47-60; Craig Clairborne and Pierre Franey, "Southern Cuisines," *The New York Times Magazine: Home Entertaining,* Part 2 (6 May 1984):42-46; Roy Reed, "Down Home in Acadia," *The New York Times Magazine: The Sophisticated Traveler,* Part 2 (9 October 1983):94, 95, 117, 118.

9 Fred B. Kniffen, *Louisiana: Its Land and People* (Baton Rouge: Louisiana State University Press, 1968), 7. Also, C. Paige Gutierrez, "The Social and Symbolic Uses of Ethnic/Regional Foodways: Cajuns and Crawfish in South Louisiana," in B.L. Keller and K. Mussell, eds., *Ethnic and Regional Foodways in the United States: The Performance of Group Identity* (Knoxville: The University of Tennessee Press, 1984), 172.

10 See, for instance, Thad St. Martin, "Cajuns," *Yale Review* 26 (Summer 1937):861.

11 The change in the perception of Cajuns was far from being immediate and generalized. It is very clear when I compare my 1981 results to those of the "Projet Louisiane," a research project conducted in 1978 by researchers of three Canadian universities (York, McGill and Laval). I personally made 79 interviews then, under the guidance of Dr. Dean Louder, in two towns of southern Louisiana: Lafayette, CODOFIL home town, located at the centre of the culture region; and Westwego, on its eastern edge. In 1981, the "I don't know" answers, hesitation and derogatory definitions of Cajun vanished. In 1978, 11 percent of the respondents gave a derogatory definition of Cajun (three percent, Lafayette; 16 percent, Westwego), and 19 percent did not give an answer or hesitated (13 percent, Lafayette; 22, percent Westwego). Also, while genealogical definitions of Cajuns were overwhelming in 1981 (79 percent), they were much less important in 1978 (37 percent).

12 For Blacks, this conclusion is confirmed by my own fieldwork and also by Robert Maguire's dissertation, "Hustling to Survive: Social and Economic Change in a South Louisiana Black Creole Community," Department of Geography, McGill University, 1987. For Indians, confirmation comes from Alain Larouche's article, "Les Cadjins du Canal Yankee: Problème d'identité culturelle dans la paroisse Lafourche," *Cahiers de Géographie du Québec* 23, 59 (septembre 1979): 281-302; and Daniel Bernier, *Entrevues par questionnaires avec les Indiens de la paroisse Terrebonne* (Québec: Document non-publié du "Projet Louisiane," Département de géographie, Université Laval, 1978). However, it is important to note that the Creole identity for Black Francophones is contested by the White Francophones in Louisiana. This situation is confirmed by my own results as well as those of Virginia R. Dominguez, presented in "Social Classification in Creole Louisiana," *American Ethnologist* 4, 4 (1977).

13 Carolyn Ramsey, *Cajuns on the Bayous* (New York: Hasting House, 1957).

CECYLE TREPANIER

14 The latter is still promoted for tourists. See, for instance, Louisiana Travel Promotion Association and the Louisiana Office of Tourism, *The World's Fair, New Orleans, 1984: The Most Exciting Place to Be in the World* (New Orleans: Promotional Tourist Brochure for the World Fair, 1984), 32-33.

15 For instance, books published in the 1970s, and widely diffused, represent the Cajuns' territory by Acadiana or the French Triangle, in other words, all of French Louisiana. See Glenn R. Conrad, ed., *The Cajuns: Essays on their History and Culture* (Lafayette: Center for Louisiana Studies, University of Southwestern Louisiana, 1978); and Rushton, *The Cajuns: From Acadia to Louisiana.*

16 Kit R. Christensen, "Multiculturalism and Uniculturalism: A Philosophical View," *The American Review of Canadian Studies* 15, 2 (Summer 1985):205-212.

17 Raymond Breton, "Le multiculturalisme et le développement national au Canada," in A. Cairns and C. Williams, eds., *Les dimensions politiques du sexe, de l'ethnie et de la langue au Canada* (Ottawa: Ministre des Approvisionnements et Services Canada, 1986), 70.

18 Eric Waddell, "Language, Community and National Identity," in A.-G. Gagnon and J.P. Bickerton, eds., *Canadian Politics: An Introduction to the Discipline* (Ontario: Broadview Press Ltd., 1990), 617.

19 Media in Quebec, especially newspapers, have been quick to point out that Quebec could become the Louisiana of the north if the province did not move to protect more efficiently the French language, given the overwhelming presence of English north of the Rio Grande. For one of the best examples of this demonstration, see Rodrigue Tremblay, "La 'Louisianisation' du Québec," *La Presse* (30 janvier and 2 février 1987):B3.

96

Part IV

Ethnicity and the Arts

A Poetics of Ethnicity

FRED WAH

Stances toward writing that have arisen out of an ethnic response demonstrate inventions of alignment and resistance. Immigrant, ethnic and Native writers in Canada have utilized most of the available public aesthetics in order to create a more satisfying space within which to investigate their particular realities. For some writers this entails an alignment with mainstream and traditional strategies, while for others the tactics of refusal and re-territorialization offer a more appropriate poetics.

I'm using the term *poetics* here not in the theoretical sense of the study of or theory about literature, but in its practical and applied sense, as the tools designed or located by writers and artists to initiate movement and change. "That is," as the American poet Charles Bernstein imagines, "poetics as a sort of applied poetic, in the sense that engineering is a form of applied mathematics." The culturally marginalized writer will engineer approaches to language and form that enable a particular residue (genetic, cultural, biographical) to become kinetic and valorized. For writers in Canada like Joy Kogawa and Rohinton Mistry the stance is to operate within a colonized and inherited formal awareness while investigating their individual enactments of internment and migration. But others, such as Roy Kiyooka and Marlene Nourbese Philip, who are operating from spatial allocations similar to Kogawa and Mistry, have chosen to utilize more formal innovative possibilities. This second group of writers seems to me to embody an approach that might properly be called something like "alienethnic" poetics. This poetics, while often used for its ethnic imprint and frequently originating from that desire, is certainly not limited to an ethnic, as they say, "project"; the same tactics could as well be used for other goals. Feminist poetics, for example, has arguably contributed the most useful strategies to the ethnic intention.

Margaret Atwood's notion that "we are all immigrants to this place even if we were born here" and quoted by Rosemary Sullivan in "Who are the Immigrant Writers and What Have They Done?" seems only to "universalize" the types, that we "many" are really only "one." A "poetics of ethnicity" would be, then, in Atwood's and Sullivan's view, simply the poetics, the whole, inclusive thing. But a practical and applied "poetics" is a singular and personal toolbox, and a writer who seeks to articulate a distinctive ethnic and, as I shall suggest, ethical sensibility requires particular, truthful and circumstantial poetics, the right tools.

For example, in his essay "The Ethnic Voice in Canadian Writing" (264-265), Eli Mandel rebounds from Atwood's claim to point to a particular "ethnic strategy": it is not only that as strangers we find ourselves in a strange land, but with the burden upon us as well . . . of living simultaneously in doubleness, that is difficult enough. To articulate that doubleness simply intensifies the pressure, the burden. But there is a further step in which what Atwood calls "inescapable doubleness" turns into duplicity, a strategy for cultural identification that I take to be the ethnic strategy, the "voice" I'm trying to identify.

The duplicitous voice, then, is what's needed and gets placed in the ethnopoetic toolbox. As indicated by Mandel (266), Robert Kroetsch subsumes the identity question into fiction's role, and Linda Hutcheon, in her introduction to the recent *Other Solitudes: Canadian Multicultural Fictions* (5), cites Aritha Van Herk as claiming fiction as a "refuge" from multicultural or ethnic "displacement." Fiction's double-dealing hand is seen as the result of a move from the familiar to the foreign.

In her article "Dialogism and the Canadian Novel," Sherrill Grace lists some of the chicanery available in the novelist trickster's bag of: double-voicing and polyphony; refraction of words, voices, and characters; parody; polemically coloured autobiography and confession; hybrid languages; carnivalization; inserted genres such as diaries, letters, found documents; Kroetsch's syncretic "provocation of the word by the word" (121). She adds:

At first glance, it would seem that politically, geographically, and linguistically Canada, unlike the United States, constitutes the perfect dialogistic space. To paraphrase Bakhtin in the *Dialogic Imagination,* we believe that we lack a truly unifying mythology; we behave as if politically decentered, and we try to allow for (or actualize) ethnic and linguistic diversity. As a result, "verbal-ideological decentring" should occur here because, as a "national culture," we have never had a "sealed-off and self-sufficient character" and have always thought of ourselves as "only one among other cultures and languages." (131-132)

Why then, asks the non-aligned writer, the fighter, does the monologic tradition dominate in fiction? What is this longing for unity? This desire for centres?

I've noticed, in the jockeying for the position of voice debate, that the term *ethnic* has been shunned as "incorrect" or "unusable" as a description of non-mainstream, visible/invisible minority, marginalized, race, origin, Native, or otherwise "Other." Linda Hutcheon, for example, argues for the use of the term *multicultural* as a more inclusive term instead of *ethnic,* which "always has to do with the social positioning of the 'other,' and is thus never free of relations of power and value" (2). To me, her rationale is similar to Atwood's view of a generic immigrant experience. Hutcheon admits that the issues associated with the term *ethnic* are, in fact, "the very issues raised by the structure of this book, as well as by the individual voices within it" (2). Though Hutcheon claims to want to challenge "the hierarchy of social and cultural privilege," (2) her apparent contradiction threatens to nullify the move.

But for me, this Greek-Indo-European term has provided significant poetic accommodation. The etymon *eth* surfaced for me many years ago when I struggled with the notion of *earth* and *ethos.* Here's the poem that provided me with a set of lasting keywords.

Eth means why any one returns
every one all over the place they are in
entwined into the confluence of the two rivers
into the edges of a genetic inscription
and our homes and loves now night
spreads out up the valleys
into the many-forgotten messages and arrangements
carried there the character sticks
hunger (n.p.)

So the tools of "place," "genetic inscription," "home," "love," "message" and "hunger" have clung like dirt to those roots.

This is also, of course, the Deleuze/Guattari term of *re-territorialization* seen by Barbara Godard in Lola Tostevin's "The Place becomes

Writing..." and Smaro Kamboureli's gloss on Tostevin's language as "the graph of place" (Godard, 160) and her own writing as "dealing with the self as 'the place of language'" (Williamson, 34). The "nomadology" (Deleuze and Guattari) of the ethnic writer, that is, the figuring out where she is, where to go, how to move, not just through language but actually in the world, is an investigation of place, as well as of placement in said place. For some, this is a reclamation project, and who could blame them, the Natives. Jeannette Armstrong calls it the "Blood of My People" (*Telling It,* 57):

forward   a red liquid   stream   that draws
ground upward   that shakes   earth and dust   to move
to move   a long line   before settling
quietly   back   into   soil

Because here she's writing within English and not the purity of her own Okanagan Salish, that "gap" in Armstong's poem is reflective of the nomadic cut and refusal to settle into English's placement of the syntactic morphology, and more basically and politically, both the imaginary nation and actual geo-morphology.

Furthermore, "place" is "home" or "cave"; proprioceptive, proprius, proper to one's self, the cave of self. But that ethos-ethnos leads to "ethic" – right way. As I came to it in a prose-poem, a lot of my old keywords tumbled forward.

Music at the Heart of Thinking Ninety

On the weekend I got into anger talk about landscape and the hunger of narrative to eat answer or time but space works for me because place got to be more spiritual at least last felt now this watery genetic I suspect passions like anger suprafixed to simply dwells I mean contained as we speak of it believe me I'd like to find a new word-track for feeling but language and moment work out simply as simultaneous occurrences so I don't think you should blame words for time-lapse tropism eg ethics is probably something that surrounds you like your house it's where you live.

Ethnic, ethic. A kind of anagogical exegesis of text that is a poetics of reading writing and is particularly attractive to the ethnic sensibility because of the continuous movement, nomadically, as well as that world-sense of Truth-slash-El Dorado Quest for and including traditional notions of value, Idealism, Positivism, Moralism and even the present political/religious economism. That's a mouthful but what I'm trying to indicate is that the truth-track for the poetics of ethnicity vis-à-vis its sister dangling root, ethic, that is, "where you live," is also "Other," a larger poetics term particularly attractive to contemporary ethnopoetics. Octavio Paz writes:

> As to the discovery, I shall begin by saying that the concrete life is the real life, as against the uniform living that contemporary society tries to impose on us. [Andre] Breton has said: la véritable existence est ailleurs. That elsewhere is here. Always here and in this moment. Real life opposes neither the quotidian nor the heroic life; it is the perception of the spark of the otherness. (Clarke, 151)

To write (or live) ethnically is also to write (or live) ethically, in pursuit of right value, right place, right home, otherness. Himani Bannerji's editors claim that "her ethic of individual responsibility, counterpointed by her recognition of external forces which imprison, is the coherent element in poems treating such topics as the cultural construction of woman and wife, . . . and the immigrant's vibrant connection to her homeland" (*Shakti's Words,* xi). The poem they're referring to is a powerful indictment of apartheid that Bannerji intervenes as "apart-hate."

Michael Thorpe, in a recent assault on Arun Mukherjee's *Towards an Aesthetics of Opposition,* is bothered by a poetics of the "Other." He asks, "Why would anyone not driven by material necessity . . . emigrate to and remain in an alien country and society in which they feel condemned to adopt a posture of opposition?" (4). Professor Thorpe, and many others who are attracted to notions of alignment and "shared common values" (1), might well feel disturbed by a poetics of difference. For the writer addressing an ethnicity directed at other values, the naming and re-territorialization is fundamental to creative action, and so any move to articulate a re-found territory requires this other-side-of-the-tracks stance.

This is always threatening to the "other" other-side-of-the-tracks because, at least here in Canada, it is politically and ideologically tied to the redress and rewrite of the apple of John A. MacDonald's eye – the current debate on "national unity." The moral exegesis of place-poetics argues, as Myrna Kostash does, for example, for a named and correct tool of "otherness":

FRED WAH

I had the very odd experience of finding myself entered in the Oxford Companion to Canadian Literature as "Kostash, Myrna. See: Ukrainian Writing." Odd, because, it seems to me that over some 20 years of writing I have made a contribution not just as an ethnic but as a woman/feminist, an Albertan, a Canadian, a non-fictionist, organization activist, teacher – why should the "Ukrainian" component of all this activity be the one to characterize me? Odd, too, in that I have no idea what "Ukrainian writing" is supposed to mean in my case; I write only in English and address an English-speaking audience. What on earth does it take to become a Canadian writer, a contributor to and practitioner of CanLit, if not books written in Canada by a Canadian for Canadians? Could it be that, given my origins outside the Anglo-Celtic and Franco founding nations, I shall never be considered to belong because I wasn't there at the beginning when the naming took place? That CanLit is a category and a practice hijacked and held captive by a very exclusive gang of men and women who all come from the right side of the tracks? (18-19)

She then goes on to negotiate for the position of the "potent" as she rejects the attempts at "assimilation" from the multicultural right side of the tracks. The exclusion, she points out,

. . . is painful and exciting, for it is in those "interstices" of cultures that we have become writers. In other words, we may not wish to belong to the club. We may wish to live with tension and distress. We may wish to remind ourselves, over and over, that we live on the wrong side of the tracks, on the edge of town. (19)

Kostash is indicating the position of applied, chosen, desired and necessary estrangement that has become a primary unit of composition for many Canadian writers as they seek to de-territorialize inherited literary forms and language, as they seek a heat through friction. This is a poetics of paradox. "Our disgraces are our graces," Charles Olson used to remind us in his seminar on poetics. We know ourselves by our resistances.

Milagros Paredes: "And I move . . . not forward, but in all the directions my questions take me. I move tentatively, having always to remind myself that surrendering to my confusion will lead me to some kind of clarity" (*Fireweed,* 77).

This principle of synchronous foreignicity, akin to biology's Gaiic catastrophism, of embracing antithesis, polarity, confusion and opposition as the day-to-day household harmony, is a necessary implement in art that looks for new organizing principles, new narratives.

Jamelie Ismail: "Read this book from right to left, reader dear (n.p.).

Himani Bannerji: "A whole new story has to be told, with fragments, with disruptions, and with self-conscious and critical reflections. And one has to do it right ... [there's that "ethic" at work]. ... Creating seamless narratives, engaging in exercises in dramatic plot creating, simply make cultural brokers, propagators of orientalism and self-reificationists out of us. My attempt here has been to develop a form which is both fragmentary and coherent in that it is both creative and critical – its self-reflexivity breaking through self-reification, moving towards a fragmented whole" (*Fireweed*, 134) [italics mine].

And, appropriately this week, we might hear Edward Said:

A part of something is for the foreseeable future going to be better than all of it. Fragments over wholes. Restless nomadic activity over the settlements of held territory. Criticism over resignation. The Palestinian as self-consciousness in a barren plain of investments and consumer appetites. The heroism of anger over the begging bowl. ... To do as others do, but somehow to stand apart. To tell your story in pieces, as it is. (150)

Anger. You can feel a bit of it, too, in Himani Bannerji's statement. And that "anger" in my own prose-poem above ("On the weekend I got into anger") is the proprioceptive response to the genetic other, a posed biotext in response to some ancestral ghosts. But I'm not alone. Here's Winnipeg poet Di Brandt:

I have tried everything, obedience, disobedience, running away, coming back, forgetting (blanking it out), recalling it again out of the dark, killing it off, translating, leaving it. sometimes it's like a glow running through me, around me, to the horizon like an aura, sometimes it's like a scar, throbbing, on my sleeve. sometimes i visualize it as a suitcase i drag around with me, centuries old, unwieldy, cumbersome, my people's words, handcuffing me, binding me, & then again, i open it in a new place & it's filled with coloured scarves, playthings. Mennonite hymns can still make me weep. there is so much re-visioning i've had to do in order to stay alive: i feel so much anger for the way we were made to suffer, as children, as women, swallowing our desires in secret, submitting to the will of the fathers and God & fate, learning our own silence. i feel so angry when i see Mennonite women trying to forget (blank out) their lives as they grow old, because there was so much suffering in them, the way they have learned at great cost not to speak. sometimes i feel like screaming for them, sometimes i feel like screaming at them. sometimes i long to go back to my grandmother's garden, filled with gooseberries & strawberries & blackberries & crab-apples & rhubarb & red currants & blue currants & raspberries & blackberries, & all the children, aunts & uncles, my family. i hate having to choose between my inherited identity & my life: traditional Mennonite versus contemporary Canadian woman writer, yet how can i be both & not fly apart? (*Prairie Fire*, 183)

Of course this is still part of the ethos, the right place, the "community."

This is Wednesday morning in Calgary, 27 February. External Affairs Minister Joe Clark phones me and asks me to participate in a discussion he's holding with some other artists on Saturday night in Calgary vis-à-vis "national unity." What he wants is our "imagination," our Image Nation. He says he's concerned about the body of much of the discussion on "national unity" drifting too heavily toward "laws" and "legislation" and such "business." While he talks to me I keep thinking, Why isn't he somewhere else doing something about peace in the Mid-East? Why isn't he busy deconstructing Canada's surreptitious arms economy? And just before he phoned, I was reading Himani Bannerji's poem "Apart-Hate" (*Shakti's Words,* 13-14). It's only a page, let me read it to you.

In this white land
Where I wander with scape-goats
there are laws

Apart-hate

In this whiteland
rocks blackhands gold and diamond
blood oozes from the mouth

Apart-hate

In this whiteland
Chinese coolies, black slaves, indian indentures
immigration, head tax, virginity tests

Apart-hate

Sudden attacks in the dark
in the dawn with cops and dogs
White Cop plays with her mouth – resuscitates

London Pretoria Toronto

Apart-hate

Reagan extends his whitehand from the whitehouse
fingers cash sells arms
the shop smells of blood, vomit and gunpowder
"divestment hurts the blacks"

106

Apart-hate

In this white land
skin is fingered like pelt
skin is sold and the ivory of her eyes

the category human has no meaning
when spoken in white

Apart-hate

You can imagine the resin in my own imagination at the time. I told Mr. Clark that, unfortunately, I'd be at a conference on multiculturalism in Winnipeg that evening. Don't get me wrong. I appreciate being asked. I wish, in some ways, I could be there, mouthing my own disjointed diatribe against the centre. I wonder if I would be able to talk about the non-aligned poetics of ethnicity; Kostash's deep need for opposition; Uma Parameswaran's "question" (*Shakti's Words*, 66) at the end of every word; Di Brandt's anger; Roy Kiyooka's "unwelcome but salutary silences . . . [and] tied tongue" (*West Coast Line*, n.p.); Gerry Shikatani's "the sign / mouth becomes / to throw / all weapons / into the cave of words (frontispiece); Kristjana Gunnars's *Carnival of Longing*; Roy Miki's "fear . . . in the face of racism"; his "museum of mirrors on the far side of town" (both from draft version); Marie Anharte Baker's racing "to write I write about race why do I write about race I must erase all trace of my race I am an eraser abrasive bracing myself embracing"; Marlene Nourbese Philip's question, "If no one sings the note / between the silence / . . . / is it still music?" (15); the community in Sky Lee's *Disappearing Moon Cafe*; Claire Harris's "Grammar of the Heart" . . . "How here to say the unsayable" (54); Jim Wong-Chu "lost . . . / on earth / above the bones / of a multitude / of golden mountain men" (21); Lee Maracle's trickster Raven, "another trick tucked within her wings"; Daphne Marlatt's "you, caught out in a language that sounded strange, stranger yourself, deprived of words that spoke what you knew" (94); David Arnason's "writing as carpentry" (*Border Crossings*); Phyllis Webb's "Leaning . . . / *slumped one degree from the horizontal / the whole culture leaning . . . / . . . / And you, are you still here / tilted in this stranded ark / blind and seeing in the dark (58-59).*
Nicole Brossard's "intention," she says,

107

... was to make trouble, to be a troublemaker in regard to language but also with values of my own embodied by a writing practice that was ludic (playing with words), experimental (trying to understand processes of writing), and exploratory (searching). You see, it brings us back to my values: exploration (which provides for renewal of information and knowledge), intelligence (which provides the ability to process things), and pleasure (which provides for energy and desire). (77)

Well there's the rub, Joe. The tactical imagination of a "national unity" is, for some writers, a "disunity." And the ethnopoetics toolbox isn't even only "ethnic," at least in the sense of racial. These tools are shared, it seems, by writers who are marginalized, invisible, experimental, political, in short, in need of any tool that might imagine, as the poet George Oppen believed, the unacknowledged world.

REFERENCES

Arnason, David. "War Journals: A Meditation." *Border Crossings* 10, 2 (April 1991): 9-14.

Atwood, Margaret. "Afterword." *The Journals of Susanna Moodie.* Toronto: Oxford University Press, 1970.

Baker, Marie Anharte."Raced out to Write This up." *Secrets from the Orange Couch* 3, 1 (April 1990).

Bernstein, Charles. "Optimism and Critical Excess (Process)." *Writing,* 23-24 (Fall-Winter 1989): 63.

Brossard, Nicole. "Poetic Politics." In Charles Bernstein, ed., *The Politics of Poetic Form,* edited by Charles Berstein, 73-86. New York: Roof Books, 1990.

Clarke, John. *From Feathers to Iron.* San Francisco: Tombouctou, 1987.

Fireweed, special issue on Asian-Canadian women, issue 30 (Spring 1990).

Godard, Barbara. "The Discourse of the Other: Canadian Literature and the Question of Ethnicity." *The Massachusetts Review* 31, 1 and 2 (Spring-Summer 1990): 153-184.

Grace, Sherrill. "Listen to the Voice: Dialogism and the Canadian Novel." In *Future Indicative,* edited by John Moss, 117-136. Ottawa: University of Ottawa Press, 1987.

Gunnars, Kristjana. *Carnival of Longing.* Winnipeg: Turnstone Press, 1989.

Harris, Claire. *The Conception of Winter.* Toronto: Williams-Wallace, 1989.

A Poetics of Ethnicity

Hutcheon, Linda, and Marion Richmond, eds. *Other Solitudes: Canadian Multicultural Fictions.* Toronto: Oxford University Press, 1990.

Ismail, Jam. *Sexions.* Kitsilano: self-published, 1984.

Kostash, Myrna. "Pens of Many Colours." *The Canadian Forum* (June 1990): 17-19.

Lee, Sky. *Disappearing Moon Cafe.* Vancouver: Douglas and McIntyre, 1990.

Mandel, Eli. "The Ethnic Voice in Canadian Writing." In *Figures in a Ground,* edited by Diane Bessai and David Jackel, 264-277. Saskatoon: Western Producer Prairie Books, 1978.

Maracle, Lee, "Trickster Alive and Crowing." *Fuse* 13, 1 and 2 (Fall 1989): 29-31.

Marlatt, Daphne. "In the Month of Hungry Ghosts." *The Capilano Review* 16/17 (1979): 45-95.

Miki, Roy. *Saving Face: Poems Selected 1976-1988.* Winnipeg: Turnstone Press, 1991.

Prairie Fire, special issue on new Mennonite writing, 11, 2 (Summer 1990).

Said, Edward. *After the Last Sky: Palestinian Lives.* New York: Pantheon, 1986.

Shakti's Words: An Anthology of South Asian Canadian Women's Poetry, edited by Diane McGifford and Judith Kearns. Toronto: Tsar, 1990.

Shikatani, Gerry. *1988.* Toronto: Aya Press, 1989.

Sullivan, Rosemary. "Who are the Immigrant Writers and What Have They Done?" *Globe and Mail,* 17 October 1987.

Telling It Book Collective, eds. *Telling It: Women and Language Across Cultures.* Press Gang, 1990.

Thorpe, Michael. "Opposition, Multicultural Apartheid or Connection?" *The Toronto South Asian Review* 9, 1 (Summer 1990): 1-10.

Wah, Fred. *Earth.* Canton, N.Y.: Institute of Further Studies, 1974.

Webb, Phyllis. *Water and Light.* Toronto: Coach House Press, 1984.

West Coast Line, edited by Roy Miki, No.3 (Winter 1990), contains "One Signature: Kumo/Cloud/s and Sundry Pieces" by Roy Kiyooka.

Williamson, Janice. "Sounding the Difference: An Interview with Smaro Kamboureli and Lola Tostevin." *Canadian Forum* (January 1987): 34.

109

FRED WAH

Wong-Chu, Jim. *Chinatown Ghosts*. Vancouver: Pulp Press, 1986.

Toward a Theatre beyond Multiculturalism

PER BRASK

The title of this paper is partly intended as an ironic statement, since the current professional theatre in Canada rarely reflects in production or staffing the demographic composition of this country. As a result, the experience to which many theatre subscribers may frequently be treated at our larger and most prestigious theatres is a curious one. With few exceptions the world portrayed on the stage seems glaringly White in comparison to the world most urban Canadians inhabit on the other side of the proscenium arch and its fourth wall – a wall that seems to become less and less figurative as the stage seems to announce its desire not to get involved in the world of its audiences.

In another sense the title of this paper is to be taken quite seriously – however, I'd encourage a smile in response to the angelic "beyond." It is probably obvious to anyone visiting our mainstream theatres on a regular basis that the policies of multiculturalism have had little effect. So the time may have come to look seriously at what the multiculturalism policy of Canada in section 3(1) item (g) lists as the federal government's desire to "promote the understanding and creativity that arise from the interaction between individuals and communities of different origins."[1] In other words, the time has come to take a serious look at the strategies of interculturalism in the production of theatre.

The Canadian theatre looked at as an entity has suffered severely during the past decade in particular; many theatres have disappeared due to lack of funding, many have been unable to attract a sufficient audience, and many have reduced their operations. In the title essay in his insightful book on the state of the Canadian theatre, *Producing Marginality,*[2] Robert Wallace has described the manner in which the confluence of the "universalist" biases of newspaper reviewers, the narrow pool of jurors for arts awards juries, the increasing influence of business ethics in the production of theatre enforced by boards of directors drawing their members from the business community, has created a situation in which "particularist" and innovative approaches to theatrical production automatically become marginalized. Wallace decries the state of the English-speaking theatre in Canada and casts a hopeful and ultimately romantic glance toward the imagistic theatre being produced in Quebec. As much as I agree with Wallace that the strategies of the imagistic theatre in Quebec and elsewhere provide significant examples of theatrical renewal, it must be said that the theatre in Quebec remains as much predominantly an expression of White culture as in the rest of the country. However, in this paper I will concentrate on the professional theatre in English-speaking Canada.

Another reason for wishing to speak about a theatre beyond multi-culturalism is that, whether or not the policies of multiculturalism were intended to produce cultural segregation, the result has often been perceived, in particular by artists from non-White backgrounds, to be a *de facto* segregation. In her carefully argued article, "The Multicultural Whitewash: Racism in Ontario's Arts Funding System,"[3] Marlene Nourbese Philip showed how jury composition combined with an insidious distinction between the artistic community and the so-called multicultural community reproduces the structure of the *status quo* and prevents new voices from being heard. This structural form of discrimination is also found within theatre organizations where representational aesthetics survive unchallenged and where the notions of Canadian cultural nationalism of the 1960s and '70s are still being implemented – that this cultural nationalism should have developed into a highly questionable ideology is perhaps ironic, but it is certainly not the first time in history that an initially progressive force turned into its opposite. After all, as Alan Williams recently stated in an interview in *Ellipsis* . . . , "the theatres which started in the early seventies, which built themselves up, and have grown up with a kind of rhetoric about doing Canadian plays, authentic Canadian-ness – one of the problems with that generation when they talk about this is that they mean sort of Scottish descent."[4]

The net result of this at least seemingly unicultural endeavour of the Canadian theatre in the face of the radically changed demographic nature of the country is, I believe, that the theatre has become increasingly irrelevant and decreasingly able to participate in the discourse around the story called Canada. The very subscribers that I mentioned at the beginning of this paper are more likely in their daily cross-cultural negotiations and conflicts to live a more immediately dramatic life from what they see portrayed on most stages. As Douglas Arrell has pointed out in his article, "Paradigmatic Shifts at the Box-Office: Winnipeg Theatre Responds to Changing Critical Values,"[5] the time is long past when audiences, by consciously or subconsciously applying the ideals of the New Criticism, searched for messages about the universal human in plays from faraway lands. Now it seems that declining attendance records may indicate a desire for a more immediate and particular encounter with what occurs on a stage.

Performers and writers from visible minority groups are also slowly – as their numbers increase – expressing their discontent at being sidelined in the theatre. In 1989 the two performers' associations ACTRA and Equity hosted a symposium on non-traditional casting in order to discuss the ways in which the lives of non-White performers could be improved. At that conference it was revealed that, whereas in the United States non-traditional casting – sometimes referred to by the unfortunate term *colour-blind casting* – is an established method of work in some theatres, most of the Canadian producers attending seemed to have major problems conceiving of casting, for example, a Black or Brown Juliet against a White or Yellow Romeo. And, though some may have severe reservations about this type of casting on legitimate semiotic grounds, I would suggest that a theatrical production exists in relation to a specific audience and not to a self-contained semiotic system. In fact, this is what allows someone like Richard Schechner to produce Chekhov's *The Cherry Orchard* in India with an Indian cast employing more than one presentation and performance strategy. It is clear that, in order to get to a point of intercultural production in mainstream theatres, a desire to look toward non-traditional methods of casting must be aroused. But if that desire cannot be awakened, perhaps need will eventually make it necessary for the professional theatre in Canada to react. In 1988 the research firm Multifax outlined at a meeting of the Canadian Centre for Philanthropy a possible future in which by the year 2000 less than 10 percent of Toronto's five million people would be of White Anglo-Saxon Protestant descent.[6] It may not be totally unreasonable to suggest that the same trends could be projected across English-speaking Canada. If that is, indeed, a likely future, then the theatre in this country has a great deal of restructuring and rethinking to do in the next few years. Only a few professional theatres have responded to this changed and changing reality, like the Firehall Theatre in Vancouver, by presenting plays written by visible minority writers and by actively recruiting members from visible minority groups and providing training if necessary.

The increasing differentiation of Canada's cultural life, and the disappearance of a meta-narrative of what Canada is, has led important critics such as Robert Kroetsch to announce: "I am suggesting that in Lyotard's definition, Canada is a postmodern country."[7] And, as Linda Hutcheon states in *The Canadian Postmodern*, "the postmodern 'different,' then, is starting to replace the humanist 'universal' as a prime cultural value. This is good news for Canadians who are not of Anglo or French origin – that is, for a good portion of the country's population today, . . . postmodernism offers a context in which to understand the valuing of difference in a way that makes particular sense in Canada."[8] But, though the meta-narrative that produced a particular history of Canada may be crumbling, giving way to a productive and delightful polyphony, let us not lose sight of the fact that all this is happening in a context of a capitalist nation. The notions of nationhood and capitalism are both powerful narratives. Indeed, the story of capitalism in its ongoing-ness is in the process of subsuming and including all other narratives – becoming, if not a meta-narrative in the sense that it is the source of all legitimation, then certainly in the sense that it is able to be a source of levelling between a variety of narratives. In this context it becomes important to me that strategies be found that allow both intercultural expression and fighting against the globalization processes of the capitalist narrative. In the search for such strategies one would do well in heeding the observations of Jean-François Lyotard, who states in his essay "Lessons in Paganism" that "history consists of a swarm of narratives, narratives that are passed on, made up, listened to and acted out; it is a mass of little stories that are at once futile and serious, that are sometimes attracted together to form bigger stories, and which sometimes disintegrate into drifting elements, but which usually hold together well enough to form what we call the culture of a civil society."[9] And later on in the same essay he says, "But histories and policies are like cultures; they are their own references and they determine their own enemies. It may sometimes be possible to unite or even combine efforts

114

and effects, and to both recount and implement particular narratives but it goes against reason, and reason is pagan, to totalize them on any lasting basis."[10] With these quotations as caveat I will describe a couple of production strategies, developed by specific theatres in many cases for purposes other than the ones I suggest they may be used for, which I believe could be employed in order to develop the narrative of interculturalism.

Before I proceed, I wish to make it clear that in searching for models of intercultural production I have been much inspired by the work of Rubena Sinha, who with her Fusion Dance Theatre in Winnipeg has spent the last few years creating dance works that involve many different styles and cultures, and who has managed to a very large extent to devise shows in which the different cultures remain equal without losing their specificity. It must be the aim of an intercultural production strategy to arrive at a solution in which the category of "the other" keeps shifting focus among the participants. Cultures now designated in Canadian parlance as multicultural, "other," would therefore no longer be viewed as quaint additions that serve the function of adding spice to an otherwise bland experience of life. It is therefore also clear that intercultural possibilities increase in direct proportion to the variety of performance experience encouraged and maintained in the many cultures that make up this country. For that reason I fully agree with Linda Hutcheon when she writes in the introduction to *Other Solitudes: Canadian Multicultural Fictions* that "to keep multiculturalism from becoming just a complacent cliché, we must work to grant everyone access to the material and cultural conditions that will enable the many voices of contemporary Canada to speak – and to be heard – for themselves."[11]

In selecting the two models that I wish to discuss here, I have attempted to find ways of producing that would allow for the greatest amount of interplay and interaction between the elements and the players. I have therefore rejected such highly lauded intercultural work as that of American director Lee Breuer and that of British director Peter Brook. In their searches for multiplicity and equivalence, in Breuer's case, and that which is the "original" human, in Brook's case, they seem – for all the excitement and innovation their works admittedly do represent – to come dangerously close to an insidious form of cultural imperialism, as Daryl Chin has charged in his article "Interculturalism, Postmodernism, Pluralism."[12]

The work of British director Mike Leigh and the model of work he has produced, on the other hand, seem to me to be most valuable in a Canadian production context. Leigh created, during the late 1960s and early 1970s, a method of play development that leaves a great deal of freedom to the individual actors. It is this aspect of his model that would allow for involving a variety of cultural perspectives without entering into the touchy issues around appropriation. In this process a play is developed through improvisations, the basis of which is similar to life-drawing classes in art school. Each actor becomes responsible for evolving a character separate from the other actors, and with the feed-back of a director and/or a writer. After a while, the various characters meet each other in improvisation, and slowly patterns of behaviour begin to emerge, as well as dramatic encounters. After some months of this type of investigation it is then possible to write a script based on the improvisations. This model of work has been used effectively by other groups, such as the Hull Truck Theatre, one of whose members, Alan Williams, introduced the method to Canada when he settled here in 1981 and subsequently founded the Rude Players. In an intercultural context, this model seems attractive because, in it, power rests with the performers who also become the source for the creation of the production. The traditional production system – in which a play is selected, then a director, then a designer and then a group of actors who rehearse for three to four weeks after which their rendering of the selected text is put before an audience – and its privileging of the text and subsequently the director's interpretation of that text, which leaves the actor in a peculiar situation as mediator, is abrogated here.

The other model I wish to introduce is one evolved by Reidar Nilsson, who founded the Tukak' Theatre as an Inuit company in Denmark in 1975. Since this theatre was the first seriously to use theatre in the contemporary sense of the term to develop shows based on Aboriginal experiences, it quickly attracted Sami as well as Canadian Native artists. Tukak's work derives from Reidar Nilsson's earlier work with the Odin Theatre, whose founder, Eugenio Barba, did his early work with Grotowski, who was much influenced by the writings of Artaud. The work of the Tukak' is therefore focused in the actor's physical expression and the ability of the human body to produce images. Much of the material Tukak' uses to react to is mythological. Shows are formed through sometimes verbal, sometimes non-verbal improvisations and movement designs. The stage here is considered a space where the production of images takes place rather than a space where the spoken word rules. In this way the work is often dance-like, but always there is a focus on dramatic tension and conflict in the imagery. This method of work can also be encountered with Sami groups like Dalvadis in northern Sweden, which consists of three performers – a Sami, an Inuit and an Iroquois. And, the Beaiivvas Theatre in northern Norway, which employs actors of Sami, Inuit and Norwegian background. This model seems attractive to me for the same reasons as the Mike Leigh model does, in that it allows for the freedom of performers from different backgrounds to draw on those backgrounds in contribution to a work that investigates co-existence.

I am not suggesting that the models I mention here are always used as democratically as I have rendered them. I am simply suggesting that they seem sufficiently open to be used in this manner.

Clearly there are many other ways in which intercultural work could be produced, and the most effective ones will only be arrived at through concrete, day-to-day trial and error. However, I firmly believe that any model must be open and profoundly non-hierarchical in its practice – which is not to say that people should become so paralyzed by niceness and accommodation that the work cannot proceed. They must avoid appropriation and cultural imperialism, except as topics, while being conscious and critical of the manner in which global capitalism wishes to see us all as merely "human." In other words, intercultural work must involve a critique of itself. The work then also becomes a reflection upon how it was produced.

In recognition of this last statement I want to clarify that I am aware that the models I have proposed here and the manner in which I have proposed them are – from a philosophical standpoint – Western in origin, and this may express Eurocentrism on my part. This, however, does not, I believe, invalidate them; rather, I see the matter as a contribution in the sense discussed by Leszek Kolakowski, who in his essay "Looking for the Barbarians: The Illusions of Cultural Universalism" states, "We affirm our belonging to European culture by our ability to view ourselves at a distance, critically, through the eyes of others; by the fact that we value tolerance in public life and scepticism in our intellectual work, and recognize the need to confront, in both the scientific and legal spheres, as many opinions as possible; in short by leaving the field of uncertainty open."[13]

NOTES

1 The Canadian Multiculturalism Act, assented to 21.7.1988.

2 Robert Wallace, *Producing Marginality* (Saskatoon: Fifth House Publishers, 1990).

3 Fuse Magazine (Fall 1987).

4 "Tempered Nostalgia," *Ellipsis . . . : The Newsletter for Manitoba Playwrights* (Fall 1990).

5 Canadian Theatre Review 66 (Spring 1991): 20-25.

6 Liam Lacy, "Soul-searching in 'Hong-Couver,'" *The Globe and Mail,* Saturday, 8 July 1989.

7 Robert Kroetsch, *The Lovely Treachery of Words* (Don Mills: Oxford University Press, 1989), 22.

8 The Canadian Postmodern (Don Mills: Oxford University Press, 1988), ix.

9 Andrew Benjamin, ed., *The Lyotard Reader* (Oxford: Basil Blackwell, 1989), 134.

10 *Ibid.*, 152.

11 Linda Hutcheon and Marion Richmond, eds., *Other Solitudes: Canadian Multicultural Fictions* (Don Mills: Oxford University Press, 1990), 15-16.

12 In *Performing Arts Journal* 33/34 (1989): 163-175.

13 Leszek Kolakowksi, *Modernity on Endless Trail* (Chicago: The University of Chicago Press, 1990), 22.

The Cult of Minorities in Recent Canadian Literature: Multicultural Configurations of Native, Ethnic, Immigrant and Womanist Writers

PAUL MATTHEW ST. PIERRE

In this paper I examine the cult or community of minorities among contemporary Canadian writers and explore some of the peripheral, alternative and neglected voice- and text-panels or -plates of a new kind of Canadian literary mosaic. The oral traditions of Aboriginal story-tellers are the extra-textual foundation of Canadian literature. The aural traditions of ethnic writers give new cadences to Canadian literature and sensitize our ears to non-status dialogue. The scribal traditions of immigrant writers working alternately in their native tongues and in Canada's official languages give Canadian literature a palimpsest quality. The transcriptive traditions of womanist writers engaged in writing-over or retelling our literature relegate some documents in the Canadian canon to BAK-file status. Native writers such as Maurice Kenny, Tom King and Tomson Highway, ethnic writers such as Joy Kogawa, Adele Wiseman, Kristjana Gunnars and Sky Lee, immigrant writers such as Meena Alexander, Rienzi Crusz and Uma Parameswaran, and womanist writers such as Margaret Atwood, Audrey Thomas, Susan Swan and Jane Rule help to piece together a new Canadian literary mosaic, forming various word- and culture-configurations and providing an alternative to the standard Canadian literary canon and a practicable model for Canadian multiculturalism.

119

PAUL MATTHEW ST. PIERRE

THE CULT OF MINORITIES AMONG CONTEMPORARY CANADIAN WRITERS

The founding nations of Canada, English and French, and the dominant cultures of Canada, Anglophone and Francophone, together form a vast majority over Native, ethnic, immigrant and womanist communities and subcultures. But historical events have upset the majority/minority balances in Canadian culture and multiculture. After the Battle of the Plains of Abraham in 1759, for example, the French founding nation became (as it remains) a minority within the English founding nation, even though to this day Anglophone and Francophone cultures enjoy equal foundational status. Under its recent Péquiste and current Liberal regimes, the province of Quebec is dedicated to maintaining its linguistic and cultural majority over Anglophone and immigrant minorities, and, after the discord of Meech Lake, to renegotiating its shared-foundational status, and even, drawing on the findings of the Allaire Report and the Bélanger-Campeau Commission, to repudiating its minority status within the Canadian dominion. Despite these constitutional rumblings, French and English founding nations together form a cult of majorities, an exclusive liaison of special interests and special standings. This cult of majorities is essentially a remnant of the bilingualism, biculturalism and cultural pluralism policies of the 1960s.

In its present multicultural configuration, Canada can be seen as a cult of minorities, a liaison of many cultural communities, none of them taking precedence over any other, at least in theory, not the English over the French, the French over the English, or the English and the French over any other ethnic, cultural or linguistic group. Each of these groups is a minority in a community of minorities, enjoying at once equal and special status.

In Canadian literature, a similar cult of minorities has arisen in the past two decades, counterbalancing the cult of majorities that Hugh MacLennan, quoting Rainer Maria Rilke, termed *two solitudes*: "Love consists in this, / that two solitudes protect, / and touch, and greet each other." Canadian literature no longer comprises just two solitary literatures, English, or Canadian, in the one solitude, and French, or Québécois and Acadian, in the other. In its linguistic plurality, multicultural Canadian literature is English and French, Dene and Inuktitut, Korean and Cantonese, Ukrainian and Urdu, and so on, each language or order of discourse having the same currency as all the others. Every

120

language, even English and French, is a minority language; every language is *inuk titut,* or person-speech. The cult of minorities in Canadian literature also manifests itself in ethnicity, the ethnicities of Chinese society in West Coast literature (Sky Lee), West Indian society in Toronto literature (Neil Bissoondath), and so forth. Aboriginal writing contributes a complex set of tribal and linguistic minorities to Canadian literature's multicultural configuration. Even though Canadian women could hardly be considered a minority demographically, womanist writing, revisionist writing primarily by-women-about-women-for-women, is essentially minority literature in Canada, up against a patriarchal majority in publishing, a patrician readership, the patronage of government grants, the patrimony of a grey-bearded Canadian literary canon, and a patriated constitution. Thus, in helping to constitute a new mosaic of Canadian multiculturalism, the cult of literary minorities exploits other voice- and text-panels and -plates, held together not by the mortar of legislation or the mortar-boards of academia but by their simple proximity to one another, the condition of what I call *post-contiguity,* which is part way between the state of contiguity and the phenomenon of superimposition.

ORAL TRADITIONS AND ABORIGINAL STORY-TELLERS: THE EXTRA-TEXTUAL FOUNDATION OF CANADIAN LITERATURE

In these heady times of constitutional debate in Canada, the English and French founding nations are engaged in nation-building, or more accurately the process of razing-and-raising the nation, what in architecture is called *deconstructivism* and in literary criticism *deconstruction.* In our self-destructive rush to become American—you recall the great American immigration sweepstakes of a few years ago – we essentially adopt the attitude of Hamlet: "O that this too too sullied flesh would melt, / Thaw, and resolve itself into a dew, / Or that the Everlasting had not fixed / His canon 'gainst self-slaughter" (I.ii., 129-133). For "the Everlasting" here, we might well substitute the contemporary folk-heroes Ti-Jean de Shawinigan, and Clyde, who went to the wells once too often!

Meanwhile, everyone else in multicultural Canada, from Albanians to Zimbabweans, is lobbying to have their distinct societies, language groups and regional interests protected at the constitutional negotiating table, at the same time fearing they will fall into the lingering shadows of our two solitudes.

121

Somewhere deep within the alphabet of Canadian multiculturalism are to be found the Aboriginal peoples, some half a million Indians, Inuit, and Métis, whose ancestors settled (that is, invented) this land *at least* 12,000 years before the Vikings and John Cabot and Jacques Cartier. Twelve millenia are enough to set even W.B. Yeats spinning, but sometimes it seems the closest we come to taking a turn in the eons of Canada is an occasional Trudeauesque pirouette for the now of politics.

In their antiquity and nativity, Aboriginal peoples are inviolably a founding nation, and much more emphatically so than either the English or the French. Even though, after 350 years of European settlement, Aboriginal land claims are a complex issue legally, the ethical matter of Aboriginal title seems fairly straightforward. One would hope that an early round of the anticipated post-Meech constitutional negotiations might well entrench Aboriginal title and recognize Indians, Inuit, and Métis as founding peoples making up a founding nation, or even many founding nations. But, in the meantime, as we wait for the other shoes of Lucien Bouchard's *Bloc Québécois* and Preston Manning's Reform Party to drop, the somewhat mean-spirited Canadian psyche will have to undergo considerable healing before we as an essentially migrant nation will be prepared to embrace the practicable reality of Aboriginal nationhood.

Four recent collections of Aboriginal writing will certainly help to acquaint Canadians with the kind of social conditions and political preconditions that Indian, Inuit and Métis people face every day. Each of these books – personal narratives, social documents and works of literature – will undoubtedly play an important role in opening up the Canadian forum for autochthonous voices.

Geoffrey York's *The Dispossessed: Life and Death in Native Canada* (1990) is an ambitious social history of contemporary Native life and the state of nativity throughout this nation. York manages to disseminate a wealth of both soft and hard evidence through an anecdotal, testamentary style and in banks of statistical data. In the end, York's data are a disheartening litany of violence, alcohol and chemical addiction, and physical and mental abuse, often punctuated by suicide and premature death. This compelling, sobering study is at once a printout of a multicultural tragedy and a blueprint for post-Oka militancy.

In Our Own Words: Northern Métis Women Speak Out (1986), by sociologists Dolores T. Poelzer and Irene A. Poelzer, is a collection of informal conversations with Métisse from northern Saskatchewan. Here the focus is less on a national tragedy than on the kind of local domestic problems and community struggles that seldom receive media coverage. In the poignant immediacy of its personal narratives, the Poelzers' study confronts us with off-track Métisse communities, communities in reserve, that we can never expect to see while fast-tracking the Trans-Canada and the Alaska highways.

Thomas King's edition *All My Relations: An Anthology of Contemporary Canadian Native Fiction* (1990) offers a representative selection of recent Canadian Native writing, such as Thomas King's neo-traditional fable, "The One about Coyote Going West," Shirley Bruised Head's metafictional dialogue-story, "An Afternoon in Bright Sunlight" and an excerpt from Tomson Highway's celebrated play, *The Rez Sisters*. The anthology as a whole is remarkable for its literary range and its multicultural scope, and specifically for raising Native issues that have sweeping implications.

In their edition *Writing the Circle: Native Women of Western Canada* (1990), Jeanne Perreault and Sylvia Vance cover the sweep of poetry and fiction from the West and inscribe some important new names into the canon of Canadian literature, such as the short-story writers Loretta Jobin and Norma Gladue, the poets Emma LaRocque and Christina Rain, and the folk-tale tellers Jessie Winnipeg Buller and Clare E. McNab. Perreault and Vance's anthology of Native writing outlines a sort of counter-canon of Canadian nativity.

These and many other Aboriginal titles, notably Jacqueline Peterson and Jennifer S.H. Brown's edition, *The New Peoples: Being and Becoming Métis in North America* (1990), lay claim to an at-once new and ancient literary land, and to an oral heritage that finally can be inscribed without losing its orality.

MULTICULTURAL VOICES OF WOMEN IN CANADIAN FICTION OF THE EARLY 1980S: WRITING-OVER, OVERWRITING AND TELLING AS RETELLING

The traditional focus of Canadian literature has been visionary, based on visions of a vast land that transcends horizons, on luminous perceptions of climatic phenomena such as the aurora borealis, and on prophetic projections of Canadian culture against the push-and-pull of British and French, American and Pacific Rim cultural imperialism. The postmodern focus of Canadian literature, however, is decidedly re-visionary. Native, ethnic, immigrant and womanist writers are dedicated to revising and rewriting Canadian literature and Canadian literary history, to acknowledging minority contributions to the literature that have gone unrecognized, and to envisioning the land, climatic phenomena and cultural projections in original ways, and thus offering Canadians new modes of perceiving the realities of their literature.

During the years 1980 to 1985, our newly patriated constitution was matriated by Canadian women writers who underscored the diversity of Canadian literature and the multiplicity of Canadian culture. Canadian literature is most obviously diverse in its bilingual, and increasingly polyglottal, make-up.

In *Les Fous de Bassan* (1982), translated by Sheila Fischman as *In the Shadow of the Wind* (1983), and transliterated into film by Yves Simoneau as *Les Fous de Bassan* (1988), *Québécoise* novelist Anne Hébert explores this diversity with delightful irony, setting her tale in an English-speaking hamlet called Griffin Creek, in the Gaspé.

The Francophone-Anglophone diversity of Canadian literature is not exclusively a phenomenon of Quebec and Canada without Quebec. In parts of the Prairies and the Maritimes (especially New Brunswick), as well as in other parts of Canada outside Quebec, the Francophone presence is strong, and it finds some expression in literature. (One thinks of the Saint-Boniface writers Gabrielle Roy and Annette Saint-Pierre.) The most eminent living Francophone writer outside Quebec is the Acadian novelist Antonine Maillet. Her fiction chronicles Acadia from the seventeenth century to the present, often with a fastidious attention to cultural detail, although sometimes with romantic abandon. But whether she is writing historical, romantic or realist fiction, Maillet is preoccupied with the sense of adventure that pervades Acadian culture and that can be detected even in modern Acadian French, with its daring seventeenth-century cadences.

Another source of diversity in Canadian fiction is writing that falls outside the cultural traditions of two founding nations and nation-languages. Between 1980 and 1985, several women novelists and story-tellers distinguished themselves in this way as peculiarly ex-claustral writers.

Beatrice Culleton is a Métisse whose Aboriginal heritage seems to distinguish her both from French culture and from the English language. Her novel *In Search of April Raintree* (1983) is partly an examination of this mixed heritage, and partly an attempt to find a place for Métis in the Canadian mosaic. A first-person confessional narrative, the novel gives voice not only to an engaging character who proves herself a woman of independence, but also to a culture that hitherto has found little expression in Canadian literature. Such is Culleton's accomplishment that *In Search of April Raintree* gives Métis the kind of voice that need never be silent again, a voice-paradigm for future generations.

Bharati Mukherjee was born in India and is now resident in the United States, but she lived and wrote in Canada between 1966 and 1980. Her fiction explores a curiously Indian sense of exile, both within India itself and around the world. Her Canadian focus is on immigrants' problems of adjustment to a new land and on the danger of becoming absorbed by cosmopolitan values. In "The World According to Hsü," a story from her collection entitled *Darkness* (1985), Canada is at once home and a distant place of refuge for a Canadian professor and his Indian wife caught in a coup while on holiday in Africa. Such is the shared sense of displacement of native-born and immigrant Canadians. To the degree that it is generational, Canadian multiculturalism might be seen in this way as an interpersonal phenomenon and a personal experience of multiple displacement.

Canadian literature's multiplicity occasionally extends south of the forty-ninth parallel. Jane Rule and Audrey Thomas are more accurately expatriate Americans writing Canadian literature than expatriate American writers living in Canada. Both started their writing careers in Canada, and, as it happens, both have lived in the community of writers on Galiano Island.

Jane Rule is concerned principally with social minorities and alternative communities, and has a special interest in lesbian relationships. In her novel *Contract with the World* (1980), somewhat in the manner of Hébert in *Les Fous de Bassan*, Rule takes six characters and allows them to tell the same story collectively, but from their own perspectives. The characters, who are artists and their friends, find within their small community an audience for story-telling and, within shifting personal relationships and allegiances, outlets for the passions of art and love.

In both her novels and her short stories, Audrey Thomas examines the constitution of the contemporary family. She explores its broken boundaries to determine how the family manages to hold itself together, if only in fragments, and why external forces hostile to the family seldom manage to infiltrate it completely. For Thomas, the most stirring remnant of the nuclear family is the woman who, although alone, her children and husband having left, remains conscious of her motherhood and her role as a "real mother," as in her 1981 story collection entitled *Real Mothers.*

Like Audrey Thomas, Alice Munro is a short-story writer devoted to analyzing domestic politics. Her particular concern is with women at their profound moments of initiation and exclusion, when they are introduced to the world of men, the experience of male contact, and to sex with men, and when these female-male bonds are broken (through disloyalty, divorce or death) and women are sometimes left as lonely as they were as adolescents.

Marian Engel's death in 1985 and the publication of her only story collection, *The Tattooed Woman* (1985), fittingly punctuate this half-decade of diversity and multiplicity among the (sub)culture of Canadian women writers. Engel did more than any other writer in this period to reclaim a cultural place in which women might write. The writer's place is no longer a garrison in nature or a garret in town. The writer's place is in literature. In her title story, "The Tattooed Woman," a disturbing allegory about a woman who systematically tattoos herself, mutilating her body to bring to the surface the scars of her unhappy marriage, Engel delineates the situation of women in general, including women writers, whose fiction makes a kind of permanent mark in Canadian letters and traces disturbing patterns in Canadian culture. Engel reminds us that Canadian women writers make up a subculture only to the extent that they endeavour to subvert the traditional mosaic-version of multicultural Canada.

Joy Kogawa is an alternate voice in Canadian fiction, a writer of Japanese descent, essentially outside Canada's two founding cultures, yet at the same time, in her novel *Obasan* (1981), confronting them head-on with their own history. *Obasan* considers whether people can change their course through cultural history or their destiny in cultural history, or whether, on the contrary, people are just hurtling through time, propelled by an irresistible force of nature. Kogawa gives us cause to ponder our horrific pasts and futures; she gives us occasion to denounce the false records of history, beginning, like the author herself, with language. *Obasan* reflects the broadly political concerns of other women writers in the first half of the patriated-matriated 1980s, and their dedication to new word-constructs as means of permanently effecting important social change.

If, by the end of the novel, Kogawa does not succeed in erasing the memory of her own forced migration and concentration-camp exile, she does manage to effect a subtle change in it, to neutralize it by rendering it more manageable and tolerable, by articulating it and thus holding an ex-claustral word-construct over it. In this regard, Kogawa is able to write over Japanese-Canadian history.

Writing over history is a dual process. In this case it involves writing over an historical record, the White version of Japanese war involvement, by superimposing one document over another, as with a palimpsest of old or a modern-day computer file, thus relegating the inaccurate or obsolete document to a kind of old-MS or BAK-file status. Kogawa has taken the colonial, racist, xenophobic historical record and defaced it, spilling blood on the constitution of official history and disrupting its semiotic code. She has shattered a word-ensignia and imposed a new code of tentative historical authenticity on it. Writing over history can also mean writing history again, however, and in this sense Kogawa can be seen as writing an alternate version of Japanese-Canadian history. By rewriting history, she places two historical records side by side, overlapping them slightly in areas of common truth and shared vision.

The Handmaid's Tale (1985) is Margaret Atwood's most resolutely North American, apparently extra-multicultural, novel to date. With its littoral New England setting and parochial American characters, it makes only glancing references to Canada. Atwood's Republic of Gilead is a United States of America projected into the near future, a country whose structures, in the totalitarian nuclear winter of "the catastrophe" (which is Atwood's phrase for a gathering of atomic, political, moral and psychosexual failures from across the globe), appear to have collapsed under the weight of its own history. Atwood's vision is essentially one of a society after the collapse of multiculturalism and the rise of uni-culturalism, or post-communitarianism. Here the cult of female minority is one of forced devotion to man as the engenderer of culture, who propagates a majority of one gender over the other.

Atwood's sombre dystopian narrative is tempered with the optimism that language is inviolable, that at best it can change people's minds, and at the very least work the illusion of warding off the future. Atwood's plea for multiculturalism, and in particular gender equity, is directed essentially at present-day culture in Canada, not so much the *status quo* as the *quid pro quo*, the exchange of something for something, in this instance the prospect of uniculturalism for the imperfect protean reality of multiculturalism, the exchange of bicameral cultural majorities for

127

the dream-we-are-presently-dreaming of a parliament of minorities and a cult of minimism.

Anne Hébert, Antonine Maillet, Beatrice Culleton, Bharati Mukherjee, Jane Rule, Audrey Thomas, Alice Munro, Marian Engel, Joy Kogawa, Margaret Atwood and the other women writers who published novels and stories in the reformative years from 1980 to 1985 inaugurated a multicultural movement in the aurora borealis of Canada's new constitutional age. By the end of the decade, womanist fiction was well-established and well on its way to resetting the balance between the patrilineal development of biculturalism (male and female) and an unlined path through multiculturalism (gender equity). Through these writers' efforts, the unmarked multicultural path remains open to all women and men writers of fiction in Canada, and to all people making up the cult of minorities.

In postmodern and *fin de siècle* Canadian literature, the new word- and culture-configurations of Native, ethnic, immigrant and womanist writers are helping to establish a new kind of Canadian literary mosaic, consisting not of small pieces of coloured tiles set in stone but of an assemblage of overlapping images, as in aerial photography, in this case moveable frames or plates of narrative that form a series of composite pictures of culture. The condition of multiculturalism in Canada, therefore, is beyond mere contiguity or contact, the sharing of an edge or a boundary like the Ottawa River or the perimeter of a reserve. The true condition of Canadian multiculturalism is post-contiguity, a condition of cultural intersection and part-superimposition, one culture touching and overlapping but not overtaking the other. These areas where one culture extends over another, where they protect and overlap and greet each other, like a turbaned Sikh in the RCMP or, as we shall see one day, a Native minister of Native Affairs, are the horizons, the auroras, and the projections of a Canada of alphabetic multiculturalism, a forest of word-signs beyond the legislated symbols of vertical and horizontal mosaics, a cult of minorities and a new Canadian mosaic of the minim.

REFERENCES

Primary Sources

Atwood, Margaret. *Bodily Harm.* Toronto: McClelland and Stewart, 1981.

_____. *Bluebeard's Egg.* Toronto: McClelland and Stewart, 1983.

_____. *The Handmaid's Tale.* Toronto: McClelland and Stewart, 1985.

Birdsell, Sandra. *Night Travellers.* Winnipeg: Turnstone, 1982.

_____. *Ladies of the House.* Winnipeg: Turnstone, 1984.

Bissoondath, Neil. *Digging up the Mountains.* Toronto: Macmillan, 1985.

Culleton, Beatrice. *In Search of April Raintree.* Winnipeg: Pemmican, 1983.

Engel, Marian. *Lunatic Villas.* Toronto: McClelland and Stewart, 1981.

_____. *The Tattooed Woman.* Markham: Penguin, 1985.

Gallant, Mavis. *Home Truths: Selected Canadian Stories.* Toronto: Macmillan, 1981.

_____. *Overhead in a Balloon: Stories of Paris.* Toronto: Macmillan, 1985.

Hébert, Anne. *Les fous de bassan.* Montreal: Editions du Seuil, 1982. [*In the Shadow of the Wind.* Trans. Sheila Fischman. Toronto: Stoddart, 1983.]

King, Thomas, ed. *All My Relations: An Anthology of Contemporary Canadian Native Fiction.* Toronto: McClelland and Stewart, 1990.

Kogawa, Joy. *Obasan.* Toronto: Lester and Orpen Dennys, 1981.

Lee, Sky. *Disappearing Moon Cafe.* Vancouver and Toronto: Douglas and McIntyre, 1990.

MacLennan, Hugh. *Two Solitudes.* Toronto: Collins, 1945.

Maillet, Antonine. *Crache à Pic.* Montreal: Leméac, 1984.

Mukherjee, Bharati. *Darkness.* Markham: Penguin, 1985.

Munro, Alice. *The Moons of Jupiter.* Toronto: Macmillan, 1982.

Perreault, Jeanne, and Sylvia Vance, eds. *Writing the Circle: Native Women of Western Canada.* Edmonton: NeWest, 1990.

Peterson, Jacqueline, and Jennifer S.H. Brown, eds. *The New Peoples: Being and Becoming Métis in North America.* Winnipeg: University of Manitoba Press, 1985.

Poelzer, Dolores T., and Irene A. Poelzer. *In Our Own Words: Northern Métis Women Speak Out.* Saskatoon: Lindenblatt and Hamonie, 1986.

Rule, Jane. *Contract with the World*. New York: Harcourt Brace Jovanovich, 1980.

Smith, Ray. *Cape Breton is the Thought Control Centre of Canada*. Toronto: Anansi, 1969.

Swan, Susan. *Unfit for Paradise*. Toronto: Christopher Dingle, 1981.

_____. *The Biggest Modern Woman in the World*. Toronto: Lester and Orpen Dennys, 1983.

Thomas, Audrey. *Real Mothers*. Vancouver: Talonbooks, 1981.

_____. *Intertidal Life*. Toronto: Stoddart, 1984.

York, Geoffrey. *The Dispossessed: Life and Death in Native Canada*. London: Vintage, 1990.

Secondary Sources

Aitken, Johan Lyall. *Masques of Morality: Females in Fiction*. Toronto: Women's Press, 1987.

Atwood, Margaret. *Second Words: Selected Critical Prose*. Toronto: Anansi, 1982.

Birney, Earle. *Spreading Time: Remarks on Canadian Writing and Writers*. Montreal: Véhicule, 1980.

Blodgett, E.D. *Configuration: Essays on the Canadian Literatures*. Downsview: ECW Press, 1982.

Bowering, George. *The Mask in Place: Essays on Fiction in North America*. Winnipeg: Turnstone, 1982.

Cagnon, Maurice. *The French Novel of Quebec*. Boston: Twayne, 1986.

Davey, Frank. "Alternate Stories: The Short Fiction of Audrey Thomas and Margaret Atwood." *Canadian Literature* 109 (Summer 1986): 5-14.

Flynn, Elizabeth A. "Gender and Reading." *Gender and Reading: Essays on Readers, Texts and Contexts*. Ed. Elizabeth A. Flynn and Patrocinio P. Schweickart. Baltimore: Johns Hopkins University Press, 1986. 267-88.

Frye, Northrop. *The Bush Garden: Essays on the Canadian Imagination*. Toronto: Anansi, 1971.

_____. *Divisions on a Ground: Essays on Canadian Culture*. Toronto: Anansi, 1982.

Goldie, Terry. *Fear and Temptation: Images of Indigenous Peoples in Australian, Canadian and New Zealand Literatures*. Montreal: McGill-Queen's University Press, 1988.

Grace, Sherrill E. *Regression and Apocalypse: Studies in North American Literary Expressionism*. Toronto: University of Toronto Press, 1989.

Hutcheon, Linda. "'Shape Shifters': Canadian Women Writers and the Tradition." *The Canadian Postmodern: A Study of Contemporary English-Canadian Fiction.* Toronto: Oxford University Press, 1988. 107-37.

Hutcheon, Linda, and Marion Richmond, eds. *Other Solitudes: Canadian Multicultural Fictions.* Toronto: Oxford University Press, 1990.

King, Thomas, Cheryl Calver, and Helen Hoy, eds. *The Native in Literature.* Oakville: ECW Press, 1987.

Kroetsch, Robert. *The Lovely Treachery of Words: Essays Selected and New.* Toronto: Oxford University Press, 1989.

Lessing, Doris. *Prisons We Choose to Live Inside.* CBC Massey Lectures. Toronto: CBC Enterprises, 1986.

Malak, Amin. "Margaret Atwood's *The Handmaid's Tale* and the Dystopian Tradition." *Canadian Literature* 112 (Spring 1987): 9-16.

New, W.H. *Dreams of Speech and Violence: The Art of the Short Story in Canada and New Zealand.* Toronto: University of Toronto Press, 1987.

New, W.H., ed. *Native Writers and Canadian Writing.* Vancouver: UBC Press, 1990; special issue of *Canadian Literature* 124-125 (Spring-Summer 1990).

Petrone, Penny. *Native Literature in Canada: From the Oral Tradition to the Present.* Toronto: Oxford University Press, 1990.

Rich, Adrienne. "When We Dead Awaken: Writing as Re-Vision." *On Lies, Secrets and Silence: Selected Prose 1966-1978.* New York: Norton, 1979. 33-49.

Ricou, Laurence. *Vertical Man / Horizontal World: Man and Landscape in Canadian Prairie Fiction.* Vancouver: UBC Press, 1973.

Shakespeare. *The Tragedy of Hamlet, Prince of Denmark.* The Signet Classic Shakespeare. Ed. Edward Hubler. New York and Toronto: New American Library, 1963.

Trehearne, Brian. *Aestheticism and the Canadian Modernists: Aspects of a Poetic Influence.* Kingston: McGill-Queen's University Press, 1989.

York, Lorraine M. "The Habits of Language: Uniform(ity), Transgression and Margaret Atwood." *Canadian Literature* 126 (Autumn 1990): 6-19.

The Use of a "Mother" Tongue: German-Canadian Poetry in Multicultural Canada

GERHARD STILZ

German writing in Canada looks back to a tradition of more than 200 years. From the early Protestant colonies in Lunenburg, Nova Scotia (1753), and the settlements of disbanded soldiers after the American Revolution, down to the refugees from Fascism in the 1930s and '40s, a variety of closely knit German-speaking communities (Amish, Hutterite, Mennonite, Catholic and Lutheran) sprang up during the nineteenth and early twentieth centuries in Ontario and in the prairie provinces. They cultivated their communal traditions in their own language and thus, in spite of the pulls and pressures of history, left significant traces on the literary map of Canada. During the post-war years, however, the emphasis of German-Canadian literary production has shifted from texts of immediate religious and communal utility to the artistic expression of sensitive, often isolated individuals (many of whom found their way to Canada in the mass migration movement of the 1950s). In this paper I set out to investigate why and how some of these recent German-Canadian writers were able to withstand the attraction of the more dominant (usually Anglo-) Canadian literature. I conclude with the question of whether "multi-culturalism" offers a real chance for the minority writer abroad to resist a second (i.e., cultural) emigration.

The concept of "multiculturalism" seems to offer a liberal solution to communal conflict and strife. From a European perspective, it has greatly helped to disentangle the latent or open antagonisms in Canada and elsewhere between people of different ethnic origins and mental roots. Our symposium discusses both the reliability and the fallacy of

133

these assumptions mainly on a social level. Whether "multiculturalism" is an equally soothing and pacifying idea for an individual who is existentially caught between two or more cultures is a more involved question. Beyond general sociological or political considerations, a possible answer can best be approached through literature, the subtlest and most distinct medium of individual self-expression. Since 1945, Canadian literature has presented many instances of this conflict, due to a considerable influx of immigrants from all over the world. They brought their cultural baggage along, their ways of living, dressing, eating and speaking, singing and feeling, and were usually exposed to one of the two dominant "solitudes" of the new country, the English or the French. Unless these immigrants were immediately received by some intact community of countrymen, they were thus faced with a need for a "second emigration" – that is, cultural adaptation and transformation in order to fit in with a new environment. Some of the immigrant writers resisted this "second emigration," at least in their creative works. They did so for various reasons – and this is where I have to limit my scope. I will speak of a few German immigrants to post-war Canada, who, blessed and burdened with a cultural tradition that had led from Romantic idealism to the reality of Auschwitz, would still not discard their literary heritage and tenaciously kept on rewriting, repairing and reconstructing the language of Luther and Goethe, Kafka and Brecht, albeit in a new country. This they did, knowingly or not, against a background of German-Canadian writing[1] that had anticipated some of the post-war immigrants' problems but had also essentially differed in many respects.

My selection will trace this cultural and linguistic conflict in poems which, implicitly or explicitly, reflect the medium and the process of writing poetry and might, therefore, be termed "poetological."

The first poet to be presented on this backcloth is, in fact, a forerunner of the post-war immigrants. Jakob Warkentin Goerzen was born in Ukraine and came to Canada in 1927, where, with his Mennonite parents, he was received into a traditional German-speaking community. He studied in Edmonton during the war and entitled his dissertation "Low German in Canada." His poem "Englisch und Deutsch" ("English and German") expresses a still-unbroken, romantic attitude to his native tongue.

ENGLISCH UND DEUTSCH

In der englischen Sprache
Prägte ich Stunden des Schauerns;
In der deutschen ergoss sich die Seele
In Zeiten der Freude, des Trauerns.

Auf Englisch sah ich den Mond
Im Osten die Staffeln erklimmen,
 Sah auch das Schwelen gespenstig
In dunkelnden Gründen verglimmen.

Doch sprach erst die Liebe,
Sangen die lustigen Vöglein im Walde,
Lebte der Frühling von neuem,
Lebte die blühende Halde:

So sprühte die Sprache
Des wahrlich Erhaben und Schönen,
Da mussten die Mutterworte
Doch alles adeln und krönen!

ENGLISH AND GERMAN

In English I passed
Hours of awe.
In German my soul spoke
In times of joy and woe.

In English I saw the moon
Climb her steps in the east
And saw the spectral glow
Fade in the darkening furrow.

Yet when love spoke,
When the gleeful birds sang in the wood,
When spring took a new lease,
When the hillside blossomed again:

Then sparkled the language
Of the truly beautiful and sublime,
Then all must be ennobled and crowned
By the words of the mother tongue.
(Jakob Warkentin Goerzen; translated by G. Stilz)

GERHARD STILZ

The poem is not very lucid in its imagery and not fully disciplined in its metre. The most difficult word is *Schauern* (line 2). It is supposed to characterize the poet's feelings as far as they can be expressed in English. Stanza 2 enlarges on these feelings, which obviously are in some way opposed to the expressive qualities attributed to German, namely joy and sadness. If anything can be derived from the images of the rising and the setting moon (that are said to lend themselves to English) it is the feeling of awe and terror. Goerzen obviously takes them to be the mixed modes of external, strange and unclear perceptions. In contrast, the German language is said to express the deep inner feelings of the soul (stanza 1), of love and spring (stanza 3), of the truly sublime and beautiful (stanza 4). In Goerzen's praise of his German native tongue as the language of the soul and of the true metaphysical, vital feelings link up with popular romantic notions of language that had been once formulated by Herder and Humboldt and had been trivialized and conserved in traditional communities and national institutions well beyond the turn of the century. What Goerzen's eulogy does not take into account is the perversion and exploitation of language by German fascism. His statement can therefore be regarded as a naive poem, the innocent repetition of a cliché within a secluded traditional community.

A much more deeply involved concern for the German language and its immediate past is formulated in Ernst Loeb's poem "Meine Sprache" ("My Language"). Loeb, who was born in Andernach on the Rhine in 1914, had escaped Hitler's racism to the United States in 1936, where he was able to study. He remained passionately committed to German language and literature, particularly to Goethe and Heine. He taught at various American and Canadian universities and was finally offered a chair at Queen's University, Kingston, Ontario. His poem "Meine Sprache" starts, not unlike Goerzen's encomium, with notions of purity and primaeval perfection that he found in his German native tongue. But then a complaint follows, full of pathetic woe, of the defilement and prostitution of the German language by liars, brutes and murderers.

MEINE SPRACHE

So warst du mein:
In deines Frühlichts vergoldendem Strahl
Lag erster Wachheit Wonne und Qual, –
So perlenrein.

Du warst das All:
Warst Form, in die sich das Herz ergiesst,
Die Perle, die Gottes Welt umschliesst, –
Noch vor dem Fall.

So kam die Nacht,
Die dich, von heiliger Flamme durchglüht,
Hinab in den Dunstkreis der Lüge zieht, –
Zur Dirne macht.

Wie weh das tut
Denn dich, die mir mitten im Herzen stand,
Dich sah ich in grober, schuldiger Hand, -
Getaucht in Blut.

Wie nagt die Pein,
Dass Niedrigkeit dich in Klauen hält,
Der Schmutz ihrer Seele dein Licht verstellt, –
Und bist doch mein!

Denn das weiss ich:
Aus Tiefen sich sehnend, höhenwärts,
Das wunde, wartende, jubelnde Herz
Spricht nur durch dich . . .

MY LANGUAGE

You were mine:
In your early morning's gildening ray
I first became aware of bliss and pain, –
Pure like a pearl.

You were the cosm:
The form in which my heart unfolds,
The pearl that God's world ever holds, –
Before the Fall.

Thus came the night
That dragged you, glowing with a holy flame,
Down into shadowy mists of lies and shame, –
Made you a whore.

I'm deeply hurt:
For you, encompassed in my mind,
I saw you roughly handled and confined, –
Submerged in blood.

My pain persists,
For base usurpers wield your might,
Their dirty minds obstruct your light, –
And yet you are mine.

For this I know:
From lowest depths new life will start,
My sorely waiting, exultant heart
Needs only you.

(Ernst Loeb; translated by G. Stilz)

The style and the images in Loeb's complaint still rely on the romantic pathos that had been used and perverted by the Fascists. Loeb tries to reclaim and revive the transcendent quality that rings in such metaphysical turns of phrase as "von heiliger Flamme durchglüht" (stanza 3), "dich, die mir mitten im Herzen stand" (stanza 4), "der Schmutz ihrer Seele dein Licht verstellt" (stanza 5). He obviously hopes that the old romantic idealism of German poetic language can be re-established by simply insisting on it, in spite of the perversions that it had allowed and been subjected to. Consequently, Loeb ends his poem by declaring solemnly and emphatically that his German native tongue, in spite of the defilement it has suffered, will remain the language of his heart. And his idealistic style confirms his trust in the survival of the romantic tradition, even after the Holocaust (stanza 6). Loeb's poem has its touching and heroic qualities, but it is a desperate and therefore a doubtful attempt to redeem a language and, moreover, a poetic style, that had become an easy prey to Fascist ideology. This redemption is sought exactly in those emotional clichés and clouds of pathos that had invited its perversion. Loeb's poem is therefore a complaint, a confession and a confirmation, but it is not a profound criticism of language.

We get somewhat closer to a revised style when we read the two poems by Anton Frisch. He was born, the son of an Austrian father and a Hungarian mother, in Italy in 1921 and educated in England and Canada, where he arrived in 1940. He wrote and published poems in English, French and German, and being nowhere quite at home, he is certainly not as "resistant" in the choice of his creative language as some of the other German-Canadian poets are. Nevertheless, Anton Frisch realized that a reconsideration of linguistic implications, of style and literary traditions, is necessary in order to arrive at valid and authentic cultural statements in a new land. This can be best shown in his two poems dealing with German songs.

The first one, "Deutsche Lieder," is very short and contains only one single statement which, however, is reflected in poetic form:

Deutsche Lieder klangen durch die kalten
Winterabende am Sternensee.
Nordlichtbrände brannten und die alten
Worte schallten überm Schnee.

Hier im Norden, freilich, klingen Lieder,
Deutsche Lieder, seltsam fremd und weh.
Auch der Wald erkennt kaum wieder
Halbverwischte Spuren im Schnee.

German songs were ringing through the cold
Winter nights on starry lake.
Polar lights were glowing and the old
Words resounded on the snow.

Here up North, however, sounds of song,
German song, are strangely sad and out of place,
As the forest hardly recognizes
Tracks in snow that change their face.

(Anton Frisch; translated by G. Stilz)

An experience is described here that has often been expressed by other Canadian poets as well: the alienation of human words in the vast country. Anton Frisch feels this effect to be particularly stirring in a German context. Songs sung during a cold winter night in the Canadian North sound unusually strange and woeful to him. They seem to have changed from their homey character beyond recognition. A sense of cultural insufficiency and disorientation is encountered in an exposed environment. Traditional techniques of finding comfort and reassurance, like the singing of old and familiar songs, seem inappropriate and ineffective. The last line ("Halbverwischte Spuren im Schnee") carries the poetic sting. Although it rhymes – as the preceding lines do – it is at odds with the metrical pattern of the poem, thus closing the song on a stumbling, discordant note of loss.

Frisch's other poem, "Es flossen einst die Tränen," is even more reflective and poetically vital. It adapts and transforms Wilhelm Müller's famous *Volkslied* "Am Brunnen vor dem Tore" set to music by Franz Schubert:

Es flossen einst die Tränen
Am Brunn beim Lindenbaum.
Der Wind sang durch die Blätter
Ein Lied vom Lebensraum.

Dann klang durchs Land der Schande
Ein anderes, grausig Lied:
Du Volk im Deutschen Lande,
Du warst's, das uns verriet.

Und Kindeskindern klang noch
Dies Lied der Schande nach.
Die Lind am Brunnen sang es,
Sang von der Deutschen Schmach.

Und wenn nach vielen Jahren
Die Welt das Lied vergisst,
Siehst eine Linde? Weine,
Wenn du ein Deutscher bist.

Tears were flowing once
At the well near the linden tree,
The wind sang through the leaves
A song of lebensraum.

Then another, a terrible song
Was heard in the land of shame:
It is you who betrayed us,
You people in Germany.

This song of shame kept ringing
With us, the grandchildren.
It was sung by the linden tree
Near the well, singing of German shame.

And if, after many years
The world should forget this song,
Should ever you see a linden tree –
Weep, if you are a German.

(Anton Frisch; rough prose translated by G. Stilz)

Anton Frisch takes up the romantic *Volkslied* quality of poetic diction, he repeats the nostalgic images of the well and the city gate, the linden tree and the wind singing through its leaves (stanza 1). Then (stanza 2), he questions the cosiness of this romantic reminiscence by referring – in the same metre – to the terrible song of *Lebensraum* that has exploited and betrayed the German idealist cultural tradition. German songs (he continues, in stanza 3) have thereby become songs of shame. Literary images, themes and genres, even language itself, are now reverberating the barbarity of a fallen civilization. And the vague nostalgic sadness that used to accompany the old romantic song will now, he says (stanza 4), to Germans become a very real cause for weeping whenever they see a linden tree.

In this poem, Anton Frisch succeeded in giving shape to the awareness that the German cultural tradition could not simply be continued or revived after the war along the old idealist lines. Like the post-war generation at home, a German writer abroad had to accept and reflect on the ruin. Only by acknowledging shame and guilt could he possibly arrive at a new status of credibility and integrity. That this remarkable statement should have been expressed in the lines of its criticized object, the *Volkslied,* is certainly a significant and a redemptive feature. Quite obviously, this poetic gesture could be effectively produced only in German.

The new language that is needed to come to terms with an old and troublesome cultural tradition has perhaps been best and most convincingly explored among post-war German-Canadian writers by Walter Bauer (1904-1976). In him we find a most creative conjunction of linguistic and poetic sensibility (schooled in the free verse of German expressionists) with a personal concern for a new beginning governed by a strong sense of responsibility for the future of humanity. Walter Bauer, born in Merseburg, had been a successful novelist and poet in Germany before and during the war. Suspicious of social-democratic allegiances, he could not help being drafted into the German army. After years of grinding war experiences on the Western and Eastern fronts (which he

141

set down and published in his diaries in a quiet, modest and clear language anticipating Heinrich Böll), he welcomed the end of the war as a liberation, as a "second creation of the world." He had a good start in the post-war German literary scene with a collection of European tales and biographies of Nansen and Livingstone, but when in 1951 emigration to Canada became possible, he left Germany in order to begin a new life in a new world. Starting as a dishwasher in Toronto, he made his way through various jobs and occupations until he was offered the post of a language teacher at the University of Toronto. His poems, diaries and prose sketches[2] are a meticulous and subtle record of his feelings as an immigrant, as a German burdened with tradition and as a human being trusting in a better future for humankind. Walter Bauer himself wrote only very few poems in English, but much of his work has been translated by his student and friend Henry Beissel.[3] Walter Bauer epitomizes the predicament and the development of the German-Canadian writer after the war.

Soon after his arrival, he expresses, in his poem "Canada," an awareness of the cold message that is native to this "new" country. The first experience is disillusion:

KANADA

Diese Erde beschenkt dich nicht
Mit der Weisheit Platons,
Aristoteles lebte hier nicht.
Dante wanderte nicht hier durch das Inferno,
Begleitet vom brüderlichen Virgil.
Und Rembrandt? Nicht hier der Glanz des grossen Herrn
Und dann der betrunkene ungekannte König im Exil.

CANADA

This earth does not bestow
The wisdom of Plato.
Aristotle did not live here.
Nor did Dante pass here through the inferno
In the fellowship of Virgil.
And Rembrandt? Not here the glamour of great lords
And the drunken unknown king in exile.

(From *The Price of Morning*, translated by H. Beissel)

Canada turns out to be older than Europe. It does not bestow the human wisdom of classical European culture. But it has different news in store, as Bauer points out in this poem:

The arctic expresses the sum total of all wisdom:
Silence. Nothing but silence. The end of time.

This, for a start, is a terrible discovery ("Bitter and icy and not to everybody's taste"). It corresponds to the cold *horror vacui* that other poets (and ordinary people) have experienced in the vastness of Canada. But, to Walter Bauer, it is a welcome message. Having left behind a world too complicated, this is a basis on which he can start anew, searching for the fundamental truths of life. First, however, he must find himself, and he does so in Toronto,[4] which is discovered to mean "meeting-place," derived from an Indian word. Walter Bauer meets himself, and others, but, above all, his own self. And, as an unknown immigrant, he uses his isolation to "reconcile himself to his own existence." This highly important step of taking stock of his own identity did not prevent him from learning a new language. But it was, above all, his own language that needed to be re-learnt, reshaped and cleansed, and which had to be imbued with a clear sense of direction.

On this basis, Walter Bauer is able to draw distinctions in his troubled German past. In his poem "Ich lebte dort, jetzt leb ich hier," he realizes that his father and mother represented the age-old conflict in Germany between loving care and cold discipline:

Ein alter Emigrant sagt:
ICH LEBTE DORT, JETZT LEB ICH HIER
Dazwischen liegt das Meer – doch nur das Meer?
Ich leb in einem andern Land, einst lebt ich dort,
Vertauscht man, wenn man ging, nur Haus und Ort?

Mein altes Land, vertraut und lieb,
Es ist mir lieb, wie mir die Mutter war,
wenn ich sein gedenke, denk ich: Mutterland.
Als Vater hat es mich geschlagen und verbannt.

Als Mutter sagt' es: "Lieber Sohn."
Als Vater schrie es: "Beug dich, stummer Knecht,
Geh!" – und ich ging – "Stirb!" – und ich starb
mit tausenden im Grab.

143

GERHARD STILZ

Dem Vaterlande danke ich's, wenn ich den Vater
nicht mehr hab.

Das Mutterwort war Liebeswort,
Es hüllte mich in Wärme ein, so Tag wie Nacht,
Es schenkte mir die Erde, Licht und Fluss
und ersten Kuss
Und alles, was mir unvergesslich bleiben muss.

Das Wort des Vaters fuhr mich an,
Das Vaterland nahm mir den Bruder und den Freund,
Es peitschte und verwarf mich, überflüssigen Sand,
Es prahlte, brannte, hängte – in der Geschichte
ist das Gross und Ruhm genannt.
Mein Mutterland wird nie in mir vergehen,
Jedoch mir bangt davor, das Vaterland zu sehen.

An old emigrant says
I lived there, now I live here,
In between is the sea – but only the sea?
I live in a different country, once I lived there,
Did I swap, when I went, only my house and place?

My old country, intimate and dear,
It's dear to me as my mother was,
Yes, when I went I remember it, I think: motherland.
As a father it has beaten and banished me.

As a mother it said: "Dear son."
As a father it shouted: "Bend down, dumb servant,
Go!" – and I went – "Die!" – and I died
With thousands in the grave.
I owe it to the fatherland, if I don't have a father any more.

Mother's word was love's word,
It shrouded me in warmth, day and night,
It presented me with the earth, with light and river
And with the first kiss
And everything that will be unforgettable to me.

The word of my father attacked me,
The fatherland took my brother and my friend,
It flogged me and rejected me, superfluous sand,
It bragged, burned and hanged –
Which is called great and glorious in history.

144

My motherland will never fade in me,
But I am scared of seeing my fatherland again.

(From *Klopfzeichen;* translated by G. Stilz)

The emotional reorientation from a "fatherland" to a "motherland," with all its implications for language, culture, human interaction and personal allegiances, is shown to be vital for the German post-war generation. It is important that hope can be seen in the "motherly" virtues of Germany: hope in the "mother" tongue. Walter Bauer feels encouraged not to let Auschwitz be the last word, neither in letters nor in deeds. Opposing Adorno, he suggests, in "Verses from a University":

After Auschwitz
Someone said, there is
Nothing left. –
After Auschwitz
I dare say, whisperingly,
There is
The beginning of human words.
The search for them will now
Never cease.

(From *Lebenslauf,* p. 118; translated by G. Stilz)

Walter Bauer suggested this in German, the language of Auschwitz. And he further motivated and explained his matured love of the German language in his sequence "Interview with an Elderly Man":

Ob er eine Sprache
Besonders liebe? –
"Ja. Die Sprache meiner Kindheit.
Die Sprache der Quellen tief in mir
In der Erde von Jahrtausenden.
Die Sprache meiner Eltern und
Meiner ersten Liebe und mancher danach.
Die Sprache meiner alten Freunde,
Die Sprache, die in mir fließt wie mein Blut
Atmet, lacht, klagt,
Die zu meinen Zeiten geschunden wurde.
Die Sprache, in der das Waser des kleinen Flusses rann.
Die Sprache, in der die ersten Frühlinge kamen.
Die Sprache, in der die Männer des zwanzigsten Juli

145

Neunzehnhundertvierundvierzig
Die Würde des Menschen verteidigten.
Die Sprache, in der Mildred Harnack vor ihrer
Hinrichtung rief: Und doch liebe ich Deutschland.
Ja. Die Sprache meiner späteren und letzten Jahre,
In der ich vieles frisch zu sagen lernte.
Die Sprache, die mich als Gast empfing und reich bewirtete,
Mir Brot und Wasser gab und manche guten Dinge.
Die Sprache, in der ich zu Studenten spreche,
Zu Freunden, zu Unbekannten.
Die Sprache, die mir grossmütig erlaubte,
In ihr zu Hause zu sein
Als Gast, als Emigrant, als Freund der Welt."

Whether he liked one language
In particular?
"Yes, the language of my childhood.
The language of the springs deep in myself
In the earth of milleniums.
The language of my parents and
Of my first love and many more after.
The language of my old friends,
The language that flows in me as my blood,
Breathes, laughs, wails,
Which was ill-used in my time,
The language in which the water in the rivulet ran.
The language in which the first springs came.
The language in which the men of the twentieth of July
Nineteen hundred and forty-four
Defended the dignity of man.
The language in which Mildred Harnack cried
Facing her execution: And yet I love Germany.
Yes. The language of my later and last years,
During which I learnt much to say in a new way,
The language that received me as a guest and hosted me abundantly,
Gave me bread and water and many good things,
The language in which I talk to students,
To friends, to strangers,
The language which permitted me generously
To be at home in it
As a guest, as an emigrant, as a friend of the world.

(From *Interview with an Elderly Man;* translated by G. Stilz)

Here the redeeming factors for German are not only that it is the
native tongue he was born into or that it is the language of his old friends,

but he makes it clear that the language that has suffered together with him has also been the language of others who suffered even more and, under adverse circumstances, paid with their lives. And he finally praises English as his second language for having allowed him to be at home in it, as a guest, as an emigrant, as a friend of the world. All this Walter Bauer explains in simple, plain words, whose cadences are assembled in unpretentious free verse, very close to prose. What he aims at is a new poetry of honesty, sincerity, of individualism and humanity. Walter Bauer relies on his native tongue for poetic expression, but he keeps his mind open and transcends provincialism and nationalism in the light of intercultural human compassion. "I don't understand the language," he opens one of his poems. And he concludes:

I speak only my mother tongue
another one passably, others not so well
But I understand, it seems, all languages.
If I look across the world
And the world becomes one.

(From *Klopfzeichen*, p. 72; translated by G. Stilz)

In this review of a few post-war German-Canadian poets, I have moved away from the defense of German as a language that, of an imposing European tradition, allows the poetic expression of the "truly sublime and beautiful," and I have arrived at the plea for German as a language that, rising from cinders and silence, is plain, clear and precise but can still serve as a provisional home and meeting-place for isolated emigrants.

Whether the contemporary Canadian policy of "multiculturalism" will strengthen creative activities in this field is difficult for me to forecast. Authors having arrived in Canada at a young age, but also the young generation of Mennonite writers, have, with a very few exceptions, decided to follow the "laws of the market" and write in English. A creative revival of German writing in Canada seems rather unlikely at the moment. The multiculturalism policy will and should, however, facilitate the necessary research and documentation on German-Canadian writing – a task that has barely been outlined. The historical approach, however sentimental it may appear, will add valuable insights to the awareness and full appreciation of Canada's difficult identity.

GERHARD STILZ

NOTES

1 The study of German-Canadian history and literature has in recent years attracted a notable number of scholars in several Canadian universities. Although substantial archival efforts and a considerable amount of research into textual sources are still needed, much valuable ground has been recovered since the 1970s. For basic materials, introductions and case studies of German-Canadian writing, I would like, above all, to refer to Rudolf A. Helling, *A Socio-Economic History of German-Canadians*, Beihefte zur Vierteljahresschrift für Sozial- und Wirtschaftsgeschichte, Nr. 75 (Wiesbaden: Steiner, 1984); Heinz Kloos, ed., *Ahornblätter: Deutsche Dichtung aus Kanada* (Würzburg: Holzner, 1961); William de Fehr et al., eds., *Harvest: Anthology of Mennonite Writing in Canada* (Altona, Manitoba: Friesen, 1974); Georg K. Epp, ed., *Unter dem Nordlicht: Anthologie des deutschen Schrifttums der Mennoniten in Kanada* (Winnipeg: The Mennonite German Society of Canada, 1977); Lawrence Klippenstein and Julius G. Toews, eds., *Mennonite Memoirs: Settling in Western Canada* (Winnipeg: Centennial Publ., 1977); John L. Ruth, *Mennonite Identity and Literary Art* (Scottdale, Pa.: Herald Press, 1978); Frank H. Epp, *Mennonites in Canada 1920-1940: A People's Struggle for Survival* (Toronto: Macmillan, 1982); Peter Liddell, ed., *German-Canadian Studies: Critical Approaches* (Vancouver: Canadian Association of University Teachers of German, 1981); Hartmut Froeschle, ed., *Nachrichten aus Ontario* (Hildesheim: Olms, 1981); Walter Riedel, ed., *The Old World and the New: Literary Perspectives of German-Speaking Canadians* (Toronto: University of Toronto Press, 1984); Hartmut Froeschle, *Die Deutschen in Kanada: Eine Volksgruppe im Wandel*, Eckart-Schriften, Heft 101 (Wien: Österreichische Landsmannschaft, 1987); *Deutsch-Kanadisches Jahrbuch / German-Canadian Yearbook*, ed. Hartmut Froeschle (Toronto: Historical Society of Mecklenburg, Upper Canada, 1 [1973] ff); Karin Guerttler und Friedhelm Lach, eds., *Deutsch-Kanadische Studien: Annalen*, Vols. 1-6 (Montreal: Université. de Montréal, 1976-1987); Deutsch-Kanadische Schriften, Reihe A: Belletristik, eds. H. Boeschenstein, G. Friesen, H. Froeschle, 1(1978) ff.; Reihe B: Sachbuecher, eds. H. Froeschle, V. Peters, 2 (1981) ff.; A comprehensive bibliography of German Canadiana compiled by Hartmut Froeschle and Lothar Zimmermann is forthcoming.
2 Walter Bauer, *Klopfzeichen: Gedichte* (Hamburg: Tessloff, 1962); *Fremd in Toronto: Erzählungen und Prosastücke* (Hattingen: Hundt, 1963); *Ein Jahr: Tagebuchblätter aus Kanada* (Hamburg: Merlin, 1967); *Lebenslauf: Gedichte 1929 bis 1974* (München: Desch, 1975).
3 "Eight Poems Written in English," by Walter Bauer, are included in the obituary issue of *The Tamarack Review* 76 (Toronto: University of Toronto Press, 1977). The bulk of Henry Beissel's authorized translations has been published in *The Price of Morning* (Vancouver: Prism, 1968) and *A Different Sun* (Ottawa: Oberon Press, 1976).
4 "Toronto heisst Treffpunkt," *A Different Sun*, p. 27.

Folklore as a Tool of Multiculturalism

CAROLE CARPENTER

With the establishment of the federal multiculturalism policy in 1971, folklore rapidly became a primary means of demonstrating the cultural character of this country, of displaying interest in and concern for the diversity of cultural groups within our borders seeking recognition, and, overall, of proselytizing the mosaic concept of Canadian culture. Yet, this concentration – amongst the public, scholars and politicians alike – arose in a country that had never accepted such grass-roots, common traditions of the average citizen as a legitimate expression of culture generally, let alone of its own national culture.

In this paper I explore the roots of this paradox; the reasons for the various uses of folklore by government, scholars and members of different cultural groups; and, most significantly, the effect of this use on the way Canadians view themselves and their culture. The particular ways in which folklore has been employed have promoted differences and dissension over commonalities and cohesion despite the great potential for the reverse. Further, Canadian folklore scholarship as well as cultural studies more broadly have suffered because of the prevailing approach to multiculturalism. Canadians think of their culture in terms of rhetoric rather than reality, and are the poorer, quite immediately and personally, in their sense of identity as a result. The direct consequence is that Canadians have an unrealistic or unrealized understanding of themselves and others as cultural beings and cannot, therefore, achieve true, functional multiculturalism, though they espouse it as their cultural ideal.

The history of this situation, the related evolution of Canadian folklore studies, and the specific uses of folklore in supporting and promoting multiculturalism, have been documented at length elsewhere.[1] Here it is important first to clarify what the scholarly folklorist means by the term *folklore*, then to summarize the historical situation and indicate its direct applicability to the dynamics of contemporary Canadian culture.

Folklore can perhaps be best understood by the non-specialist as the oral traditions of a people. In current scholarly usage, it includes all those cultural artifacts – be they oral, material or behavioural – that exist amongst a group of people who learn them through oral/aural means or through observation and imitation, and who identify with and through these artifacts, which they consider traditional. The term *folklife* is frequently employed in reference to the material culture, customs and general way of life characteristic of a folk group, the specification of which will become clear in the course of this discussion.

A profound and pervasive association of folklore with ethnicity has typified Canadian attitudes toward and dealings with this cultural material. Yet there long have been many Canadians for whom ethnicity is not a major aspect of their identity. Some may be scions of early settlers, while others are more recent arrivals who, for a variety of reasons, have actively rejected their heritage cultures.[2] Still others consciously seek to acquire a Canadian identity or feel that they have one. The French Canadians are a case in point here, for they do not see themselves as preserving a foreign ethnicity. Rather, their "homeland" – the heartland of their culture – is Quebec, and the cultural patterns of their distinct society are far less retentions of old-world traditions than they are indigenous creations and adaptations of cultural artifacts transported here and transformed to suit the new circumstances.

As a consequence of the equation of folklore with ethnicity, there have long been many Canadians identified with the mainstream[3] who have associated folklore with exotic, sometimes alien, certainly distinctive others who are, then, considered to be the folk. Linguistic, regional or religious subcultures are included amongst these others, all of whom are marginal, so that those who have been the norm, have been in control and have wielded cultural clout have generally considered folklore to be the quaint and charming traditions of someone else, not themselves. Consequently, Canadians-at-large have been, and today continue to be, less culturally aware than is desirable since they fail to recognize and celebrate their own oral traditional heritage (only part of which for anybody is ever ethnic). This failure makes them considerably less likely to develop a real appreciation for the traditions of minorities within their midst, and leaves most Canadians basically ignorant of their operative culture and unfulfilled as cultural beings.

Culture involves much more than ethnicity, but Canadians often do not associate their strong attachments to various regional, international, life-cycle, occupational and other groupings as part of their personal cultural identification. Yet, such they are, and, for many Canadians, strong they are as well. For instance, because of their age, teenagers across Canada share much in common culturally despite their differing heritage traditions; or that farmers throughout our country have similar patterns of life and in some ways share much the same orientation to their precarious existence whatever their ethnicity.

If Canada is ever to foster anything approximating actual multi-culturalism, then the concept of culture must come to be appreciated in its fullness so that groups defined by any number of shared factors (such as geography, language, age, religion, education, gender, occupation, race, religion, economics) are recognized as viable cultural entities, that is, the possessors of distinctive cultural traditions potentially if not actually equal in value or significance to any that are ethnically defined. All such groupings could be considered by modern folklorists to be folk groups. Canadians – each and every one of us – would then be the folk, possessors of lore and practitioners of customs, as we have been to this date, despite our protestations and lack of awareness. This approach would foster unity while celebrating diversity and combating the dissension and divisiveness evident from 20 years of ethnically defined multi-culturalism.

Throughout our history, however, we Canadians have developed a particular concept of culture that has impeded this pluralistic and essentially humanistic approach. It is imperative that we understand the nature and evolution of our distinctive set of ideas about what culture is, how it operates, and what it means in order that we appreciate its effect on the nation and the necessity to change our established mindset.

The British who found themselves in Canada as administrators or settlers typically considered culture to be that which civilizes human-kind, elevating people above the beasts. The Renaissance and the Age of Reason had clearly established in Europe an equation between culture and the tradition of Western civilization such that culture necessarily *was* the great books, the great works, the great creations of great minds.

It was some *thing*; it was quantifiable; it was acquirable. Along with the mercantile economy, it evolved into a commodity – to be marketed, hoarded, displayed and studied. Some people had more of it than others; indeed, some humans were barely distinguishable from the beasts because they had so little acquaintance with the perceived greatness of civilization.

With such a definition in mind, then, the British conquerors of New France and their descendants naturally assumed that there was nothing worthy of being considered real culture in most of Canada[4] once the French elite left (except perhaps the Church, which, it must be noted, the British handled very carefully, indeed, and the language, which the Quebec Act of 1774 in theory supported). All that might be termed *folklore* – the surviving peasant traditions, the oral historical records that certainly existed, the indigenous celebrations, the family customs and the overall ways of being that had developed in Canada – was certainly not valued by those in authority as worthy of remembering, of preserving and considering as culture. Real culture it was not: there basically was none in Canada except that which was transported here. To paraphrase Northrop Frye,[5] cultural head office was considered to be someplace else.

So it was with the traditions the Loyalists imported from the rebelling southern colonies. Their stories, their ways of doing or making or of entertaining themselves – all their processes of living – were not valued except insofar as they could be documented or were specifically seen as preserving British culture in North America. As a result, the oral histories of migration to Canada, the accounts of the exploits of colourful characters in the War of 1812 and the like have merited but passing references in published works.[6] Canadians with British connections generally came to feel that the pioneer era was not to be remembered in ritual and lore; it was to be overcome and discarded as the country developed into a civilized place.

As the nineteenth century progressed along with industrialization, the traditional peasant way of life faded into oblivion in Britain. Social Darwinists saw this evolution as right and mete, for British culture was viewed as the pinnacle of human achievement and dominant by merit as well as might. Such ideas reinforced the colonial mentality well-entrenched in Canada and kept any notions of culture as an indigenous way of being from emerging in this country in contrast to the ideas positively nurtured in the United States. French Canadians nostalgically remembered their oral traditional culture of *l'Ancien Régime*, but

152

British-based notions of culture prevailed when the nation was officially born and afterward well into the twentieth century.

The Canada First movement and similar nationalistic endeavours of the late-nineteenth and early twentieth centuries failed to dislodge culture from its elitist orientation.[7] Mainstream Canadians still basically thought of culture in elevated terms and denigrated the grassroots, the oral, the common, as insignificant if not downright backward. We conceived of ourselves as young, for we thought of ourselves as culturally immature: there was not much actual greatness here, and we seldom recognized what it was anyway until outsiders celebrated our achievements. Our brand of colonial "cultural cringe" cut us off from our own personal roots, causing us to deny the existence of a Canadian way of life and making us unwilling to accept who we really were or are and what our culture actually was or has come to be. What can be identified as "Canadianness" has seemed to be a phantasmagoria if not a nothingness. Folklore frequently functions in other nations to foster and exemplify national identity,[8] but not so – at least not adequately – for Canadians.

Prior to the multicultural policy, Canadians generally paid attention to their folklore rather selectively. Amongst distinctive regional, linguistic or ethnic groups, folklore was often considered an important means of cultural articulation in the face of majority superiority and/or mainstream domination. Folklore was, in essence, a means to establish and preserve the garrisons typical of Canadian society[9] and increasingly exemplified in ethnic boundaries.[10] Oral traditions were not popularly associated with being Canadian, whatever that meant. Canadian institutions – governments in particular – did, however, display a notable willingness to attend to folklore when it was deemed pragmatic to do so. Still, there was no grass-roots movement to develop Canadianness through folklore. That effort, when it came, was government-derived, politically motivated, and pragmatic rather than passionate.

In the search for means to express our national identity around the 1967 Centennial, Canada followed the romantic nationalist tradition of western Europe in recognizing the need to have indigenous and/or national traditions – our own folklore. The sources, strength and effects of such movements in Germany, Italy, Finland and Ireland in the nineteenth and early twentieth centuries are well-documented elsewhere.[11] Suffice it to say here that folklore has been a powerful factor in fostering and expressing nationalism – some nations were arguably born through folklore.[12] We can today see such movements at work in the

Baltic States, for folklore was a primary means of keeping Latvian, Lithuanian and Estonian identification vigorous throughout the Soviet domination.

Multiculturalism provided the power elites of our country with a source for supposedly Canadian traditions, but at a cost then unknown and as yet untold. Canadians were informed what their identity ought to be (for instance, through the government propaganda programs in the early 1970s that variously proclaimed "our identity is in our diversity, our unity in our multiplicity"). The citizenry as a whole did not feel this Canadianness, did not identify with and through it; rather, in keeping with Canadian respect for authority, they accepted intellectually what they were told from above. Paradoxically, in the search to express identity, the people of Canada lost a sense of owning their culture.

Canadians adopted multiculturalism with seeming alacrity. Certainly there had been any number of individuals and groups clamouring for such an official orientation that would recognize and support the cultural artifacts of their particular sub-cultures.[13] But their commitment to the cultural ideal was insular and not insignificantly based on ethnocentric self-interest rather than, as certainly was possible, any vision of common experiences, of cooperative constructive endeavour here. Minority cultural groups (as they were then known) sought to command attention, recognition and, perhaps most important, funds through demonstrating the extent of their distinctive heritage traditions preserved in Canada. What resulted was large-scale (even if unrecognized) reinforcement of the cultural cringe – real culture once again was seen to be primarily that which was brought from elsewhere. Noted Canadians such as Margaret Atwood might say, "We are all immigrants here,"[14] but some people evidently felt and demonstrated the immigrant condition much more than others. Yet, these demonstrations were supposed to represent Canadianness for everyone.

Folklore rapidly became much more visible throughout the nation, with government, scholars and the public attending to it in various forms. Government policy supported research, publication and preservation by various institutions (most notably for our concerns here, the Canadian Centre for Folk Culture Studies), as well as a wide range of community activities within the groups themselves. One has to wonder why there was this apparent willingness – both official and popular – to recognize folklore as so significant, given the prevailing attitudes in the culture.

Pragmatism prevailed, obviously, for it was easy through folklore to demonstrate interest in a wide variety of cultural groups quickly, and this interest was not deemed likely to compromise either the basic structure of the country or its everyday life, as the contemporaneous alternative of operative bilingualism and biculturalism surely would have.[15] The mosaic concept of the culture clearly offered a definitive means of expressing some of the deepest demands of the Canadian psyche – specifically, to be different from Americans, to be able to say what we are by comparison, and to point to evidence supporting the differences easily and concisely. There were scholars available or engageable to deal with the folklore of many groups, and there was in place even a section (albeit small and, therefore, potentially containable) of the National Museum devoted to this material. The different cultural groups were obviously positively disposed to such attention, for they had brought folklore variously at times and in amounts as part of their cultural baggage of immigration, and a considerable portion of what remained as distinctive about the particular groups and treasured by them was, in fact, their oral traditional heritage.

The immediate effect of this government involvement with folklore I have discussed in depth elsewhere.[16] Several key points are, however, pertinent to the argument here. The period from 1971 to 1975 was largely positive and expansionist, but the type of attention paid the various traditions, and the studies done of them, were problematic for the long term in that the emphasis was typically on description rather than analysis. These problems were evident to scholars by the later seventies, but the social climate did not foster scientific scrutiny of multicultural artifacts. Few, indeed, were the efforts to explain why certain traditions had been maintained or transformed in their adaptation to Canada and what they meant here today. The orientation was on preservation rather than acculturation so that the interactions with what was here were effectively deemed irrelevant. The imported cultural artifacts were, through such selective scholarship, envalued over the indigenous, adapted, or adopted cultural traditions. Canadian or Canadianized culture was once again denigrated. Meanwhile, folklore became more evident in the culture-at-large, officially sanctioned and supported by government rhetoric proclaiming our diversity. Ethnicity was heightened, forming the basis for later problems that were developing, unrecognized by most.[17]

155

Amongst declared as well as decreed "ethnics,"[18] various reactions emerged. There was a sense of freedom to pursue their cultural persuasions, which, humanistically, was laudable. In terms of cultural dynamics, though, this *laissez-faire* attitude often impeded adaptation and encouraged many recent immigrants and their offspring to believe that what they brought to this country was all that was here, and that there was, in effect, nothing here (as, according to legend, Cabot's Portuguese navigator said upon sighting Canada, thereby naming it). Yet, these beliefs were not borne out by reality, as such Canadians frequently recognized upon returning "home" to their lands of origin, where they felt and were considered to be rather foreign: something evidently had happened to them and their traditions in Canada.[19] Further, in any definable ethnic group, there were distinctions, a diversity of sub-groupings, which frequently went at best under-recognized in the public displays and representations that tended to stereotype the entire group. Many supposed ethnics were alienated by such forced identification.[20] The experience in Canada of many minority-group members did not match the official cultural line and the activities that were bred from and supported by that rhetoric.

There was, though, and still is, a very positive and distinctively Canadian aspect to the retention and recognition of heritage cultural traditions in our country: that is, a sense of being in touch with one's roots, of being in a continuity of culture/civilization. This orientation has been characteristic of Canada from earliest times. It was especially well-established through the active choices made at the time of Loyalist settlement (and later variously reinforced) to pursue a destiny distinct from the United States – a destiny of continuing tradition rather than breaking it and beginning anew (or, at least, believing that the nation has done so as Americans tend to do). This sense of cultural connectedness merits cultivation, for it represents the reality of the human condition and is a characteristic of Canadianness that makes our culture especially humane.

Within Canadian society-at-large, by the mid-1970s, there was passive participation in many traditions, but failure to recognize ownership of many, if any, of them. Consequently, there was widespread cultural disenfranchisement except as ethnic. The equation of culture with ethnicity was intensified, leaving many Canadians with the feeling of being without culture apart from American-derived, media-based pop culture. Such feelings result in the bizarre classroom situation I have frequently encountered wherein it is necessary to convince students that they personally possess culture apart from or superseding ethnicity. My students tend to accept and spout forth the rhetoric, and to characterize this nation's culture variously as a mosaic, a tossed salad or a fruit bowl, but to understand little the dynamics of the culture within which they live – what it is and how it operates for them. As a result, my Canadian culture courses are in good measure studies in cultural dynamics and exercises in personal cultural empowerment, made necessary because the Canadian way of life is not widely understood and appreciated owing to a narrow insistence on multiculturalism that precludes recognition of what actually exists in this country and for its people.

After 20 years of the policy, there is operative multiculturalism in notably few aspects of our culture. Culinary customs are the single biggest success, for a diversity of food characterizes the everyday lives of most Canadians. Yet, notably few are those who recognize this cultural trait as distinctively Canadian or particularly significant. The elements of the tradition are not unique, and we as a people are on a quixotic quest for that which is ours alone in order to declare some thing, some pattern, some ideas to be that most elusive of cultural traits – Canadian. At the same time, we officially encourage cultural continuity. Small wonder we are in a state of cultural confusion, still searching for an identity that fits, a Canadianness that resonates with historical reality as well as the contemporary situation.

Folklorists know well the limitations of many studies conducted in the halcyon days of multicultural funding. Much of the research was not motivated by scholarly demands, but rather directed at socio-political ends. Folklore studies in this nation have suffered as a result. Neither the material under study nor the discipline itself has enjoyed significantly greater scholarly recognition or appreciation as a result of work with a multicultural focus. Canadian scholars are not at the forefront of folklore studies in multicultural milieux; they are not shaping cultural policy as a result of their multicultural research; and they are not at the cutting edge of public folklore work internationally. Rather, the Candian Centre for Folk Culture Studies (CCFCS) has been radically reduced in staff and, increasingly over the past 15 years, restricted to museum curatorial activities. In the same period, the American Folklife Centre at the Library of Congress (established in 1975) has developed into an international leader in the conservation and appreciation of intangible heritage. The multicultural stance adapted by the CCFCS did not serve to preserve its government support beyond its fulfilling a political goal, nor to enhance its reputation either at home or abroad, nor to develop informed appreciation of the materials it studies.[21]

But all is not lost. It is in the very nature of folklore to be intensely specific to given peoples and places at the same time as being universal in its characteristics, use and functions. Therefore, just as folklore has been used to reinforce cultural boundaries in this country and has been abused by governments for their own ends, so it could in the future be employed to demonstrate the commonalities amongst the diverse and distinct groupings of Canadians. An example is provided by a recent project undertaken by the Ontario Folklife Centre under contract with the Archives of Ontario. Entitled "Being Here: Stories of Settlement in Ontario during the Past Century," the study involved some 500 interviews with persons age seven to over 90, of various cultural backgrounds, across the province.[22] The stories told by this diverse sampling of the population displayed remarkable thematic consistency. Obviously, the experience of immigration – despite details that specify it to persons, times, places – is a shared cultural process that could effectively create a basis for communion amongst disparate elements.

Such an approach would transcend the artificiality of ethnic exclusivity or uniqueness as articulated by various groups and commonly perceived in Canada as a result of the multicultural programming to date. It would become obvious that each distinguishable group has a myriad of traditions that are variations upon themes played out in slightly different modes by each other group, and that all are responsive to and at least somewhat affected by the larger entity in which they exist. Certainly, this orientation would be truer to the reality of the oral tradition around the world throughout human history. It would provide a foundation, too, for appreciating other cultural groupings as mentioned earlier, and, potentially, for realizing our culture on a personal basis. Each Canadian would thereby be enabled, according to his or her will at different times in varying circumstances, to identify with and through a constellation of cultural expressions yet know that she or he shared this diversity of identities with others all operating within a distinguishable system – Canadian culture. Then there would be functional multiculturalism. Then folklore would be appreciated as it ought be by all those who possess it, that is, by everyone. Then folklorists could pursue their studies in accord with the nature of the material rather than in response to the dictates of the socio-political milieu.

Folklore is a powerful cultural tool because it belongs to the people. Folk wisdom says: "Let me make the songs of my country and I care not who makes the laws."[23] The test of time suggests that strongest is the nation where the laws are in harmony with the songs.

NOTES

1 See, in particular, my articles, "The Ethnicity Factor in Anglo-Canadian Folkloristics," *Canadian Ethnic Studies,* special issue on ethnic folklore in Canada, 7, 2 (1975): 7-18; and, "Folklore and Government in Canada," in *Canadian Folklore Perspectives,* ed. Kenneth S. Goldstein (St. John's: Memorial University, 1978), 53-68; and my book, *Many Voices: A Study of Folklore Activities and Their Role in Canadian Culture* (Ottawa: National Museum, 1979).

2 The reasons for such rejection are many and well-documented by immigration scholars both in Canada and elsewhere. Factors in the emigration circumstance (such as religion, politics and economic malaise) may be highly significant for some persons and the same factors along with others (for instance, host society acceptance, family connections and access to opportunity) may be very important in immigration. The significant point here is, however, that by no means all persons who have immigrated to Canada themselves or whose ancestors came here have a commitment to maintaining the ethnicity of their heritage. Indeed, it is worth noting that many Canadians today have decidedly mixed backgrounds and would be hard-pressed to identify with one ethnicity over another.

3 Of late not commonly used in this country, this term refers to the culture that emerged here, based in the traditions of the two founding European peoples and incorporating their responses to the land and the third founding group, the Native peoples. This culture has evolved over time, but has continued to exist as that to which immigrants must (at least to some extent) and do (despite widespread popular belief to the contrary) adapt. Though its normative aspect is disputable, its existence is not, for this culture is clearly represented in, if nothing else, the set of laws that exist as a shared set of beliefs (one of the primary definitions of culture) governing all Canadians.

4 The Nova Scotia colony was naturally an exception, for a considerable number of highly civilized British people were established there, though the substantial Highland Scottish settlement was considered amongst the under- or uncivilized.

5 From his television documentary, "Journey without Arrival," CBC, 1976.

6 For instance, the volume edited by Arthur Bousfield and Garry Toffoli, *Loyalist Vignettes and Sketches,* published by the Governor Simcoe Branch, the United Empire Loyalists' Association of Canada (Toronto, 1984) to celebrate the bicentennial of Ontario, contains tantalizing remarks, but nothing more about the infamous William Butler or about family stories concerning the rescue of a migrating ancestor whose ship went down en route to Canada. Because they were not documentably verifiable, such accounts did not qualify as historical data and were not valued as culture worthy of preservation even though people themselves cared enough to pass the narratives on by word-of-mouth.

7 One of the best examples is the failure of the First World War battle for Vimy Ridge to enter the national consciousness through narratives as the Gallipoli debacle certainly did for Australia. The success of Albert Facey's autobiography, *A Fortunate Life* (Ringwood, Victoria: Penguin Books Australia, 1981) is an excellent example of the Australians' fascination with the average citizen's story of their great national disaster, which virtually any school child in that nation can recount. Our great victory at Vimy, meanwhile, is largely unknown to Canada's youth, whatever claims Pierre Berton may make in *Vimy* (Toronto: McClelland and Stewart, 1986) for it having been our passage into nationhood.

8 Again Australia offers an excellent example here. The Australian national character is rooted in folklore: in a distinctive Australian dialect; in well-known folk songs; in oral narrative and beliefs about the idealized bush hero. As argued by Russel Ward in *The Australian Legend,* 2nd edition (Melbourne and

159

New York: Oxford, 1975), this lore has been a major, popular and successful factor in the development of a sense of Australianness amongst the people themselves. This argument is expanded by Richard White in *The Invention of Australia* (Sydney/Boston: Allen and Unwin, 1981).

9 As repeatedly and forcefully argued by Northrop Frye directly with respect to Canadian literature in his "Conclusion," *A Literary History of Canada*, Carl Klink, ed. (Toronto: University of Toronto Press, 1976), pp. 821-849, and as evident throughout Canadian culture in *The Bush Garden: Essays on the Canadian Imagination* (Toronto: Anansi, 1971), pp. i-ix.

10 See Fredrik Barth, *Ethnic Groups and Boundaries: The Social Organization of Culture Difference* (Boston: Little, Brown, 1969), for an explanation of ethnic-group boundaries and their maintenance that pertains directly to the dynamics of contemporary Canadian multiculturalism.

11 See, for example, William Wilson's *Folklore and Nationalism in Modern Finland* (Bloomington: Indiana University Press, 1976); and chapter 4, "International Relations and National Distinctions," in Carpenter, *Many Voices*.

12 As claimed by W. Edson Richmond for Finland in "The Study of Folklore in Finland," in *Folklore Research around the World*, R.M. Dorson, ed. (Bloomington: Indiana University Press, 1965).

13 The fact that there were so many minority-cultural representations to the Royal Commission on Bilingualism and Biculturalism in the late 1960s is evidence of this support.

14 In her "Afterword," *The Journals of Susannah Moodie* (Toronto: Oxford University Press, 1970), p. 62.

15 This argument is developed at length in chapters 7, "Identity, Diversity and Unity," and 8, "The Jigsaw Puzzle," of my book, *Many Voices*.

16 See my article, "Folklore and Government in Canada."

17 It is possible that, had the federal government established a multicultural advisory group earlier, contemporary problems of incipient racism, inter-ethnic antagonism, and public opposition to the multicultural policy might have been better anticipated. However, at a later stage, ethnic groups exercised less critical judgement than lobbyist concern.

18 According to Wsevolod W. Isajiw, "ethnicity refers to: an involuntary group of people who share the same culture or to descendants of such people who identify themselves and/or are identified by others as belonging to the same involuntary group" (*Ethnicity* 1 [1970]: 123). This definition has certainly been in operation in Canada where membership in a given ethnic group might not be a matter of choice and personal identification, as evident in the demand for ethnic specification on the Canada census forms.

19 Students in Canadian culture courses I have taught over the past two decades at York University (a particularly diverse campus culturally) have frequently commented on their experience of this phenomenon and its contribution to a realization of their own Canadianness which, at least in part, prompted their desire to study the culture.

20 A vocal and articulate example is Deepa Mehta, a contemporary filmmaker whose first and prize-winning feature film, *Sam and Me* (1991), explores inter-cultural tensions and racism in Canada. Mehta, who is of East Indian heritage, denounces what she calls the "folk-dance syndrome," which serves conveniently to categorize ethnics through a limited view of their heritage traditions. She calls for a recognition of the character complexities within distinguishable groups as necessary to their acceptance as full human beings. See Catherine Dunphy's report of an interview with Mehta, "Exploring Canada's Polite Veneer of Racism," *Toronto Star*, 1 September 1991, pp. C1, 8.

21 I explored the historical reasons for this situation in my recent article, "Politics and Pragmatism in Early North American Folklore Scholarship," *Canadian Folklore / canadien* 13, 2 (1991): 1-15.

22 The collection is housed in both the Ontario Folklore-Folklife Archives located on York University's campus in North York and in the Archives of Ontario, Toronto.

23 As cited on the title page of the first edition of *Old Time Songs of Newfoundland*, edited and published by Gerald S. Doyle (1927).

Part V

Living Canada's Ethnic Diversity

Challenges in Measuring Canada's Ethnic Diversity

PAMELA WHITE

Canada's census is the most complete source of data on the country's ethnic and cultural groups. It is my intent in this paper to discuss some of the problems and challenges Statistics Canada encountered during the testing and content determination phases of the 1991 census (Pryor, et al. 1991). I will also include a brief postscript that describes the media and public responses to the 1991 census ethnic-origin question that occurred during the 1991 enumeration period (May-June 1991).

WHAT IS ETHNICITY?

For several decades, the search for definitions of ethnicity has preoccupied scholars from various fields, especially sociology, psychology and anthropology (for some selective examples see: Cohen 1978; Herberg 1989; Isajiw 1974; Karklins 1987; Lachapelle 1980; Lauwagie 1979; Ryder 1956; Smith 1984; Stephan and Stephan 1989; and Woon 1985). The problems of "objective" versus "subjective" perspectives, ethnic groups vis-à-vis statistical aggregates, ethnic boundaries, and what referents (ancestry, group identification and/or interaction, common values, geography and so forth) determine ethnicity surface throughout the literature. Any review of the literature brings the conclusion that there is no consensus on what criteria determine ethnicity.

The issue is confounded by a very distinct conceptual dilemma both in terms of the concepts themselves and the notions or definitions given to these by the population who are the respondents to any inquiries in this regard. Ancestry, ethnic origin, race, cultural origin and ethnic or cultural identity lead to partitions that can compose, in turn, a "minority," further classified, for example, as ethnic, racial or visible minorities. Such a situation could probably be defined without too much exaggeration as a conceptual maze. As a result, the literature is filled with the notion that this array of concepts involves what are called "soft concepts" or "soft data" with the inference that such concepts are lacking in logical taxonomy, exclusive categories or a singular dimension for measurement. In fact, there are some who hold the view that essentially race and ethnicity cannot be measured accurately (Petersen 1987, 188).

Ethnicity, as one of these concepts, has been pointed out as lacking replicability and shared meaning. Moreover, it has multiple dimensions and overlapping categories. Further, as ethnicity is socially constructed (Lieberson 1985), ethnic identity has relevance within dimensions of time and space. Thus Lieberson and Waters (1988, 252) view it as both a status and a process. They note: "At any given time, we are more likely to see the ethnic state of affairs reported by the population – it is less easy to see the process of ethnic change that is also going on."

Therefore, ethnicity is a classic example of subjectivity in definition because it is based on various grounds, including language, country of birth, country of residence, colour, race and religion. Indeed, for many people in various current societies a question about ethnicity elicits legitimate multiple responses and changing responses over time as the grounds for individual respondents shift.

No doubt, another brave and unrealistic assumption is to assume that ethnicity, however defined, is something that every respondent possesses (Bogue 1985, 364). Lieberson (1985), for example, considered non-responses and the write-in of American in the 1980 United States census to be a logical ethnic ancestry answer for that sector of the population which no longer sees any relevance in the origins of its ancestors or as symptomatic of someone whose family ethnic history had been lost through intergroup marriage, divorce and adoption. This corresponds to the point made by Smith (1984, 122) who notes that in any society a considerable proportion of the population is not able or does not want to respond to questions on ethnic background.

CANADA'S CENSUS ETHNIC QUESTION

Unlike Canada, other countries have only come more recently to collect ethnicity data on their national censuses. For example, the United States census in 1980 and 1990 included questions on race, Hispanic background and ancestral origin (Farley 1991). The 1991 census of Great Britain uses an ethnicity question to distinguish the ethnic minority groups from the rest of the population (Bhrolchain 1990; Sillitoe and White 1990). The Australian census in 1991 did not include an ethnic ancestry question, though one had been part of the 1986 Census (Cornish 1989).

The collection of Canada's ethnic origin data has a long history. The first question appeared on the 1757 census of what is now Nova Scotia. Since Confederation, such a question has been included in every census excepting 1891.

Canada's census ethnic question formats have changed considerably since Confederation. These question-changes are covered in a recent Statistics Canada publication (1991) entitled *Historical Ethno-Cultural Questions.* Interested readers should consult this source, as this paper will not review questions prior to the 1981 census.

Since 1981, Canadians have been able to report more fully their ethnic or cultural origins. The condition requiring the tracing of origins along the "paternal ancestral line" was dropped in 1981, and multiple responses have been accepted since that time. In 1986, for example, 28 percent of Canadians reported being of mixed ethnic background.

In their book, *From Many Strands,* Lieberson and Waters (1988) identify four components of American ethnicity: (1) a person's ancestral roots if he or she could actually trace back to when his or her ancestors came to the New World; (2) what the respondent believes his or her ancestry to be; (3) the ethnic groups with which the respondent identifies; and (4) what others consider the person's ethnicity to be.

Prior to 1986, especially as the question asked respondents to consider their origins on first coming to this continent, the emphasis of the Canadian census question was on the ethnic or cultural roots of the population. In fact, the census question probably prompted respondents to report what they believed or understood and were willing to indicate about their ethnic background.

Thus, in light of the Lieberson and Waters criteria, the Canadian census had a subjective notion of ethnicity, but one with an emphasis on the concept of ethnic roots, ethnic ancestry and origin. Identity was not a focus of the Canadian census. However, in 1986 with the removal of the "on first coming to this continent" temporal reference, ambiguity was created as there was greater emphasis on the idea of "belonging" or affiliation. The divergence in 1986 from the "roots" emphasis to one tied with belonging led Statistics Canada to separate the notion of the roots and ancestry view of ethnicity from that of identity and belonging in the extensive testing conducted prior to the 1991 census.

REVIEW OF 1991 CENSUS TESTING OF ETHNICITY QUESTIONS

Both ancestry and identity questions were tested. However, this was not the only change made to the question during the various testing phases.[1] Question formats were tested, including the use of open-ended and mark-in entry response options. Different groups were included in the list of examples shown on the question. The notion of ancestor was given a reference point, that of parents and grandparents. A variety of testing methods were employed, including focus groups, and modular and multi-stage probability samples tests.

Statistics Canada also held meetings in almost every major city in Canada, and users were invited to give their views regarding the 1991 census content (Statistics Canada 1990). Briefly, one can summarize the public consultation and test results on the ethnic questions as the following:

1. There was no consensus among users regarding preference for ethnic ancestry data as opposed to ethnic identity data. This lack of consensus was obvious at the public meetings, in the written briefs, and among focus group participants.

2. There was no consensus on the format of the question. This included options such as open-ended, mark-box, and list of groups that should be shown as mark-boxes and/or as examples on the questionnaire.

3. Response burden was an issue. When response burden was increased, for example, requiring all respondents to write-in their ethnic and cultural origins and identities, the non-response rate increased.

4. There was a strong tendency on the part of respondents to report Canadian as their ethnic origin and as their ethnic identity.

"CANADIAN" ETHNIC ORIGIN AND IDENTITY

As societies mature and evolve, there is an increasing likelihood that statisticians will be confronted by great variations in responses from the population regarding ethnicity and origin. Some, whose families have been in the country for many generations, believe that their origins or background are not in another place or region of the world, they see themselves as "indigenous" to the society within which they live (Horowitz 1989).

Certainly, Canada is not alone in having to deal with the conceptual roots and fluidity of such a concept as "Canadian." "American," "Australian," "Yugoslav" and "Soviet" are parallel concepts in country situations of multiple ethnic composition that have brought the need to address this increasing dilemma (Anderson and Silver 1989; Horn 1987; Lieberson 1985; Lieberson and Waters 1988).

A review of the instructions to Canadian census enumerators reveals that up until 1951 Canadian and American were not to be listed as ethnic origins (Statistics Canada 1991). Since 1951, both groups have been included in the list of ethnic origins collected by the census. In 1961, "Canadian" appeared in the list of pre-coded entries provided to the enumerator. In response to petitions made before the minister by groups such as the St. Jean Baptiste society who feared that the French count would decline should a substantial number of French Canadians report *"canadien(ne),"* the instructions were changed just six months prior to enumeration. Respondents could still report "Canadian," but this group would not be included in the list of origins read to each respondent by the enumerator.

The reporting of "Canadian" resurfaced as an issue during the release of the 1986 census data on ethnicity. Focus group testing in Toronto, Montreal and Vancouver in 1988 confirmed the tendency on the part of respondents to report "Canadian." In response to the focus group results, the First National Census Test (November 1988) included "Canadian" in the list of mark-in origins shown on the questionnaire (see Appendix 1). The counts for "Canadian" in the First National Census Test (multi-stage probability test, sample size of 80,000 households) ranged from 36 percent in the ancestry question to over 50 percent in the identity question. Please note that "Canadian" was shown on the question as the last entry and after 15 mark-in entries and two write-in spaces (see Appendix 1).

This "Canadian" response (see Appendix 2) came at the expense of British, French and other European groups, all populations of long residence in Canada. Moreover, the group who reported a Canadian ancestry differed from the group having a Canadian identity. In the fall of 1988, over half of those who reported "Canadian" ancestry were Francophones from Quebec. As for "Canadian" ethnic identity, 67 percent reported English as their native tongue, 28 percent reported French as their native tongue, and five percent reported a native tongue other than English or French. As well, the geographic distribution was more representative of the country. Regarding the high Francophone Canadian response, it is important to remember that this test occurred before the failure of Meech Lake.

The Second National Census Test (sub-set of the Labour Force Survey sample, which included 8,000 households) was conducted during the fall of 1989, and contained open-ended ethnic ancestry and ethnic identity questions. On one-half of the sample, "Canadian" was included in the list of example ethnic groups shown on the question (see Appendix 1). The results of this test included the following:

1. Non-response levels were in the 16- to 25-percent range;
2. "Canadian" was reduced in the sample not in receipt of the "Canadian" questionnaire (see Appendix 3);
3. Of those who did respond, a pattern similar to that which had been observed in the first test was evident. Canadian ancestry was reported by Francophone respondents living in Quebec. Canadian identity was more geographically representative of the Canadian population, but did not include a high immigrant component.

While Statistics Canada did not ask respondents why they reported "Canadian," we do have some indication from the focus group sessions and the comments entered onto the questionnaires. The reasons are varied, and include:

1. a notion of *first people*; please note that Aboriginals also reported "Canadian" as their ancestry;
2. Canadian birth of respondent or of "x" generations of ancestors;
3. Canadian residence of respondent or of "x" generations of ancestry;
4. first settlers, especially in Quebec, that is, *les canadien(ne)s*;
5. patriotism, that is, loyalty or adherence to Canada as a nation;

6. citizenship;
7. assimilated, that is, non-ethnic;
8. counter multiculturalism statement;
9. as achieved status vis-à-vis ascribed ethnicity;
10. identification as residual on rejection of other possible ethnic responses;
11. ancestry, that is, relevant previous "x" generations are considered Canadian.

What does the surge in "Canadian" tell us about the measurement of ethnicity in Canada? First, it reveals that ethnic categories are dynamic with respondent self-assessments emerging often counter to the established classification systems. This is clearly demonstrated with the "Canadian" response patterns.

This of course is not a new phenomenon, and in fact occurs for other groups. For example, some individuals of Czech or Slovak background do not agree with the collection of data on the group "Czechoslovakian." Equally, certain members of Canada's Slovenian, Serbian and Croatian communities do not agree with the collection of data on the ethnic group "Yugoslavian." Nonetheless, in 1986, more respondents reported "Czechoslovakian" (44,435) than gave "Czech" (39,635), though fewer gave "Slovak" (27,000). Similarly, "Yugoslavian" (85,575) was a more commonly reported response in 1986 than were the "Serbian" (12,965), "Croatian" (44,165) or "Slovenian" (8,120) groups.[2]

TOUGH CHOICES TO BE MADE FOR 1991 CENSUS CONTENT

Regarding 1991 census content, Statistics Canada had to make some tough choices (Petrie 1989). Respondent burden could not be increased, and indeed Statistics Canada made every attempt to reduce response burden. Also, the agency was required to meet the certain data needs that were mandated under legislation as well as to provide where possible continuity of concepts and data between censuses. The challenge facing Statistics Canada for 1991 was how to balance the needs of users, legislative requirements for data, and test results, while bearing in mind that census content could not be increased.

The decision taken was to repeat the 1986 census ethnic-origin question in the 1991 census. The benefits of this approach included comparability of data between 1986 and 1991. Given that data series was broken in 1981 and again in 1986, such an opportunity to evaluate trends was welcomed by users.

Even though the 1991 ethnic-origin question is based on the notion of ancestry, it is expected that the count for "Canadian" may well rise. In previous censuses this count has ranged about 100,000; however, it is likely to be higher than this in 1991.

The 1991 ethnic-origin question also meets the legislative data requirements of the Multiculturalism Act and the Employment Equity Act. Regarding this later data need, a race question was tested, and it did perform well in both national census tests. However, during a period of fiscal restraint, it is difficult to justify the inclusion of a question that will produce data comparable to that which can be derived from an existing question. Statistics Canada recognizes that not to include a race question may be viewed as being controversial (Stasiulis 1991), but it is one of many difficult choices the agency had to make regarding the 1991 census (Boxhill 1991).

The 1991 ethnic-origin question shows the same list of marked entries as in 1986. In 1986 over 85 percent of all responses occurred in these boxes. Statistics Canada recognizes that groups lacking a mark-in entry do not favour this approach, but it should be noted that a vast majority of the population is accounted for by this selection. Moreover, mark-in entries reduce respondent burden and census processing costs.

Please note that the mark-in entry for Blacks was retained for 1991. This group was added to the list of mark-in groups in 1986 to improve the data on visible minorities. Moreover, this question change met the recommendations of the Abella Commission on Employment Equality. Again, this is an instance where classification and terms do not meet the approval of all respondents and data users. Given the increasing tendency for Blacks to identify as Afro-Canadians, Afro-Americans and Afro-Caribbeans, clearly a more appropriate term may need to be considered and tested during content development for the next census.

However, it must be recognized that there is not a universal adoption of terms by all members of a community. For example, an association may wish respondents to self-identify as Hispanic rather than Mexican or Guatemalan, to report Greek and not Macedonian, or to give Czech or Slovak rather than to write-in Czechoslovakian. However, respondents may not wish to self-identify in this way. Respondents make choices regarding their ethnic background (Waters 1990) and the decisions they take affect census ethnic counts.

Another change for 1991 that has been made is an expansion of the list of ethnic groups shown as distinct categories. For example, we expect to be able to provide data on Canada's Afghan, Kurdish, Tibetan and Maghrebin populations. While these groups were counted before, they were not given separate codes and listed as unique groups. Again, this is another instance where the agency has attempted to better describe the ethnic diversity of Canadians. The other side of this change is an increase in data complexity, which affects the costs of data processing and retrieval.

One aspect that Statistics Canada cannot change for 1991 is the complexity of the ethnic-origin variable. Statistics Canada recognizes that multiple responses are difficult to work with, and that for any one ethnic group the single response counts represent an undercount of the population of a particular ethnic or cultural background.

Yet, multiple-ethnic response is but another facet of Canada's ethnic diversity. The nature of ethnicity is changing in this country, and ethnic groups do not stay unaltered from one generation to the next. Reconsideration by Canadian academics of the roles that multiple responses and intergroup marriage plays in multiculturalism and ethnic change would be a welcome area of research. Certainly American sociologists, including Lieberson and Waters (1988), Waters (1990) and Alba (1990), have extensively examined this aspect of ethnic diversity.

To facilitate access to census data, the 1991 census output program has undertaken major modifications that will improve the 1991 products and services[3] that will be available to users. For example, the 1991 census retrieval system is expected to deliver in a more timely manner both customized and pre-programmed tabulations. The issue of cost, which is always a factor, has not as yet been established, though certainly consortium purchases of Microdata files and data sets will reduce the overall costs for the user. Such an approach was followed to good effect in 1986, and no doubt will be repeated in 1991.

Finally, and certainly the most important: counting all Canadians. Statistics Canada translated the 1991 questionnaire in 31 different languages other than English and French. School kits, fact sheets and other information devices were developed to inform respondents about the census and its importance to all Canadians. The Regional Office staff contact numerous ethnic groups and communities across the country. Coverage is important. I know I depend on all of you to "Count Yourself In On Census Day, June 4, 1991."

PAMELA WHITE

POSTSCRIPT: SUMMER 1991

Media attention and coverage of the 1991 Census ethnicity question focused on three issues: the mark-in entry for Blacks, and the Canadian and Hispanic responses.

In Montreal and Toronto, Black groups voiced objections to the use of the term *Black*, which they viewed to be a racial term and not an ethnic one. How this will affect counts and response patterns will not be determined until the data are released in early 1993.

The Sun newspaper chain launched a series of articles on the Canadian issue in the weeks before the census. Included was a write-in ballot for the Canadian ethnic groups, to which over 5,000 readers mailed a pro-Canadian ballot to the newspaper. As well, several southern Ontario radio stations conducted phone-in talk shows on the issue of multiculturalism and "Canadian" as an ethnic group.

This "Canadian" response was not unexpected, given the attention given to the country's multiculturalism policies by the Spicer Commission (1991) and the lack of Canadian unity following the demise of Meech Lake. The effect of this media attention on respondents' reporting of ethnic ancestry in 1991 will be determined when the data are released in 1993.

The third issue concerned the Hispanic category. The Canadian Hispanic Association, in claiming to have 500,000 members, sought a mark-in entry of "Hispanic." The effect of this coverage on 1991 census counts will be known when the 1991 data are released.

It should be noted that the demands of the Canadian Hispanic Association were in direct opposition to the issue raised by Black groups in Canada. Blacks objected to the generalization of their ethnicity into one category. The Canadian Hispanic Association wanted the census to collect one Hispanic category instead of the ethnic diversity that is currently available to users, such as Mexican, Chilean and Argentinian.

In a more positive light, such media attention provides Statistics Canada with the opportunity to inform users of the data products and services that are available to them. For example, these may assist ethnic associations to use more fully the census data base that contains information on ethnic origin, place of birth and native tongue (in 1991, also religion) to develop and design user-defined ethnic variables. In this way, ethnic groups can derive variables that better suit their needs and so adjust to the changing reporting patterns of respondents.

REFERENCES

Alba, Richard D., "The Twilight of Ethnicity among Americans of European Ancestry: The Case of the Italians." *Ethnic and Racial Studies* 8 (1985): 134-158.

_____. *Ethnic Identity: The Transformation of White America.* New Haven: Yale University Press, 1990.

Anderson, Barbara A., and Brian D. Silver. "Demographic Sources of the Changing Composition of Soviet Union," *Population and Development Review* 15 (1989): 609-656.

Bonacich, Edna. "A Theory of Ethnic Antagonism: The Split Labour Market." *American Sociological Review* (October 1972).

Bogue, Donald J. *The Population of the United States.* New York: The Free Press, 1985.

Booth, Heather. "Which 'Ethnic Question'? The Development of Questions Identifying Ethnic Origin in Official Statistics." *The Sociological Review* 33 (1985): 254-274.

Boyd, Monica. *Ethno-Cultural Questions on the General Social Survey.* Statistics Canada, Centre for Ethnic Measurement, Fall 1991.

Boxhill, Walton O. *Making Tough Choices.* Statistics Canada, non-catalogues publication, 1990.

Bulmer, Martin. "A Controversial Census Topic: Race and Ethnicity in the British Census." *Journal of Official Statistics* 2 (1986): 471-480.

Cohen, Ronald. "Ethnicity: Problem and Focus in Anthropology." *Annual Review of Anthropology* 7 (1978): 379-403.

Farley, Reynolds. *Race and Ethnicity in the U.S. Census: An Evaluation of the 1980 Ancestry Question.* Ann Arbor, Michigan: University of Michigan Population Studies Centre, 1990.

_____. "The New Census Question about Ancestry: What Did It Tell Us?" *Demography* 28, 3 (August 1991): 411-429.

Gans, Herbert. "Symbolic Ethnicity: The Future of Ethnic Groups and Cultures in America." *Ethnic and Racial Studies* 2 (January): 1-20.

Herberg, Edward N. *Ethnic Groups in Canada: Adaptations and Transitions.* Scarborough: Nelson Canada, 1989.

Horn, Ronald V. "Ethnic Origin in the Australian Census." *Journal of the Australian Population Association* 4 (1987): 1-12.

173

Horowitz, Donald, L. "Europe and America: A Comparative Analysis of 'Ethnicity.'" *Revue Européene des Migrations Internationales* (1989): 47-61.

Isajiw, Wsevolod W. "Definitions of Ethnicity." *Ethnicity* 1 (1974): 111-124.

Jiobu, Robert M. *Ethnicity and Inequality.* Albany, N.Y.: State University of New York Press, 1990.

Kallen, Evelyn. "Multiculturalism: Ideology, Policy and Reality." *Journal of Canadian Studies* 17, 1 (1982): 51-63.

Karklins, Rasa. "Determinants of Ethnic Identification in the USSR: The Soviet Jewish Case." *Ethnic and Racial Studies* 10 (1987): 27-47.

Kralt, John M. *Ethnic Origin in the Canadian Census: 1871-1981.* Ottawa: Statistics Canada, mimeo, 1978.

Lachapelle, Réjean "Evolution of Ethnic and Linguistic Composition." In *Cultural Boundaries and the Cohesion of Canada*, edited by R. Breton, J.G. Reitz and V.F. Valentine, 15-43. Montreal: The Institute for Research on Public Policy, 1980.

Lauwagie, Beverly N. "Ethnic Boundaries in Modern States: Romano Lavo-Lil Revisited." *American Journal of Sociology* 85 (1979): 310-337.

Lieberson, Stanley. "Unhyphenated Whites in the United States." *Ethnic and Racial Studies* 8 (January 1985): 159-180.

Lieberson, Stanley, and Mary C. Waters. *From Many Strands: Ethnic and Racial Groups in Contemporary America.* New York: Russell Sage Foundation, 1988.

Petersen, William. "Politics and the Measurement of Ethnicity." In *The Politics of Numbers,* edited by W. Alonso and P. Starr, 187-233. New York: Russell Sage Foundation, 1987.

Petrie, Bruce. *Hansard.* Standing Committee on Multiculturalism and Citizenship, 12 December 1989.

Pryor, Edward T., Gustave J. Goldmann, Michael J. Sheridan and Pamela M. White. "Is 'Canadian' an Evolving Indigenous Ethnic Group?" *Ethnic and Racial Studies* (April 1992).

Nelson, Candace, and Marta Tienda. "The Restructuring of Hispanic Ethnicity: Historical and Contemporary Perspectives." *Ethnic and Racial Studies* 8, 1 (1985): 49-74.

Ryder, Norman. "The Interpretation of Origin Statistics." *Estadistica* 14, 53 (1956): 651-666.

Spicer, Keith. *Citizens Forum on Canada's Future.* Ottawa: Minister of Supply and Services Canada, 1991.

Stasiulis, Daiva. "Symbolic Representation and the Numbers Game: Tory Policies on 'Race' and Visible Minorities." In *How Ottawa Spends,* edited by Frances Abel, 229-267. Toronto: McClelland and Stewart, 1991.

Sillitoe, Ken, and Paul H. White. *Ethnic Group and the British Census: The Search for a Question,* mimeo. London: British Census, 1990.

Smith, Thomas W. "The Subjectivity of Ethnicity." In *Surveying Subjective Phenomena,* edited by C.F. Turner and E. Martin, 117-128. New York: Russell Sage Foundation, 1984.

Statistics Canada. Reference: 1986 Census Dictionary. Catalogue 99-101E/F, Ottawa: Minister of Supply and Services Canada, January 1987.

_____. Reference: Census Handbook. Catalogue 99-104E/F, Ottawa: Minister of Supply and Services Canada, June 1988.

_____. 1991 Census Content Development: Final Report. August 1990.

_____. Canada's Census Ethno-Cultural Questions, 1871-1991. Non-catalogue, Ottawa: Statistics Canada, Centre for Ethnic Measurement. June 1991.

_____. 1991 Census Catalogue. April 1992.

Stephan, Cookie White, and Walter G. Stephan. "After Intermarriage: Ethnic Identity among Mixed-Heritage Japanese Americans and Hispanics." *Journal of Marriage and the Family* 51 (1989): 507-519.

Waters, Mary C. *Ethnic Options: Choosing Identities in America.* Berkeley: University of California Press, 1990.

White, Pamela M. *Ethnic Diversity In Canada.* Ottawa: Statistics Canada, 1989, pp. 92-183.

_____. *National Census Test Results: Ethnic Origin and Ethnic Identity.* Ottawa: Statistics Canada. Unpublished report, 1990.

Woon, Yueng-Fong. "Ethnic Identity and Ethnic Boundaries: The Sino-Vietnamese in Victoria, British Columbia." *Canadian Review of Sociology and Anthropology* 22 (1985): 534-558.

Yancey, William L., Eugene P. Erickson and Richard N. Juliani. "Emergent Ethnicity: A Review and Reformulation." *American Sociological Review* 41, 3 (1976): 391-403.

Yinger, J. Milton "Ethnicity." *Annual Review of Sociology* 11 (1985): 151-180.

NOTES

Co-authored with E.T. Pryor, J.G. Goldman, and M.S.Sheridan, Statistics Canada.

1 1991 census ethnic origin question testing is described in greater detail in E.T. Pryor, G.J. Goldmann, M.J. Sheridan and P.M. White, "Is 'Canadian' an Evolving Indigenous Ethnic Group?" *Ethnic and Racial Studies* (April 1992).
2 Given the recent struggles in Yugoslavia, the 1991 census data may reveal different reporting patterns for the Yugoslavia groups.
3 Statistics Canada, 1991 Census Catalogue, April 1992.

Appendix 1
National census tests questions: Ethnic ancestry

NCT–1

15. What are the ethnic or cultural origins of this person's parents and grandparents?

Mark or print as many groups as apply.

01 ○ French   07 ○ Ukrainian

02 ○ English   08 ○ Dutch

03 ○ German   09 ○ Chinese

04 ○ Scottish   10 ○ Jewish

05 ○ Irish   11 ○ Polish

06 ○ Italian   12 ○ Portuguese

13 ○ North American Indian

14 ○ Métis

15 ○ Inuit (Eskimo)

Continue below →↓

Specify Band or First Nation or Tribe, if applicable (for example, Cross Lake Indian Band, Haida Nation, Inuviakut)

[_____] 1 [ ]

[_____] 2 [ ]

16 ○ Other ethnic or cultural group(s) (for example, Greek, Norwegian, Indian from India or U.K. or Uganda, Vietnamese, Filipino, Mexican, Armenian, Haitian, Lebanese, Japanese)

Specify

[_____] 3 [ ][ ][ ]

[_____] 4 [ ][ ][ ]

17 ○ Canadian

NCT–2, with Canadian

15. What are the ethnic or cultural origins of this person's parents and grandparents?

Specify up to 4 groups, if applicable.

(For example, French, English, Irish, German, Italian, Ukrainian, Jewish, Polish, Chinese, North American Indian, Métis, Inuit/Eskimo, Filipino, Indian from India, Arab, Armenian, Haitian, Mexican, Canadian, Afro-American, etc.)

See guide at end of questionnaire.

Specify ethnic or cultural groups

1

2

3

4

NCT–2, without Canadian

15. What are the ethnic or cultural origins of this person's parents and grandparents?

Specify up to 4 groups, if applicable.

(For example, French, English, Irish, German, Italian, Ukrainian, Jewish, Polish, Chinese, North American Indian, Métis, Inuit/Eskimo, Filipino, Indian from India, Arab, Armenian, Haitian, Mexican, Afro-American, etc.)

See guide at end of questionnaire.

Specify ethnic or cultural groups

1

2

3

4

16. What is this person's ethnic or cultural identity?

Mark or print as many groups as apply.

01 ◯ French 07 ◯ Ukrainian

02 ◯ English 08 ◯ Dutch

03 ◯ German 09 ◯ Chinese

04 ◯ Scottish 10 ◯ Jewish

05 ◯ Irish 11 ◯ Polish

06 ◯ Italian 12 ◯ Portuguese

13 ◯ North American Indian

14 ◯ Métis

15 ◯ Inuit (Eskimo)

➤ *Continue below* ↓

Specify Band or First Nation or Tribe, if applicable (for example, Cross Lake Indian Band, Haida Nation, Inuviakut)

16 ◯ Other ethnic or cultural group(s) (for example, Greek, Norwegian, Indian from India or U.K. or Uganda, Vietnamese, Filipino, Mexican, Armenian, Haitian, Lebanese, Japanese)

Specify

1

2

17 ◯ Canadian

NCT–2, with Canadian

16. What is this person's ethnic or cultural identity?

Specify up to 4 groups, if applicable.

(For example, French, English, Irish, German, Italian, Ukrainian, Jewish, Polish, Chinese, North American Indian, Métis, Inuit/Eskimo, Filipino, Indian from India, Arab, Armenian, Haitian, Mexican, Canadian, Afro-American, etc.)

See guide at end of questionnaire.

Specify ethnic or cultural groups

5

6

7

8

If North American Indian, Métis or Inuit/Eskimo, specify Indian Band or First Nation or Tribe (for example Cross Lake Indian Band, Haida Nation, Inuviakut)

9

NCT–2, without Canadian

16. What is this person's ethnic or cultural identity?

Specify up to 4 groups, if applicable.

(For example, French, English, Irish, German, Italian, Ukrainian, Jewish, Polish, Chinese, North American Indian, Métis, Inuit/Eskimo, Filipino, Indian from India, Arab, Armenian, Haitian, Mexican, Afro-American, etc.)

See guide at end of questionnaire.

Specify ethnic or cultural groups

5

6

7

8

If North American Indian, Métis or Inuit/Eskimo, specify Indian Band or First Nation or Tribe (for example Cross Lake Indian Band, Haida Nation, Inuviakut)

9

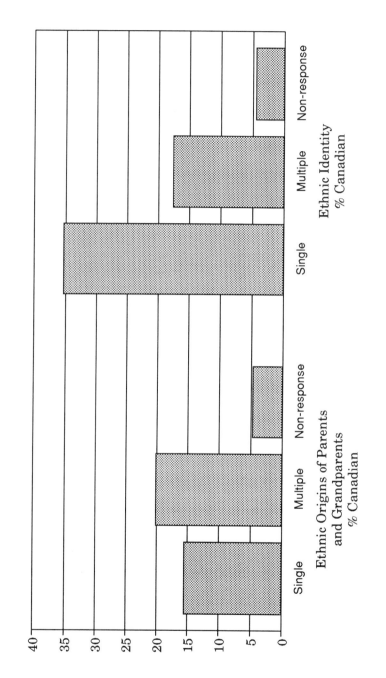

Appendix 2
Response "Canadian" to ethnic ancestry and
ethnic identity questions, First National Census Test, 1988

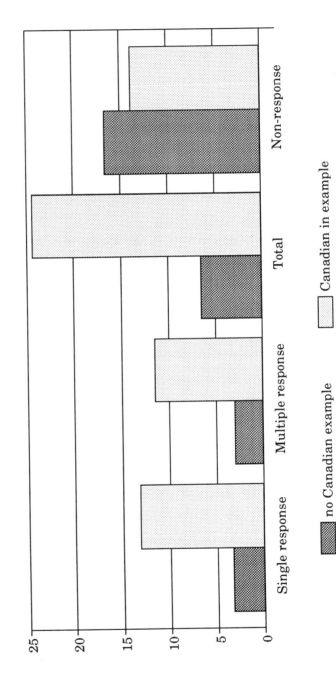

Appendix 3
Response "Canadian" to ethnic ancestry and
ethnic identity questions, Second National Census Test, 1989

Costs and Benefits of Multiculturalism: A Social-Psychological Analysis

JOHN BERRY

The Canadian policy of multiculturalism may be seen as a huge social experiment. Our historical and contemporary ethnocultural demography, as well as current patterns of immigration, virtually eliminate any possibility of successfully forging a monocultural society. We really have no choice but to accommodate our diversity in some way. The novelty of a multiculturalism policy is that it attempts a balancing act among various alternatives: the homogenization of assimilation on the one hand, and the fragmentation of separation or segregation on the other, while avoiding the pitfalls of marginalization. There are potential costs and benefits that attend this experiment that I will discuss in a later section of this paper. Before that, however, we need to consider two domains of psychological research that set the stage for this later analysis: ethnic relations and acculturation.

ETHNIC AND RACE RELATIONS IN CANADA

To a large extent, the areas of ethnic relations and acculturation have remained distinct in psychological research, but there are sufficient parallels to draw them together. First, both areas arise only in culturally plural societies. Second, they share a concern for group contact and resultant change in some basic social and psychological phenomena. Third, there is a central role for affective states (attitudes and ideologies) that indicate what people think and what they feel should be the case. Fourth, there are some obvious behavioural outcomes for individuals

183

(changes in individual behaviours and identities, and acts of discrimination). And, fifth, both lead to an outcome that ranges from being stressful and conflict-ridden through to an adaptation that accommodates the needs of people in contact, both newcomers and the larger society.

The study of ethnic and race relations is a vast topic. Rather than reviewing the current empirical knowledge about ethnic group relations in Canada, I present here some current conceptualizations and issues.

Prejudice: While prejudice is essentially a psychological phenomenon, it can become established in social norms and societal practices that may or may not any longer have negative affect or animosity underlying the practice. Hence a distinction has been drawn between personal and institutional prejudice. The former involves negative feelings by a person toward another person or group, while the latter may not; institutional prejudice is prejudice that has become conventional, but not necessarily with any personal intent to harm, injure or attack. Because of the different character of these forms of prejudice, change mechanisms would need to be different depending on whether one or the other (or both) are present.

Similarly, a distinction has been drawn between blatant and subtle prejudice. The former (sometimes called "old fashioned" prejudice) is revealed in overt acts of verbal or physical hostility (such as insults, attacks and deliberate acts of discrimination). The latter is covert (sometimes called "symbolic prejudice") and is revealed in "more acceptable" activities such as being opposed to various forms of equity or other social change programs. In the last decade, changing social norms (both informal and formal laws) have made blatant prejudice socially unacceptable, even illegal. Hence, the expression of prejudice has become subjected to normative influence (as in the case of institutional prejudice) and can no longer be considered a purely psychological phenomenon.

Security: The 1971 multiculturalism statement proposed that confidence in one's individual identity was a plausible precondition for accepting others. We have previously referred to this as the "multiculturalism assumption" (Berry, Kalin and Taylor 1977). That is, if one feels secure and that one has a place in the Canadian mosaic, then one can be open and accepting also of a place for those who belong to other groups. The alternate relationship is also possible: that developing one's own group's confidence can lead to ethnocentrism. This alternate relationship is indeed the basis of ethnocentrism theory (LeVine and Campbell 1972) in which positive own-group attitudes are often negatively correlated with attitudes toward other groups.

Contact: Ever since the classic analyses of Amir (1976) through to the present (Amir and Ben-Ari 1988) it has been established that personal experience with members of other groups can lead to either increased liking or increased hostility; the outcome depends on some specific factors. Positive outcomes are likely when there is: equal status of the groups; the presence of common goals; and when contact is voluntary and intimate. Negative outcomes are likely when there is: status inequality; competition for scarce resources; and enforced interaction. When social conditions vary, the outcome of contact will vary; hence, attitude change is a social as well as a psychological phenomenon.

Group similarity: An important element in intergroup and interpersonal attitudes is that of the similarity of the groups or persons in contact: the greater the similarity, then the greater the attraction. Whether found in experimental or in field studies, this relationship appears to be robust. It appears to apply both to psychological similarity in the case of interpersonal attraction (e.g., similar beliefs or interests) and to cultural similarity in the case of intergroup attraction (e.g., shared group characteristics, such as language, religion, values, norms). An obvious implication of this relationship is that since groups who are now arriving as immigrants in Canada are rather dissimilar from those already established in the country, less acceptance of them may be expected, at least initially. To the extent that these groups acculturate to the larger society by adopting some generally shared Canadian norms and values, then increased acceptance may result. We now turn to a consideration of such acculturation phenomena.

IMMIGRANT ACCULTURATION PATTERNS

How immigrants and ethnic groups change and adapt to the larger Canadian society is an important aspect of group relations (see Berry 1990a). As noted earlier, there are important parallels between ethnic relations and acculturation as cultural and psychological phenomena, both resulting in the possibility of outcomes ranging from positive mutual adaptations through to stress and conflict. We have also seen that not all the adaptation and change are expected to come from those newly arrived: official multiculturalism involves some adaptation on the

185

part of the larger society (referred to as "institutional change"). Thus acculturation is, in principle, a two-way street.

Acculturation was first identified as a cultural-level phenomenon by anthropologists (e.g., Redfield et al. 1936) who defined it as culture change resulting from contact between two autonomous cultural groups. In principle, change occurs in both groups; in practice, more change occurs in the non-dominant than in the dominant group.

Acculturation is also an individual-level phenomenon, requiring individual members of both the larger society and the various acculturating groups to work out new forms of relationships in their daily lives. This idea was introduced by Graves (1967), who has proposed the notion of "psychological acculturation" to refer to these new behaviours and strategies. One of the findings of subsequent research in this area is that there are vast individual differences in how people attempt to deal with acculturative change (termed "acculturation strategies"). These strategies have three aspects: their preferences ("acculturation attitudes": see Berry et al. 1989); how much change they actually undergo ("behavioural shifts"); and how much a problem these changes are for them (the phenomenon of "acculturative stress": see Berry et al. 1987).

Perhaps the most useful way to identify the various orientations individuals may have toward acculturation is to note that two issues predominate in the daily life of most acculturating individuals. One pertains to the maintenance and development of one's ethnic distinctiveness in society, deciding whether or not one's own cultural identity and customs are of value and to be retained. The other issue involves the desirability of inter-ethnic contact, deciding whether relations with other groups in the larger society are of value and to be sought. These two questions have obvious similarity with two key elements of multiculturalism policy: heritage maintenance, and social participation and sharing. These two issues are essentially questions of values, and may be responded to on a continuous scale, from positive to negative. For conceptual purposes, however, they can be treated as dichotomous (yes and no) preferences, thus generating a four-fold model (see Figure 1).

Each cell in this four-fold classification is considered to be an acculturation strategy or option available to individuals and to groups in plural societies, toward which individuals may hold attitudes; these are Assimilation, Integration, Separation and Marginalization. When the first question is answered no, and the second is answered yes, the Assimilation option is defined, that is, relinquishing one's cultural

186

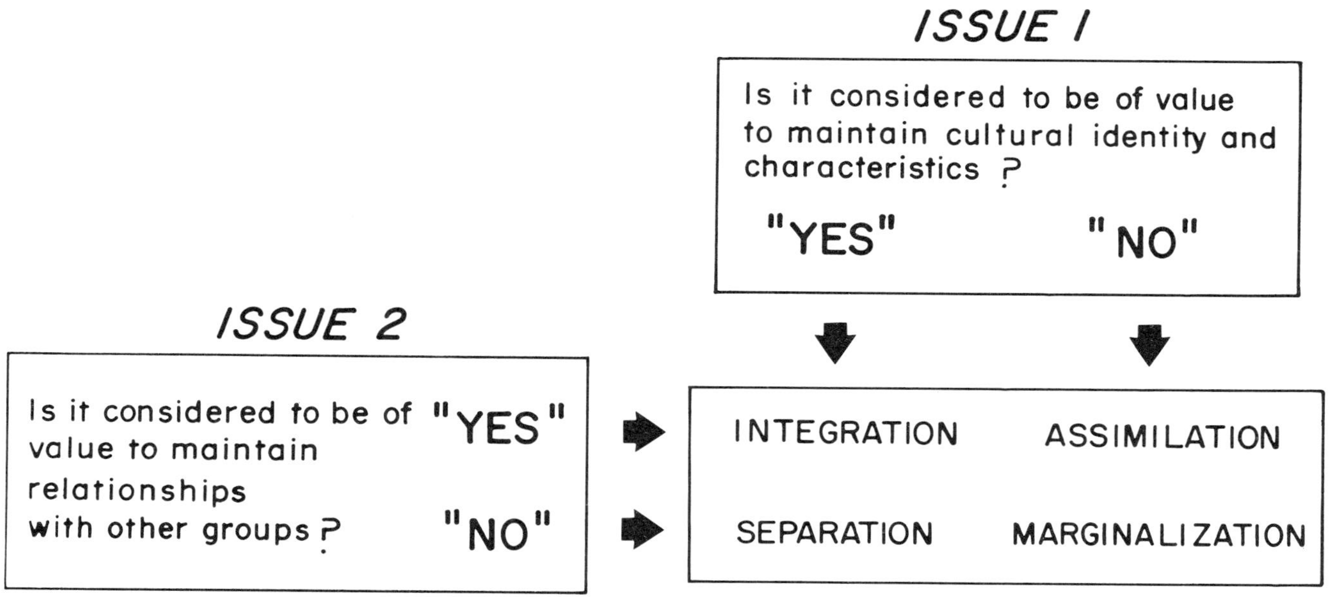

ISSUE I

Is it considered to be of value to maintain cultural identity and characteristics ?

"YES"   "NO"

INTEGRATION   ASSIMILATION

SEPARATION   MARGINALIZATION

ISSUE 2

Is it considered to be of value to maintain relationships with other groups ?

"YES"   "NO"

Figure 1: Four acculturation strategies available to individuals and groups in a plural society.

identity and moving into the larger society. This can take place by way of absorption of a nondominant group into an established dominant group; or it can be by way of the merging of many groups to form a new society, as in the "melting pot" concept.

The Integration option implies the maintenance of the cultural integrity of the group, as well as the movement by the group to become an integral part of a larger societal framework. In this case there is a large number of distinguishable ethnic groups, all cooperating within a larger social system, resulting in the "mosaic" that is promoted in Canada.

When there are no relations with the larger society, and this is accompanied by a maintenance of ethnic identity and traditions, another option is defined. Depending upon which group (the dominant or nondominant) controls the situation, this option may take the form either of Segregation or Separation. When the pattern is imposed by the dominant group, classic Segregation to keep people in "their place" appears. On the other hand, the maintenance of a traditional way of life outside full participation in the larger society may derive from a group's desire to lead an independent existence, as in the case of separatist movements. In these terms, Segregation and Separation differ primarily with respect to which group or groups have the power to determine the outcome.

Finally, there is an option that is difficult to define precisely, possibly because it is accompanied by a good deal of collective and individual confusion and anxiety. It is characterized by striking out against the larger society, and by feelings of alienation, loss of identity, and by acculturative stress. This option is Marginalization, in which groups lose cultural and psychological contact with both their traditional culture and the larger society. When imposed by the larger society, it is tantamount to ethnocide. When stabilized in a nondominant group, it constitutes the classical situation of marginality (Stonequist 1935).

Inconsistencies and conflicts between these various acculturation strategies are one of many sources of difficulty for acculturating individuals. Generally, when acculturation experiences cause problems for acculturating individuals, we observe the phenomenon of acculturative stress (see Figure 2). In a recent overview of this area of research (Berry et al. 1987), it was argued that stress may arise, but it is not inevitable. Or, as Beiser et al. (1988) have phrased it: migrant status is a mental-health risk factor; but risk is not destiny.

On the left in Figure 2, acculturation occurs in a particular situation (e.g., migrant community or Native settlement), and individuals partic-

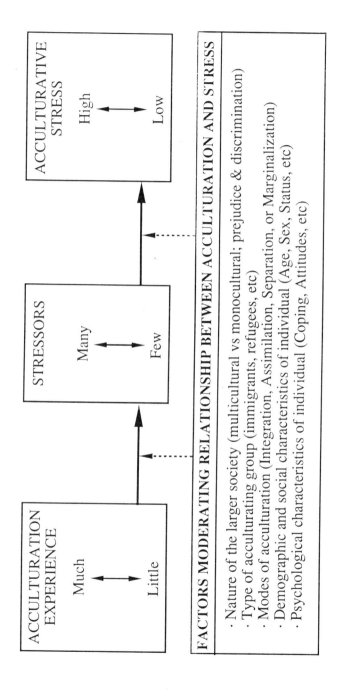

Figure 2: A model of acculturation stress.

ipate in and experience these changes to varying degrees; thus, individual acculturation experience may vary from a great deal to rather little. In the middle, stressors may result from this varying experience of acculturation; for some people, acculturative changes may all be in the form of stressors, while for others, they may be benign or even seen as opportunities. On the right, varying levels of acculturative stress may become manifest as a result of acculturation experience and stressors.

The first point to note is that relationships among these three concepts (indicated by the solid horizontal arrows) all depend upon a number of moderating factors (indicated in the lower box), including the nature of the larger society, the type of acculturating group, the mode of acculturation being experienced, and a number of demographic, social and psychological characteristics (including coping abilities) of the group and individual members. That is, each of these factors can influence the degree and direction of the relationships between the three variables at the top of Figure 2. This influence is indicated by the broken vertical arrows drawn between this set of moderating factors and the horizontal arrows.

Results of studies of acculturative stress have varied widely in the level of difficulties found in acculturating groups. Early views were that culture contact and change inevitably led to stress; however, current views are that stress is linked to acculturation in a probabilistic way, and the level of stress experienced will depend on a number of factors that will be reviewed later.

The larger society will be affected by these acculturation phenomena in a number of ways. First, if the Assimilation or Integration modes are adopted, then contact is directly involved, and, particularly for Assimilation, increased similarity will probably occur. On the other hand, in the Separation or Marginality modes, there is little contact, and similarity may also be perceived to be low. Second, since acculturative stress phenomena are generally viewed as socially or psychologically unacceptable, groups exhibiting such behaviours may well be rejected by the larger society, thus involving low contact and negative attitudes. Third, both these outcomes may well lead to the institutionalization of rejection and hostility, resulting in ghettos, educational discrimination, high incarceration, and other forms of social, economic, political and spatial discrimination.

In such a set of circumstances, the larger society may establish permanent psychological and social protective barriers, including prejudice and discrimination, and both formal and informal rules of avoidance and exclusion. Further, while attempts to reduce these barriers (through bilingualism, multiculturalism and equity policies and programs) may be promoted and accepted by economic and political elites in the larger society, popular reaction ("backlash") in the majority of the population is a distinct possibility.

SOCIAL BENEFITS AND COSTS OF MULTICULTURALISM

The analysis of the social benefits and costs of a multicultural policy takes into account both the intended goals of multiculturalism and the actual and possible outcomes that can be discerned in the published literature.

The multiculturalism policy is clearly intended to manage intergroup and interpersonal relations in Canada. The goal of this management is to encourage groups and individuals toward Integration following a mid-course between the alternatives of Assimilation and Separation, and moving away from the social and psychological pathologies associated with Marginalization. While seeking to manage and encourage in these ways, the policy also supports individual and group choice; the emphasis on human rights, social participation and equity, as well as on group maintenance and intergroup tolerance demonstrates this concern with individual freedoms. In one sense, it is a balancing act between collective rights and individual rights: collective "life style" preferences should not constrain individual "life chances."

With respect to the policy itself, there are two immediate benefits that probably result from its very existence without regard to whether it is "right" or "wrong." First, it demonstrates our social concern for and attention to the quality of human relations in Canada; the absence of a policy would presumably signal the opposite. It at least makes all people aware that their ethnocultural and individual needs are not being ignored; psychologically this may very well be a contributor to morale and self-esteem (which is one of the factors that contribute to positive group relations). This benefit may be equally important for members of the larger society, since the multiculturalism policy exists for all Canadians. Second, the policy can be construed as a "primary prevention" program (cf. Williams and Berry 1991), in which known factors are used to foster positive relations and adaptations, rather than waiting until problems appear. The intention is to give every individual and

191

ethnocultural group (whether dominant or non-dominant) a place, a sense of belonging, in Canadian society; psychologically, such a sense of place may again provide a boost to morale and self-esteem.

Beyond these two possible beneficial consequences of just having a multicultural policy, there are other general benefits that can be linked to its specific content. First is the general point of view that *diversity is a resource*. In biological-systems theory, the greater the variance on any trait, or across traits, in a population, the greater is the capacity of that population to deal effectively with changing circumstances. A population that adapts completely to its habitat, by developing an invariant or homogeneous response to it, loses its range of alternatives. This view is captured by the adage "adaptation is the enemy of adaptability." In social systems, homogeneity also reduces the ability of societies and institutions to respond to change, while diversity provides a range of choices.

Three specific instances of this general principle can be identified. In one, Canada's role as an international participant in diplomatic and political events can be enhanced by having a population in which cultural, linguistic, religious and value sensibilities are found that help Canadians understand events in other societies. Our self-image as the international "good boy" is one that most Canadians appreciate, especially when travelling or working abroad, and has come to be a valued element in our definition of what it means to be Canadian. The maintenance of ethnocultural diversity at home may be seen as an important factor in our ability to participate abroad.

A second specific instance can be identified, this one at the individual level. If the Integration mode of acculturation resembles most closely the intention of the multiculturalism policy, then personal diversity (in the sense of knowing how to live and work in two cultural worlds) gives a person flexibility and choice in daily life that those who have become assimilated or remain separated do not have; and, of course, those who have become marginalized have the fewest choices of all.

The third specific instance is also at the individual level. Just as there seems to be no limit to the number of languages a person can master, there may well be no limit to the number of cultures an individual can acquire and appreciate. Since one of the goals of our formal educational system is to provide individuals with an enriched environment, it makes sense to provide this in a living environment, rather than just through books or other mediated experience.

The second general benefit of multiculturalism is that, in principle, it permits us to better meet our international *obligations with respect to human rights,* and allows us to compare favourably in other international comparisons (such as health, education and justice). This benefit is rather intangible but, nevertheless, important. The extent to which we have actually lived up to our potential is a matter of debate. However, most would agree that there is room for improvement in many areas (Aboriginal rights, culturally sensitive health and education, and the reduction of bias in policing and the delivery of justice). The point is that, with the existence of multiculturalism policy and programs, there is an ethical framework within which to work toward the improvement of human rights and social conditions in Canada. The alternatives imply the denial of the right to be different (Assimilation), the ejection of persons who pursue that right (Segregation) or both (Marginalization).

The third general benefit of multiculturalism is the potential for promoting the *social and psychological well-being* of all Canadians. Using the acculturation strategies framework presented in Figure 1, the potential benefits of the Integration option have to be judged in relation to the potential costs of the alternatives. The argument is that Integration promotes the social and psychological well-being of all Canadians, while Segregation, Separation, Assimilation and Marginalization reduces them, even for the dominant society. To begin, I assume that there is no support for a Segregation policy: inevitable problems with international diplomacy, trade and human rights probably would not be accepted by Canadians, quite apart from the psychological and social problems that such a policy would entail (Lambley 1980; World Health Organization 1983). Similarly, while Separation is possible (since national self-determination is generally considered to be a basic collective human right), the social conflict and psychological stress associated with this option renders it less than attractive for most individuals and groups in Canada. Indeed, all ethnocultural associations and all Aboriginal groups who seek an enhanced place for themselves do so with an explicit commitment to achieving it within Confederation. I conclude that, whatever changes may take place in the direction of greater ethnocultural distinctiveness, they are unlikely to entail either Segregation or Separation as their eventual outcomes.

The second alternative, that of Assimilation, has sometimes been promoted on the grounds that the elimination of group differences will lead to the elimination of the basis for social conflict. Two direct arguments are available to counter this position. One is that, in contemporary societies that have pursued assimilationist policies (e.g., the United States: "E Pluribus Unum"; and France: "Unité de l'Hexagon"), group differences have obviously not been reduced or even disappeared. Black, Hispanic and Asian cultures have persisted in the United States, as have regional cultures (e.g., Breton, Basque, Catalan) in France. Indeed, both countries have had to make recent changes in their assimilationist stances: bilingual education in the United States, and bilingual signs (French-Breton) in France. It is also plausible to relate high levels of overt intergroup conflict (e.g., Black-White, Basque-French), and possibly similar levels of social deviance to the struggle over the right to be culturally different in assimilationist societies.

A second direct argument is psychological: individuals, even in homogeneous groups, seek to differentiate themselves one from another, even to the extent of establishing two or more distinct groups within the original population. The work of Tajfel (1978; 1982) has clearly demonstrated this phenomenon. Self-distinctiveness, leading to group distinctiveness, seems to be a fundamental psychological process; where there is a tendency to converge, there is also a tendency to diverge. The implication of this phenomenon of differentiation is that assimilationist activity is likely to be countered by differentiation activity, leading to a nullification of such a policy initiative. Assimilation is thus not only difficult to achieve, but it also appears to run counter to a fundamental psychological process.

The third alternative, that of Marginalization, has been described as an outcome fraught with social and psychological pathologies. For example, among Aboriginal peoples in the Arctic (e.g., Berry 1990b) six indicators of social and mental malaise (suicide, homicide, spousal and child abuse, and alcohol and drug abuse) along with other social indicators (e.g., incarceration) reveal an epidemic of major proportions. Most observers attribute this situation not to qualities of Aboriginal peoples, or to the larger society, but to the character of the relationships between them; this is easily identified as a classic case of Marginalization of Aboriginal peoples by the larger society. The danger of such an outcome befalling other groups is always present and clearly must be avoided at all costs.

The Integration option, the one that most closely resembles the main features of multiculturalism policy in Canada, is thus to be preferred in part on the basis of the costs associated with the alternatives. However, a strong positive case can be made for Integration on its own merits. I have already noted that confidence and a sense of place are likely to be the outcomes of the policy for both dominant and non-dominant groups. In both the intergroup relations and the acculturation literatures, increased potential for security and tolerance and reduced potential for stress were shown to flow from the Integrationist strategy. These demonstrable empirical relationships provide the most direct evidence for the social and psychological benefits of multiculturalism to be found in the literature; they are apparently robust and reliable, and will likely stand the test of future investigation.

Turning to the possible costs of the multiculturalism policy, there are three distinct arguments that have been advanced. First is an "economic" cost: the dollars needed to operate a host of programs related to the support of cultural and linguistic maintenance, of contact and participation, and of various forms of equity. Most recently this argument has been heard with respect to bilingualism in Ontario (The French Language Services Act), but has been also heard with respect to immigration, refugees, and pay and employment equity. On the basis of research on one of these issues with one involved group (Alliance for the Preservation of English in Canada: see Berry and Bourcier 1989), my conclusion is that the economic argument is merely a front for deep-seated underlying bigotry. The economic argument is a "subtle" or "symbolic" form of prejudice, and deserves to be recognized as such.

A second possible cost lies in the potential for ethnic and racial discrimination and inequality: encouraging people to remain different makes them easy targets for such action. The existence of the "vertical mosaic" was initially claimed to be evidence of discrimination resulting in inequality among ethnic and racial groups. However, Pineo and Porter (1985) subsequently considered there to be evidence for the "collapse of the vertical mosaic." In a study of educational achievement in Toronto, Richmond (1988) found that, while ethnicity was a relatively important factor in determining how far one went in school, second-generation non-British achieved more educational upward mobility than did the second-generation British.

Most recently, Breton et al. (1990) concluded that there is no general relationship between ethnicity and status: participation varies by ethnic group and by domains (economic, political and social); sometimes ethnicity is a hindrance, but sometimes it is an asset to full participation in the larger society. Of course, the presence of variability in this phenomenon means that some individuals in some groups in some situations will be the targets of prejudice and discrimination; and most would agree that this is unacceptable in a society that pursues tolerance as a general goal. However, the culprit is more likely to be specific attitudes toward specific groups in specific circumstances, rather than the general policy of multiculturalism. What is needed is a concerted attack on these instances, rather than attacking the policy as a whole.

Indeed, the current first priority of the Ministry of Multiculturalism is race relations, in apparent recognition of where the specific problems lie. Evidence shows that it is those of non-European background in Canada who are most negatively evaluated, who are least prestigious, and who are most discriminated against. Alternate explanations are possible (rooted in some possible correlates of "race," such as perceived similarity, familiarity, accent, values); these need to be examined systematically before the source of the rejection can be unambiguously identified and the specific root causes dealt with. However, such needed research should not delay the implementation of programs to reduce the overt discrimination apparent in Canada at the present time.

A third cost is the potential for increased divisiveness and a reduction of national unity. In an earlier analysis (Kalin and Berry 1982b) we concluded that there is no necessary conflict between multiculturalism and achieving national unity. The evidence reviewed suggests that, generally, Canadians are moderately tolerant of diversity, and accepting of multiculturalism; there appears to be no serious personal conflict for those who think of themselves as both Canadian and as a member of a particular ethnocultural group; and there appears to be no serious ethnic or regional conflict that is about to take the form of overt and sustained violence that periodically afflicts other plural societies (Reitz 1988). If anything, these threats to national unity may be diminished, rather than enhanced, by the multiculturalism policy, giving each individual and group at least some place in an overall national, heterogeneous society.

Other possible costs have been alluded to in relation to the increasing settlement of visible minorities in Montreal, Toronto and Vancouver. There is no current evidence of a "tipping point" in Canada (where attitudes become more negative once a certain proportion of a group is present in a community). In fact, Kalin and Berry (1982a) found generally positive relationships between ethnic concentrations and ethnic attitudes in neighbourhoods across Canada. In contrast, popular wisdom frequently assumes that urban concentrations of visible minorities are inappropriate and create conflict.

Since there is no clear empirical evidence to decide the point, theoretical positions must be relied upon. On the one hand, urban concentrations provide "targets"; but on the other, they provide "support groups." On the one hand, they may enhance "cultural maintenance"; but on the other, they may inhibit "contact and participation." On the one hand, they may generate feelings of threat and insecurity for members of the larger society; but on the other, they may create a sense of security and self-esteem for members of the particular groups. We must conclude that on theoretical grounds, as well as on empirical grounds, there is a stalemate. The one clear statement that is possible is that both empirical and theoretical work is urgently needed in order to decide the issue.

Another possible cost is related to difficulties that the larger society may encounter in adapting to the changing social reality in Canada. Both the demography and the policy responses are changing rapidly, and many apparently feel that the speed is too great and the distance too far. We know that those who are relatively older, who are less well-educated, and who have had few intercultural contacts during their lives, are likely to feel threatened by these changes. Aware of current norms about the overt expression of prejudice, many assert their views in economic ("costly"; "job loss"), or social ("race riots"; "lower quality of education") terms. While invalid, these views are important statements of legitimate underlying concerns by members of Canadian society. If treated as such, and if steps are taken to reduce the perception of threat, the potential costs will not likely materialize. However, if ignored or ridiculed, feelings of threat may well be exacerbated, and potential costs will become converted into substantial ones through organized backlash and reaction.

On balance, the benefits of multiculturalism appear vastly to outweigh the costs at the present time. This is partly due to the essential validity of some of the elements of the policy, and partly due to a process of continuing refinement of programs that have been developed to implement the policy. For example, the change in emphasis in the mid-1970s toward contact and participation, and away from group maintenance (sometimes called the shift from "cultural" to "social" activity), probably reduced the potential for increased ethnocentrism. And the more recent shift toward improving race relations as a key to managing

Canada's diversity signals an awareness of the likely major source of social conflict.

The only possible alternative to Multiculturalism (Assimilation) has not been successful elsewhere in the world, and would likely be massively resisted if tried in Canada (leading to levels of social conflict not previously encountered here). In any case, having announced ourselves to the world for two decades as officially multicultural, we are not likely to get away with changing the rules for those who perhaps came for this very reason.

It appears that the only viable and realistic course is to pursue the Integration option, guided by the policy of multiculturalism, in recognition of the psychological and social value of human diversity in Canada.

REFERENCES

Amir, Y. 1976. "The Role of Intergroup Contact in Change of Prejudice and Ethnic Relations." In *Towards the Elimination of Racism,* edited by P. Katz. New York: Pergamon.

Amir, Y., and R. Ben-Ari. 1988. "A Contingency Approach for Promoting Intergroup Relations." In *Ethnic Psychology,* edited by J.W. Berry and R.S. Annis. Amsterdam: Swets and Zeitlinger.

Beiser, M. et al. 1988. *After the Door Has Been Opened.* Report of the Federal Taskforce on Mental Health Issues Affecting Immigrants and Refugees. Ottawa: Ministry of Health and Welfare, and Ministry of Multiculturalism and Citizenship.

Berry, J.W. 1990a. "Psychology of Acculturation." In *Applied Cross-Cultural Psychology,* edited by R. Brislin. London: Sage.

_____. 1990b. "Body and Soul: Physical, Social and Psychological Health Contrasts among Aboriginal Peoples in Canada, Greenland and Alaska." Paper presented to Circumpolar Health Congress, Yukon.

Berry, J.W., and D. Bourcier. 1989. "Attitudes toward Official Bilingualism in Eastern Ontario." Paper presented at Canadian Psychological Association Meetings, Halifax.

Berry, J.W., R. Kalin, and D. Taylor. 1977. *Multiculturalism and Ethnic Attitudes in Canada.* Ottawa: Ministry of Supply and Services.

Berry, J.W., U. Kim, T. Minde, and D. Mok. 1987. "Comparative Studies of Acculturative Sress." *International Migration Review* 21:491-511.

Berry, J.W., U. Kim, S. Power, and M. Bujaki. 1989. "Acculturation Attitudes in Plural Societies." *Applied Psychology* 38:185-206.

Breton, R., W. Isajiw, W. Kalbach, and J. Reitz. 1990. *Ethnic Identity and Equality.* Toronto: University of Toronto Press.

Graves, T. 1967. "Psychological Acculturation in a Tri-ethnic Community." *South-western Journal of Anthropology* 23:337-350.

Kalin, R., and J.W. Berry. 1982a. "The Social Ecology of Ethnic Attitudes in Canada." *Canadian Journal of Behavioral Science* 14:97-109.

_____. 1982b. "Canadian Ethnic Attitudes and Identity in the Context of National Unity." *Journal of Canadian Studies* 17:103-110.

Lambley, P. 1980. *The Psychology of Apartheid.* Athens: University of Georgia Press.

LeVine, R.A., and D.T. Campbell. 1972. *Ethnocentrism: Theories of Conflict, Ethnic Attitudes and Group Behaviour.* New York: Wiley.

Pineo, P.C., and J. Porter. 1985. "Ethnic Origin and Occupational Attainment." In *Ascription and Achievement in Canada,* edited by M. Boyd. Ottawa: Carleton University Press.

Redfield, R., R. Linton, and M.J. Herskovits. 1936. "Memorandum on the Study of Acculturation." *American Anthropologist* 38:149-152.

Reitz, J. 1988. "Less Racial Discrimination in Canada, or Simply Less Racial Conflict?" *Canadian Public Policy* 14:424-441.

Richmond, A. 1988. *Immigration and Ethnic Conflict.* Toronto: Macmillan.

Stonequist, E.V. 1937. *The Marginal Man.* New York: Scribner.

Tajfel, H. 1978. *Differentiation between Social Groups.* London: Academic Press.

_____. 1982. *Social Identity and Intergroup Relations.* New York: Cambridge University Press.

Williams, C., and J.W. Berry. 1991. "Primary Prevention of Acculturative Stress among Refugees: The Application of Psychological Theory and Practice." *American Psychologist* 46:632-641.

World Health Organization. 1983. *Apartheid and Health.* Geneva: W.H.O.

Eth-Elders:
Keepers of the Multicultural Core

LEO DRIEDGER

The focus of this paper is on the growing "eth-elder" population, who represent the oldest and most salient portion of ethnic identification in Canada. The ethnic elderly over 65 years of age represent about 11 percent of the Canadian population, and this proportion is growing.

The members come from highly segregated rural and urban areas; they use their respective languages extensively; their religion is important to them; and they are practising their distinctive cultural ways and values. These eth-elders are enormously varied demographically, regionally, linguistically and culturally. They represent the multicultural core.

I present, first, some of the demographic and regional variations of Canadian eth-elders, followed by some indicators of the salience of their ethnic identification. The major contribution of this paper will be to show that these demographic, regional, cultural, residential and social class variables cluster differentially so that we have a variety of eth-elder types. These eth-elder types have varied needs, which the communications and service industries increasingly need to recognize, because more energetic, healthy, educated, professional multicultural "grey power" is on the rise. As early retirement and longevity increase, elders have new leases on second lives. They will expect more – much more.

A DEMOGRAPHIC AND REGIONAL PERSPECTIVE

At the time of Confederation in 1867, Canada was mostly a bilingual and bicultural nation made up of southern Ontario, southern Quebec, Nova

LEO DRIEDGER

Scotia and New Brunswick – a regional fraction of what is now Canada. The British (61 percent) were a majority, the French (31 percent) were a strong second charter group, and others (nine percent) represented a small minority (Driedger 1989, 92). By 1981, the British had declined to 40 percent, the French to 27 percent, and Others had increased to one-third (33 percent). Canadian demographics had changed dramatically. A look at age groups provides interesting additional information.

A DEMOGRAPHIC AND REGIONAL PERSPECTIVE

In the first two columns of Table 1 we compare those under 65 with those over 65 years of age by ethnic groups. While the British represented 40 percent of the total Canadian population in 1981, they represented almost half (49 percent) of those over age 65. The French comprised 27 percent of the total Canadian population, but were under-represented (23 percent) among the elderly. In the past, British birth rates were below the average, and French birth rates were well above the average. That too has changed, with French birth rates dropping to the lowest in Canada more recently.

Note that among the Others, who represent 33 percent of the 1981 population, the Jews, Poles, Ukrainians and Germans like the British, are over-represented among the elders. The Chinese, Italians, Native peoples and all others like the French, are under-represented. The first group are early immigrants with relatively few recent immigrants, while the reverse is true for the second group of Others. Many of these recent immigrants also have high birth rates, which is especially true also among Aboriginals, whose birth rates are among the highest.

In columns three and four we present the proportion of each ethnic group who are 65 years and older. The British (11 percent) have a higher proportion of elderly (the national average in 1981 was nine percent) and the French (7.8 percent) are under-represented. The Jewish (16.5 percent) as well as the Polish (14.5 percent), Ukrainian (13.7 percent), and German (10.3 percent) groups have more elderly than the average; the Dutch (7.5 percent), Chinese (6.7 percent), Italian (6.7 percent), all others (5.9 percent) and Natives (3.5 percent) are under-represented. There are very few Aboriginal eth-elders; the Jews have almost five times as many proportionately. This clearly shows that the elderly among the Jews are much more important demographically than among the Aboriginals – a significant difference.

202

Table 1
Elderly and non-elderly populations by ethnicity, Canada, 1981

Ethnicity	Per 100 of age group		Per 100 of total	
	0-64	65+	0-64	65+
British	39.3	49.3	88.9	11.1
French	27.1	23.0	92.2	7.8
Jewish	1.0	2.0	83.5	16.5
Polish	1.0	1.7	85.5	14.5
Ukrainian	2.1	3.3	86.3	13.7
German	4.7	5.4	89.7	10.3
Dutch	1.7	1.4	92.5	7.5
Chinese	1.2	0.9	93.3	6.7
Italian	3.2	2.3	93.3	6.7
All other	14.7	9.2	94.1	5.9
Native peoples	2.2	0.8	96.5	3.5
Totals:	100.0	100.0	90.9	9.1

Note: This table includes British, French and eight ethnic origins (single response) with the largest counts for the total population. These latter ethnic origins are arranged here by descending proportions of the aged population (last column).

Source: Statistics Canada. *The Elderly in Canada.* Ottawa: Minister of Supply and Services, 1984, table 8, p. 16.

REGIONAL ETH-ELDER VARIATIONS

The eth-elder variations by regions are also interesting, as shown in Table 2. The British dominate in the Atlantic provinces, ranging from 94 to 73 percent of the three provinces. The fourth, New Brunswick, illustrating early colonial history, is the most bilingual and bicultural, with almost two-thirds British (62.6 percent) and one-third French (31.3

percent) and very few others; it also has an officially bilingual constitution.

Quebec (76.6 percent) is as French as the Maritimes are British, again representing its French colonial past. Whether Quebec will stay in confederation is not at all certain, but they have been an important large tile in the Canadian ethnic mosaic. While the British (61 percent) have always been dominant in Ontario, that dominance is declining, with other ethnic groups now accounting for 33 percent and growing fast because of large increases of immigrants from the Third World. While 61 percent of the Ontario eth-elders are still British, the provincial population will soon include a majority of Others, already reflected in the newly elected NDP government, who draw strongly from non-charter groups.

The West is highly multicultural, especially on the prairies. No ethnic group forms a majority on the prairies, although the British, the Germans and Ukrainians are the largest groups. The British (61.8 percent) are a majority in British Columbia. The Northlands including the Northwest Territories, the Yukon and the northern parts of the western provinces are very multicultural, dominated by a variety of Aboriginal groups, although this is still less evident among eth-elders, because the Aboriginals (3.5 percent) have so few elderly.

These regional demographic data show that we have at least five eth-elder regions – the Maritimes, Quebec, Ontario, the West and the Northlands. Differences between these regions to a large extent account for variations in eth-elder needs.

ETH-ELDERS IN KEY CITIES

The regional eth-elder patterns are also reflected in the ten cities across Canada shown in Table 3. The British are a dominant majority in St. John, Halifax, Toronto and Vancouver, the French in Quebec City and Montreal, and the non-charter groups are a majority in Kitchener (heavily German), Winnipeg and Edmonton (heavily Ukrainian). While Ottawa is officially bilingual (English and French), Kitchener is unofficially bilingual (English and German) as are Winnipeg and Edmonton (English and Ukrainian). The four eastern cities are heavily unilingual and unicultural, two British and two French. Toronto will likely join the multilingual and multicultural cities soon, as the recent younger immigrant populations age.

Table 2

Distribution of ethnic elderly (55 years plus) by province, Canada, 1981

Ethnic origin	Nfld.	N.S.	P.E.I.	N.B.	P.Q.	Ont.	Man.	Sask.	Alta.	B.C.	Total
British	94.3	75.8	73.1	62.6	11.3	61.0	44.4	43.5	48.3	61.8	47.5
French	2.5	9.9	11.2	31.3	76.6	6.6	6.4	4.0	4.4	3.0	24.2
African	.0	.4	.2	.1	.2	.3	.1	.0	.1	.1	.2
Chinese	.0	.0	.0	.0	.2	.9	.4	.3	1.1	2.4	.7
Dutch	.1	2.2	.8	.6	.2	1.9	2.9	2.0	3.2	2.1	1.6
German	.1	4.7	.3	1.2	.7	5.1	10.3	17.5	11.4	7.2	5.3
Greek	.0	.1	.0	.0	.4	.4	.0	.1	.1	.2	.3
Italian	.1	.3	.2	.2	2.5	4.5	.7	.1	1.1	1.8	2.6
Jewish	.1	.4	.0	.2	2.7	2.2	2.8	.2	.6	.5	1.8
Polish	.0	.4	.0	.0	.6	2.3	4.8	2.7	2.8	1.5	1.8
Portuguese	.0	.0	.0	.0	.2	.8	.4	.2	.1	.2	.4
Scandinavian	.2	.4	.3	.5	.1	.7	3.6	6.8	6.0	4.4	1.8
Ukrainian	.0	.3	.2	.1	.5	2.5	13.8	11.2	9.7	2.8	3.1
Other single	1.1	1.6	9.7	.5	2.7	7.8	7.4	8.7	8.4	8.9	6.1
Multiple origins	1.5	3.5	4.0	2.7	1.1	3.0	2.0	2.4	2.7	3.1	2.6
Totals %	100.0	100.0	100.0	100.0	100.0	100.0	100.0	100.0	100.0	100.0	100.0

Source: Two-percent sample tape of the 1981 census, aged 55 and over, Canadian Association on Gerontology/
Association Canadienne de Gerontologie.

Table 3

Percentage of ethnic elderly (55 years and older) in 10 metropolitan centres of Canada, 1981

Ethnic origin	St. John	Halifax	Quebec	Montreal	Ottawa	Toronto	Kitchener	Winnipeg	Edmonton	Vancouver
British	91.0	73.3	3.7	15.2	48.6	53.8	44.1	40.6	41.7	56.8
French	2.4	8.7	89.4	58.7	30.8	1.8	2.5	6.4	5.5	3.2
Chinese				.4	.6	1.8	.3	.5	1.8	4.2
Dutch	.1	2.7		.2	.7	1.0	1.8	1.7	2.9	1.3
German	.1	3.6	.2	1.2	2.0	3.0	29.3	8.7	8.8	5.7
Italian	.1	.1	.1	5.0	1.9	7.4	.9	1.3	1.2	2.0
Jewish	.1	.7	.1	5.5	1.5	5.6	.2	4.8	.9	.9
Polish	.1	.3	.1	1.1	1.2	2.7	2.8	5.2	3.4	1.6
Portuguese				.4	.3	1.5	2.4	.5	.3	.2
Scandinavian	.2	.3		.1	.4	.4	.3	3.1	4.2	4.2
Ukrainian		.2		1.0	1.1	2.9	2.0	13.7	14.2	2.8
Other single	1.0	2.4	.7	5.4	3.6	11.9	5.7	7.1	7.3	9.0
Multiple	1.4	4.5	.6	1.7	3.0	2.4	3.6	2.3	2.7	2.8
Other	3.6	3.2	5.1	4.1	4.3	3.8	4.1	4.1	5.1	5.3
Totals %	100.0	100.0	100.0	100.0	100.0	100.0	100.0	100.0	100.0	100.0

Source: Two-percent sample tape of the 1981 census, aged 55 and over, Canadian Association on Gerontology/
Association Canadienne de Gerontologie.

INDICATORS OF ETH-ELDER IDENTITY

Census data are limited in the number of ethnic identity indicators that can be used, but native tongue, language use at home and religious affiliation provide some indication of variations.

LANGUAGE ABILITY AND USE

Except for Jewish eth-elders, a majority of all other groups learned their native tongues at home (Table 4). In fact, nine out of 10 in half the groups listed could speak their native tongues; this is a major store of ethnic language heritage. Except for the Jews, Scandinavians and Dutch, two-thirds or more spoke their original tongues.

Use of the original tongue at home was not quite as extensive, but still considerable. Most of the charter group eth-elders spoke their respective English (99 percent) and French (88.4 percent) languages at home. Of the other eth-elders, over half or more also spoke their original tongues including the Chinese (86.4 percent), Portuguese (86.4 percent), Greeks (76.3 percent), Italians (72.4 percent) and Ukrainians (52.6 percent). Four of the five represent immigrants who have come to Canada recently.

The eth-elders of four groups have shifted extensively to use of English at home, including Scandinavians (94.5 percent), Jews (77.5 percent), Germans (73.8 percent), and the Dutch (70.2 percent). Except for the Jews, studies show that Scandinavians, Germans and the Dutch are assimilating fast (Driedger 1975; Driedger and Chappell 1987). Jewish adherents tend to depend more on religion, family and community than on language for their identity.

RELIGION AS SYMBOLIC SUPPORT

Organized religion serves a symbolic and functional role in most societies; it has the potential to provide a sense of security, a readily available social group, and a social role for the older individual. Religious beliefs, especially among older persons, can also assist in coping with grief and death especially among older persons. Because of these apparent functions, gerontologists have been interested in the patterns of religious participation during the middle and later years of life. (McPherson 1990, 443)

Canadian data that deal with religious practice among eth-elders are limited, so we can provide religious affiliation of only those aged 65 and

Table 4
Native tongue by ethnic groups and their home language use,
aged 65 and over in Canada, 1981.

Ethnic Origin	Speak Native Tongue	Home Use of Native Tongue	Home Use of English
British	97.9%	99.0	99.0
French	92.8	88.4	11.4
Chinese	93.6	86.4	12.2
Portuguese	90.4	86.4	12.8
Greek	93.2	76.3	18.6
Italian	89.6	72.4	23.1
Ukrainian	89.3	62.6	46.5
Other single	60.9	42.5	49.0
Polish	68.7	40.0	49.9
German	62.3	24.7	73.8
Dutch	53.6	23.3	70.2
Jewish	45.2	18.1	77.5
Scandinavian	57.0	5.5	94.5

Source: Two-percent sample tape of the 1981 Canadian census aged 55 and over. Canadian Association on Gerontology/Association Canadienne de Gerontologie.

over, as shown in Table 5. What is striking is how eth-elders cluster within one or several religions; religion and ethnicity often correlate significantly. French (96.3 percent), Portuguese (96 percent), Italian (95.9 percent) and Polish (78.9 percent) eth-elders are almost all affiliated with the Roman Catholic Church. A majority of British eth-elders are either United Church (35.1 percent) or Anglican (25 percent).

Other northern Europeans such as Scandinavians (51.8 percent) and Germans (31.2 percent) are affiliated with the Lutheran Church. Ukrainian eth-elders are divided largely among the Ukrainian Catholic (37.8 percent) and Eastern Orthodox (31.5 percent) churches; among Greeks (94.1 percent) almost all belong to the Eastern Orthodox Church. Jews (97.3 percent) as an ethno-religious group are almost all of Jewish

Table 5

Affiliation of ethnic elderly (age 65 and over) with religious denominations

Ethnic origin	R.C.	U.C.	Angl.	Bapt.	Luth.	Men.	Pent.	Pres.	Unit.	Prot.	E.O.	Jewi.	East.	No
British	13.4	.0	25.0	5.8	.8	.1	1.3	10.1	35.1	4.8	.1	.2	.1	3.3
French	96.3	.0	.5	.4	.1	.0	.1	.2	1.2	.5	.0	.1	.0	.6
African	21.2		18.2	15.2			10.6	3.0	9.1	1.1	3.0		4.5	3.0
Chinese	6.4		2.5	5.0	.6	.3	1.4	3.4	14.1	2.8		.6	8.3	54.3
Dutch	15.0		7.3	4.6	1.8	12.4	2.1	5.0	18.6	26.2		.2		6.8
German	23.5	.0	3.6	5.2	31.2	10.9	2.0	2.6	12.7	4.8	.1	.1	.0	3.3
Greek	1.7		.8					.8		2.5	94.1			
Italian	95.9		.3		.2		.7	.4	1.2	.5	.1			.6
Jewish	.3		.1				.1	.1	.1	.1	.1	97.3		1.7
Polish	78.9	2.9	1.9	.4	2.5	.1		.6	3.3	1.5	2.3	2.6		2.9
Portuguese	96.0		.8		.8			.8	.8	.8				
Scandinavian	1.8		4.4	4.4	51.8		2.1	2.0	21.5	7.4	.1		.1	4.4
Ukrainian	11.5	37.8	1.8	1.4	.7	.2	1.1	.6	5.8	2.7	31.5	.3		4.8
Other single	31.5	.6	2.1	2.1	16.5	1.1	1.0	2.1	9.6	5.0	8.6	1.1	8.8	5.0

Key: R.C.–Roman Catholic; U.C.–Ukranian Catholic; Angl.–Anglican; Luth.–Lutheran; Bapt.–Baptist; Men.–Mennonite; Pent.–Pentecostal; Pres.–Presbyterian; Unit.–United Church; Prot.–Other Protestant; E.O.–Eastern Orthodox; Jewi.–Jewish; East.–Eastern Non-Christian; No–No Religion

Source: Two-percent sample tape of the 1981 census, aged 55 and over, Canadian Association on Gerontology/ Association Canadienne de Gerontologie.

religion. Interestingly, a majority of the Chinese (54.3 percent) do not claim any religion – the only ethnic group with a significant number in that category.

It is clear that certain ethnic groups are linked to certain religious groups, thus providing an ethno-religious context that makes for additional variety and complexity in the multicultural mosaic. The indicators of language knowledge and use, and religious affiliation are inadequate to provide a well-rounded view of the extent and salience of eth-elder identity, but they do hint at the complexity and variety that we can expect. These few indicators, combined with demographic and regional factors, help us distinguish eth-elder types.

REGIONAL ETH-ELDER TYPES

My demographic, regional and cultural discussion of eth-elders provides the background and data for the construction of eth-elder types. Distinguishing types will be useful to illustrate that the needs of the elderly vary, so services and social agencies need to take into account ethnic diversity in the various parts of the country. Ethnic grey power will increasingly become part of the national political, economic and social agenda in the future. Five eth-elder types have been identified, representing traditional Aboriginals, French Québécois, the dominant British plurality, European Prairie agriculturalists, and urban elders.

THE NORTHLANDS TRADITIONAL ABORIGINALS

The 413,000 Aboriginal people of Canada are comprised mostly of Native Indians; only about 20,000 are Inuit (Frideres 1983). The basic homeland of these Aboriginals is the northlands of Canada, representing about four-fifths of the Canadian land area. While many are still located in their pre-industrial aboriginal habitat, more and more are moving to the mining and logging settlements, and some are coming south. Only 3.5 percent are elderly because early deaths tend to over-compensate for high birth rates; very few enter old age. Thus, there are only about 15,000 who are over 65 years, scattered in the northlands in the food-gathering setting. Edwards (1983, 75-76) found that over half of these elderly lived below the poverty line, over half the women were widowed, and housing was inadequate and crowded. They often live with their extended families in a Native cultural setting where they speak their native tongues and follow their traditions. These few scattered Native elderly are usually far away from modern services, but in a familiar *gemeinschaft* social context with their people. They are segregated away from most modern influences, definitely a Northlands Traditional Aboriginal eth-elder type (Driedger and Chappell 1991).

These eth-elders are unique in that so very few are scattered over the vast northlands of Canada, insufficient in numbers for local institutional services to serve them efficiently. Since Aboriginals are among the poorest Canadians, they also do not have the means to provide separate services. Fortunately, many are still an important part of traditional extended families where many still have an honoured place. However, as the Aboriginal population becomes more mobile and modern, families will probably also change, and traditional support will be less readily available. Government financial support is growing but, with the exploding Aboriginal population, these financial supports are also becoming more of a burden to the various governments. As the younger population ages, these Aboriginal baby-boomers will require much larger financial attention in the future. Aboriginal eth-elders will become an increasingly larger part of the Canadian population – they are more visible racially, and will remain a distinct and increasingly larger tile in the multicultural mosaic.

FRENCH QUEBECOIS: A CHARTER MINORITY

Like the Aboriginals, French Canadians have until recently depended on high birth rates to perpetuate their demographic place of almost one-third of the population, though this has recently declined to 27 percent. Judging from declining birth rates in Quebec, they may soon comprise little more than 20 percent of the total in Canada, if they remain in Confederation. Like the Aboriginals, the French have depended little upon new immigrants for their population growth – that is why the province of Quebec now wants more power over immigration quotas. However, in many other respects, French Canadians are quite different.

The French were the first Europeans to settle permanently in New France, in what is now southern Quebec along the St. Lawrence River, some 350 years ago (Rioux 1971). New France extended along the St. Lawrence River into the Great Lakes area and downward along the Mississippi into New Orleans. It was France's largest colony for more than a hundred years, a major rival of the British, sandwiched between the British American east-coast colonies and the Hudson's Bay (fur-trading) Company in the Canadian northwest. The Northwest (fur-trading) Company operating out of Montreal extended over an area at least as large as that of the British. Since New France began hundreds of years ago, and since few immigrants have come to Quebec, there are practically no foreign-born French Québecois eth-elders in that province; they have been French Canadians for generations. Most of the elderly in Quebec are Francophone and French Canadian culturally.

New France was very rural, based on a seigniorial land system along the rivers, linked with the French Catholic parishes often named after saints, still evident among the names of villages and towns today. The French elderly in Quebec come out of the *habitant* rural setting, so that 37.7 percent of all Canadian elderly with a grade-five education or less reside in Quebec. They have retained a strong French Canadian identity and prefer to speak French. They are spatially segregated along the St. Lawrence River in a French Canadian world. These French Québecois eth-elders are a second distinct type, quite different from the Northlands Traditional Aboriginal type. While the French in Quebec account for a smaller ratio of eth-elders (23 percent) than their demographic proportion in Canada (27 percent), Quebecers over 65 years of age are also a relatively small proportion (7.8 percent) of the French, lower than the 11 percent average nationally. However, now that French birth rates are lowest in Canada, their population will age faster, so that the proportion of French eth-elders will soon increase, becoming ultimately more like the Jewish proportion of 16 percent, which is now the highest in Canada.

THE DOMINANT BRITISH PLURALITY

The British are the largest charter group in Canada, representing less than 40 percent of the population in 1986. A hundred years ago the British (61 percent) were indeed a majority, but no ethnic group is now a majority, though British elders over 65 years represent almost half (49.3 percent) of Canada's elderly. In the future, the British elderly will decline proportionately. Well over half of all the elderly in Canada with bachelor's degrees are British; and they are disproportionately represented in the higher status occupations; their English language is dominant; and they belong to the higher status Anglican and United Church denominations. While many are of higher socio-economic status, the British elderly are not a homogeneous group. There are at least three significantly different subtypes: Colonial Maritimers, Loyalist Industrialists and Prairie Agriculturalists.

Newfoundlanders, who are largely of British origin, represent the earliest British colonial past – segregated islanders who only recently joined Confederation. St. John's was a major fishing centre, and Halifax became a fortified British colonial stronghold to counteract the French stronghold at Louisbourg. The largely British origin eth-elders in the three most easterly provinces (Newfoundland, Nova Scotia and Prince Edward Island) are mostly English-speaking, they are highly conscious of their British colonial past, they are relatively segregated and isolated at the east end of Canada, they are highly oriented to the sea, of lower socio-economic status, and the most homogeneously unilingual and unicultural in Canada (even more than the French in Quebec). Their provinces are very much on the peripheral hinterland of the industrial heartland of Canada, often engaged in economic struggles as have-not provinces.

A second British eth-elder subtype are the Empire Loyalists, who are heavily concentrated in southern Ontario, the industrial heartland of Canada. These Loyalists came after the American Revolution more than 200 years ago, and created what Armstrong (1981) refers to as the Ontario Establishment. As royalists who chose to continue under British rule, many had political and economic connections with their British homeland, and received special favours and positions on the Ontario frontier settlements. These strongly royalist traditions have continued, as, economically, southern Ontario has become the stronghold of the Canadian heartland from which they have all benefited politically. Many Loyalist Ontario eth-elders are among Canada's central power elite, in contrast to their British maritime eth-elders, who are poor cousins in comparison. Thus, we have British "haves" in Upper Canada, engaged in manufacturing and agriculture in a highly urban environment, and British "have-nots" engaged in rural fishing and primary occupations in the Maritimes.

Some British eth-elders on the prairies are the descendents of the fur trade, and more recently of agriculturalists, who came roughly a hundred years ago. They tend to blend in with the northern European agriculturalists, who have created the most multicultural region in Canada. It is clear that these three British subtypes are very different socio-economically, their regional settings require very different responses, making British eth-elders in Canada quite plural.

EUROPEAN PRAIRIE AGRICULTURALISTS

When the prairies opened up for settlement over a hundred years ago, they were settled very heavily by northern Europeans such as British, French, German, Dutch, Scandinavian and, later, by eastern European, Polish and Ukrainian agriculturalists. Carl Dawson (1936) was among the first to study a dozen of these ethnic rural communities on the prairies, and more recently Alan Anderson (1972) studied such ethnic bloc settlements in Saskatchewan. Both Dawson and Anderson found that the prairies were settled in blocs by a variety of European groups, forming solid cohesive ethno-religious communities where they perpetuated their languages, cultures, institutions and folklore. Anderson (1972) found that almost all knew their respective languages and used them extensively, they were very much engaged in religious activities and ethnic voluntary associations, and continued with their ethnic focus and folkways. Hutterites did so almost exclusively, while Scandianvians somewhat less, but still significantly.

These European eth-elders became modestly well-to-do and retired in villages, or moved to small railroad towns, which from the beginning served as focal points in their rural community enclaves. Gimli, Dauphin, St. Anne, Steinbach, Winkler, Morris and Brandon would be good examples in Manitoba. A move off the farm into town usually involves a distance of only a few miles, so that they are close to their children and grandchildren, some of whom continue to farm, or work in town or a nearby city. Eth-elders usually live independently in their own homes, and many of their ethno-religious communities have built retirement homes for members who are no longer able to live alone. These communities are generally able to provide institutional care close to where many lived all their lives. More recently, such moves to town have also extended to cities such as Saskatoon, Regina, Winnipeg, Calgary and Edmonton.

The rural communities are able to provide support facilities because they are compact communities, and extended families are able to support members financially and socially, so eth-elders remain an extension of their families, churches and communities. British fishing villagers in Atlantic Canada, rural Quebecers, and rural Loyalists in southern Ontario tend to provide for their eth-elders in a similar way. However, each type and community does so within a unique and distinctive religious and ethnic context. Social contacts and services are available

214

in their familiar ethnic language, including traditional foods and folk-ways, and within familiar family and friendship networks.

URBAN ETH-ELDERS

Jewish elders represent urban eth-elders best, an urban polar type in many ways a contrast to Aboriginal elders. There are, however, a number of urban eth-elder subtypes, principally High Status Metropolitans, Low Status Immigrants, and Retired Sun-Seekers.

High Status Metropolitans are best represented by Jewish Canadians of ethno-religious communities who have become the most upwardly mobile group socio-economically. They have lived in metropolitan centres for generations, and most of them have spent all their lives in the city, which is their home of work and play. The Jews are an aging population (16.5 percent are over 65 years), they are almost all urban, highly segregated in Montreal, Toronto and Winnipeg where most of them live, they rank highest on education, occupational status and income, and on most indicators of ethnic identity they score higher than all other ethnic groups (Driedger and Chappell 1987, 53,54). The Jews are definitely an Urban High Status eth-elder type, with high ethnic and religious identity, an enormous contrast to the Northlands Traditional Aboriginal type.

Chinese eth-elders, like the Jews, have also been engaged in business, have been highly segregated, have continued their traditions and community values, but are centred more around linguistic, cultural and racial uniqueness than on religious concerns. Although different in important respects, Jewish and Chinese eth-elders have many things in common. Both communities provide strong family and communal supports, including facilities and services for eth-elders. They feel at home in the city where they have been for generations.

Low Status Immigrants, like Portuguese, Greeks and Italians have come more recently, and in contrast to the Jews are of lower socio-economic status, are largely foreign-born, South European culturally and linguistically, largely Roman Catholic and Orthodox, from large extended families, and the proportion over 65 years of age is relatively small. Like the Jews, however, most have moved into large metropolitan areas like Toronto, Montreal and Vancouver, family and community supports are extensive, religion and ethnicity are important to them, and they are also highly segregated residentially. The urban southern European eth-elders often stay with their extended families, because ethnic institutions and facilities are not as readily available (being lower class), and they do not feel as comfortable in public facilities for the elderly, which in any case they might not be able to afford.

Retired Sun-Seekers could be considered a third urban eth-elder subtype. The west coasts of British Columbia and California are very popular with prairie eth-elders – they are full of retired westerners (especially Victoria). Arizona and Florida are the choices of both Ontario and western retired émégrés. Many are middle class, so they can afford to live south in winter and north in summer, taking advantage of the best weather as seasons change. These are usually healthy, white-collar eth-elders largely from North European backgrounds, who travelled in their earlier years and like to remain mobile. Others move from Canada for more permanent residence, with shorter and longer visits back to Canada to see their children and grandchildren. Many, having lived in stable communities for a long time in Canada, find becoming a part of new communities in the sun, new churches to go to, and the excitement of making new friends, a freeing experience. They visit, swim, read, travel and socialize a lot.

SHAPING THE MULTICULTURAL ETH-ELDER RANGE

In this paper I suggest that eth-elders are keepers of the Canadian multicultural core. I have shown that Canada is a diverse ethnic country, and that eth-elders are very differentially distributed across Canada. This diversity and clustering of groups is also found in major metropolitan centres across Canada.

I have also shown that most eth-elders are able to speak their native tongues, and they use these languages extensively at home. Religion is also an important symbolic support, and eth-elders tend to cluster in the various Catholic, Protestant and Jewish religious patterns for ethnoreligious support.

I have suggested, too, that, regionally, eth-elders could be thought of as eth-elder types. These types included the Traditional Aboriginals in the northlands, the French Québécois in Quebec, the Dominant British plurality in Atlantic Canada, Ontario and the West, the European Agriculturalists on the prairies, and the Urban Eth-elders, comprised of High Status Metropolitans, Low Status Immigrants and Retired Sunseekers. The heterogeneity and multicultural diversity should be clearly evident.

Table 6
Shaping the multicultural eth-elder range

Type	Region	Ethnic Groups
Traditional Aboriginals	Northlands	Native Indians, Inuit
French Québécois	Quebec	French Canadians
British Plurals		
Colonial Maritimes	Atlantic	English, Scottish, Irish
Loyalist Industrialists	Ontario	British
Prairie Agriculturalists	West	British
European Agriculturalists	Prairies, Ontario	Germans, Ukrainians, French, Dutch
Urban Eth-elders		
High Status Metropolitans	Toronto, Montreal, Vancouver	Jews, Chinese
Low Status Newcomers	Toronto, Montreal	Portuguese, Italians
Retired Sun-seekers	British Columbia	North Europeans

In previous studies we have presented models to try to summarize this eth-elder diversity by social class and residence (Driedger and Chappell 1987, 95; and 1991, 243-248). In Table 6 I simply summarize the discussion, presenting the five types, the regions in which they dominate, and the ethnic groups which are most often represented.

It is clear that the aspirations and needs of these eth-elders vary enormously, and those who wish to relate to or serve them will need to tailor their behaviours to fit regional and ethnic contexts. Agencies serving British eth-elders in Newfoundland have a very different set of challenges than workers with Traditional Aboriginals in the north, or European Agriculturalists on the prairies. High-status Jewish Metropolitans will be able to provide for their own needs much more adequately than lower status Aboriginals in the city. Planning for rural French Québécois is much different from serving European Prairie Agriculturalists. Politicians and economists will also want to shape their appeals to this plurality of grey power, because their numbers are growing and their pocketbooks and votes will increasingly carry the margins that bring success.

REFERENCES

Anderson, Alan. 1971. "Assimilation in the Bloc Settlements of North-Central Saskatchewan: A Comparative Study of Identity Change among Seven Ethno-Religious Groups in a Canadian Prairie Region." Ph.D. dissertation, University of Saskatchewan.

Anderson, Grace. 1974. *Networks of Contact: The Portuguese and Toronto.* Waterloo, Ontario: Wilfrid Laurier University Press.

Anderson, Grace, and David Higgs. 1976. *A Future to Inherit: The Portuguese Communities of Canada.* Toronto: McClelland and Stewart.

Armstrong, Frederick H. 1981. "Ethnicity in the Formation of the Family Compact: A Case Study in the Growth of the Canadian Establishment." In *Ethnicity, Power and Politics in Canada,* edited by Jorgen Dahlie and Tessa Fernanda. Toronto: Methuen.

Canadian Association on Gerontology. 1981. *Fragmented Gods: The Poverty and Potential of Religion in Canada.* Toronto: Irwin Publishing.

Dawson, Carl A. 1936. *Group Settlement: Ethnic Communities in Western Canada.* Toronto: Macmillan.

deVries, John, and Frank Vallee. 1980. *Language Use in Canada.* Ottawa: Minister of Supply and Services.

Driedger, Leo. 1975. "In Search of Cultural Identity Factors: A Comparison of Ethnic Students." *Canadian Review of Sociology and Anthropology* 12:150-162.

_____. 1989. *The Ethnic Factor: Identity in Diversity.* Toronto: McGraw-Hill Ryerson.

Driedger, Leo, and Neena Chappell. 1987. *Aging and Ethnicity: Toward an Interface.* Toronto: Butterworths.

_____. 1991. "Variations in Aging and Ethnicity." In *Ethnic Demography,* edited by Shiva Halli, Frank Trovato and Leo Driedger. Ottawa: Carleton University Press.

Edwards, E.D. 1983. "Native-American Elders: Current Issues and Social Policy Implications." In *Aging and Minority Groups,* edited by R.L. McNeeley and J.L. Colen. Beverly Hills: Sage Publications.

Frideres, James S. 1983. *Native People in Canada: Contemporary Conflicts,* second edition. Scarborough, Ontario: Prentice-Hall.

Lieberson, Stanley. 1970. *Languages and Ethnic Relations in Canada.* New York: John Wiley.

McPherson, Barry D. 1990. *Aging as a Social Process: An Introduction to Individual and Population Aging.* Toronto: Butterworths.

Rioux, Marcel. 1971. *Quebec in Question.* Toronto: James Lewis and Samuel.

Statistics Canada. 1984. *The Elderly in Canada.* Ottawa: Minister of Supply and Services.

Multiculturalism in Health Care: Understanding and Implementation

RALPH MASI

"Observe the nature of each country; diet, customs; the age of the patient; speech; manners; fashion; even his silence. . . . One has to study all these signs and analyze what they portend." Thus, Hippocrates, writing in the fifth century B.C., recognized the importance of culture to health care. Today, one of the challenges faced by health professionals is to respond to the needs of people with diverse backgrounds in our multicultural society. Health professionals play an important role in the community, providing access both to health services and to education on health matters. Understanding cultural factors involved in health can help simplify health care and make it more effective.

DEFINITIONS

Multicultural health is defined as health care that is culturally sensitive and responsive. The definition includes concepts of ethnic and race relations, cross-cultural or trans-cultural health care.

The term *community* will be used in reference to the group of people for which the program or service is intended. It is acknowledged that within the concept of the term *community* is a specific reference to the broad cultural and racial diversity that exists within a community, and that this realization should be fundamental to any use of the term.

Culture refers to patterns or standards of behaviour that one acquires as a member of a particular group. These standards may include

221

language, behaviour, concepts, beliefs and values. A person's culture may or may not be that of his or her ethnic origin or identity.

An *ethnic group* is a group of people who share a common ancestry or history, and who have distinctive patterns of family life, language, values and social norms. A person's ethnic origin, therefore, identifies him or her as having come from a particular group background; however, he or she may have a somewhat different, or an entirely different, cultural identity as a result of having acquired other cultural patterns.

QUALIFICATIONS

Three important qualifications should be noted: References to ethnocultural groups such as "Chinese" are intended to identify an ethnocultural background, not citizenship. It must constantly be remembered that there is as much or more variation within a cultural group as there is among groups or communities. Identity is complex. Within Canada we refer not only to ethnic groups but also to linguistic groups such as "the Spanish-speaking people," or to racial groups, such as "the Black community." A member of either collective could come from anywhere in the world and have a complex identity. Similarly, a collective group such as the southeast Asians is diverse not only culturally but also linguistically.

To allow for the discussion of issues, generalizations must be made. Generalizations should not be interpreted as representing characteristics applicable to all or, in some instances, even most of the individuals within the community. Generalizations may, in fact, be completely inappropriate when applied to the individual or the circumstance. The application of generalizations in this manner constitutes stereotyping.

There may be more similarities between the health beliefs or practices of different ethnocultural groups at the same socio-economic level than there are within the same ethnocultural group at different socio-economic levels. Although socio-economic factors contribute significantly to health beliefs and practices, they are outside the scope of this article.

BACKGROUND

In 1974, under the then Minister of Health Marc Lalonde, the Government of Canada produced a report entitled *A New Perspective on the Health of Canadians*. In the report, his ministry examined methods of improving the health of Canadians; it concluded that "the Government of Canada, in co-operation with others, will pursue two broad objectives: (1) To reduce mental and physical health hazards for those parts of the Canadian population whose risks are high. (2) To improve the accessibility of good mental and physical health care for those whose present access is unsatisfactory" (Health and Welfare Canada 1974).

To be sensitive and responsive to the needs of the entire Canadian population in the 1990s, health-care professionals must be cognisant of the influences cultures play on health care, services and delivery, and the influence of the health-care professional's own culture on diagnosis, treatment and recommendations. Cultural sensitivity is of special importance to accomplish the second objective of the Lalonde report – access to appropriate mental and physical health care. In more recent years, similar objectives have been restated by Health and Welfare Canada, as well as by the World Health Organization (World Health Organization 1985; Health and Welfare Canada 1986).

Canadian society is pluralistic, comprising individuals and groups of many cultural and linguistic backgrounds. An examination of the 1986 census figures provides evidence that a significant percentage of persons in all provinces identify a native tongue other than English or French. A majority of those individuals whose native tongue is not English or French have immigrated to Canada. Similarly, in many cities, individuals identifying themselves as being of other than English or French background comprise a large percentage of the population; in Toronto, Vancouver and Winnipeg they make up the majority (Secretary of State 1990). In some provinces, people of non-British origin are a considerable percentage of the population, in Ontario's case almost half, and their origins are quite diverse.

Moreover, these figures do not accurately reflect the needs of Francophones and Native Canadians who have specific health needs within their respective communities, which may differ from those needs provided for in the community. Their needs also must be interpreted within the context of official bilingualism and Aboriginal or historical Native rights. It is also important that we realize that cultural diversity in Canada is not simply a temporary phenomenon. Demographers indicate that if Canada is to maintain its current economic position, increased immigration will be required in future to offset the declining birth rate.

It is surprising to find a relative lack of Canadian studies on the relationships between culture and health. There has been some development in the area of Native health studies: courses exist at a small number of post-secondary institutions such as the University of Regina. Some university health-professional schools now offer elective courses on the subject.

In recent years there has been a developing awareness of the need to examine the effect that culture has on health care. All provinces have hosted conferences on multicultural health care, and in 1989 the Canadian Council on Multicultural Health hosted the first national conference on multiculturalism and health care, entitled *Multiculturalism and Health Care: Realities and Needs* (Masi 1989).

However, there was still a lack of information or research in Canada. There has been some new information on the subject (Masi 1989; Health and Welfare 1988; Canadian Council on Multicultural Health 1991), but still, one must often turn to the United States for research or studies, for example, the Report of the Secretary's Task Force on Black and Minority Health (Department of Health and Human Services 1985). The need to turn to the American experience is in one sense all the more puzzling given the continued "melting pot" philosophy of the United States compared to the Canadian policy of multiculturalism.

In 1985, the Ontario Human Rights Commission commissioned a report on visible minority health-care workers. The report pointed to a number of inadequacies within the health-care field that need to be examined if we are to respond to the needs of communities in Canada. In one recommendation the authors stated, "The evidence of this study suggests that many hospitals and other health systems do not fully recognize and act on the fact that Canada has become a multicultural and multiracial society" (Head 1985). Subsequently, a report examining access to health and social services for members of diverse cultural and racial groups has again pointed to difficulties or barriers for some ethnocultural groups in gaining access to mainstream health and social systems (Doyle and Visano 1987).

Since then, a number of studies have echoed similar issues. Over the past several years, there have been a number of reports released that have examined issues relating to the provision of health-care services for the particular needs of cultural communities in Ontario.

These reports include: (1) *Ethnicity and Aging: The Report of the National Workshop on Ethnicity and Aging* (Canadian Public Health

Association 1988); (2) *Canadian Task Force on Mental Health Affecting Immigrants and Refugees: After the Door Has Been Opened* (Health and Welfare Canada 1988); (3) *Access to Health and Social Services for Members of Diverse Cultural and Racial Groups,* Social Planning Council of Metropolitan Toronto (Doyle and Visano 1987); (4) *Partnerships in Health* (Multicultural Health Coalition 1988); (5) *Multiculturalism and Health Care: Realities and Needs,* Canadian Council on Multicultural Health (Masi 1989); (6) *Equity in Health: Health Planning for the Canadian Mosaic* (Canadian Council on Multicultural Health 1988).

On reviewing the information of the conferences and studies, one will note a number of key issues that are consistently raised (Masi 1989):

1. that there be greater emphasis given to community-based health services, and less on the institutionally based ones;

2. that there be greater representation of cultural communities at decision- and policy-making levels, especially in the ones that directly affect the overall health care of the community, as well as greater representation in the health professions in general; and that special assistance in the way of funding be provided to assist individuals from disadvantaged groups to achieve this objective;

3. that the integration of multicultural or cross-cultural sensitivity and awareness skills be strongly encouraged or mandated within the health education systems – especially in the medical and nursing systems at both the under- and post-graduate levels; and that accreditation examine the appropriateness and content of the multicultural training in the health education and service institutions;

4. that qualified interpreters or intermediators be a priority in health-care services; and that appropriate recognized programs be developed to provide the necessary skills and training for such persons;

5. that there be more translated health information developed appropriate to the needs of cultural communities; and that a national clearinghouse be developed to share resources and minimize duplication of materials;

6. that research on aspects of multicultural health care be considered a greater priority; and that it be funded appropriately;

7. that the stresses involved in re-settlement be recognized to a greater degree; and that services and programs to assist in re-settlement in a culturally new environment be provided.

DEVELOPMENTS

Despite the previous lack of sensitivity or response by mainstream health systems or organizations, in the past several years there have been an increasing number of efforts in the health-care field to respond to community concerns or needs. For example, many health organizations have developed multicultural committees, others have sponsored multicultural awareness programs. Some hospitals, such as the Regina General Hospital, have started programs to examine and respond to specific community needs (Baker, Findlay and Isbister 1987). There are other examples, such as the Mount Sinai, Doctors and Central hospitals in Toronto. In Ontario, the Ontario Hospital Association has been developing a manual on cross-cultural training for health-care professionals. In the same province the Ministry of Citizenship has developed a publication entitled *Multiculturalism and Health Care: A Cultural Simulation for Health Care Professionals* to assist health professionals to better understand multicultural health issues.

Ontario is not alone in these developments. All provinces have committees or organizations on multicultural health, many of which have been undertaking projects that are intended to improve equity and accessibility to health for cultural communities.

As well, a number of professional and community organizations have been developed to address multicultural health care. These include the Transcultural Nursing Society, which was formed in 1974 and has promoted cultural sensitivity and transcultural nursing techniques (Leininger 1984). Across the country a number of provincial organizations have developed under the leadership of the Canadian Council on Multicultural Health to promote multicultural health care in each of the provinces (Canadian Council on Multicultural Health 1991).

MULTICULTRUAL HEALTH ISSUES

In my 1989 report prepared for the Canadian Council on Multicultural Health, I identified a number of areas that need to be examined in order to assist and improve ethnocultural communities' access to the health-care system (Masi 1989):

1. documentation or research on genetic, biological and metabolic variables;

2. information on genetics, cultural beliefs and practices pertinent to health care;

3. information on ethnoculturally related diseases, illnesses and physiological sensitivities for health-care professionals working within specific communities;

4. health personnel fluent or knowledgable in the language and culture of the community;

5. community representation within the health-care professions and at policy- or decision-making levels of the health-care systems or institutions;

6. awareness of religious or socially acceptable practices, beliefs or treatments that differ between the health-care provider and the community;

7. translated and acculturated information geared to the educational level of the target community;

8. programs or services that are culturally sensitive to community norms and to variations within a community;

9. health concerns or needs of a specific community that may differ from those of the mainstream society;

10. health care or programs that are accessible after work hours.

GUIDELINES FOR CULTURAL SENSITIVITY

In recent years the Advisory Committee on Health and Culture to the Ontario Ministry of Health has developed a series of guidelines to assist the development of more culturally sensitive health-care programs and services. The Ontario Ministry of Health has since extensively circulated the guidelines in the form of a consultation paper. The guidelines would, if implemented, help develop programs or services that would be sensitive and responsive to multicultural health issues. The guidelines have been well received and could form the basis for a structured approach for integrating cultural considerations within health-care services and programs.

GUIDELINES FOR THE IMPLEMENTATION OF CULTURAL SENSITIVITY AND AWARENESS IN HEALTH-CARE SERVICES AND PROGRAMS

1. Policy statement: Organizations or agencies in the field of health should identify their intent to serve the entire community through a

statement of objectives or in a policy or position statement. Any program or service that is intended to address specific racial or cultural needs should similarly identify its purpose.

2. Initiation and representation: Programs and services should involve responsible representation from the communities they are to serve. Representation may refer to individuals identified by the community to speak on their behalf. Multicultural representation can also mean that the members of a board or council, or the membership emanates from and reflects the diversity in a community. It is also important that planning recognize that there are some sectors that may be especially disadvantaged and will require specific attention (e.g., immigrant and racial-minority women and seniors).

3. Definition of the community: Health programs and services intended to serve the community should understand the diversity within the community and cultural groups. Cultural groups contain many variables. There are differences within and among racial and cultural groups including specific disadvantaged sectors within groups, which need to be acknowledged to develop appropriate services. Many factors may strongly influence the cultural values or needs of community groups, including the extent of acculturation.

4. Cultural/linguistic components: Health programs and services should be sensitive and responsive to cultural values, norms and practices as well as linguistic needs. In order to serve communities equitably, programs and services need to respond to the racial, cultural and linguistic diversity of the community.

5. Community involvement: Programs and services should involve participation by the community. If programs and services are to be effective in reaching the community, they should be supported by the community. Support from the community should also be solicited prior to the commencement of programs and services intended for the community.

6. Organizational support: Once established, services should include representation and decision-making from the communities served.

7. Employment and education: The principles of equity must be reflected in all employment practices. That includes recruitment, hiring, performance appraisal, promotion and the provision of a harassment-free work environment. Staff must be afforded opportunities for training and development to improve their knowledge of and responsiveness to cultural issues.

8. Coordination with similar interest groups: Programs and services should operate in cooperation with other existing systems, programs and services. In a multicultural society, cooperation and coordination with other existing programs and services will be necessary to minimize duplication and fragmentation of services. It is important that the organizational structure be sufficiently flexible to allow for changing needs in the community with the changing demographics and/or changing health needs.

9. Evaluation: Evaluation should be an integral part of any program or service. To assess the degree of cultural effectiveness of a program or service, community involvement in the evaluation must be a significant component. The guidelines could form an effective and practical structure for multicultural health care. Indeed, the guidelines should form the basis for any truly community based or responsive program or service.

CONCLUSIONS

To be effective, health treatments, programs, care and services must be understood by the cultural communities to which they are directed. In order that they be understood and then accepted by the individual and the community, these same health-care services will need to recognize the importance of ethnocultural background. There must also be the recognition of the roles that cultures have in the development of programs or services or in the delivery of health care itself. It is important that we know and recognize variations within communities.

As we increasingly come to terms with population mobility and our pluralistic society, the onus will be placed on health professionals to understand ethnocultural influences and to respond to them in a culturally sensitive manner. It is impossible to develop specific prescriptive responses for each ethnocultural community, but awareness together with a knowledge of strategies and techniques of transcultural or multicultural health care can assist practitioners to understand and be sensitive to ethnocultural concerns and issues in health.

The challenge presented to health professions and health-care systems in general is to make adaptations to respond to the multicultural, multilingual, multi-racial nature of Canadian society. By developing an awareness of and sensitivity to cultural influences on health (be it information, diagnosis or delivery), health care can be made more responsive and accessible.

REFERENCES

Baker, F.W., S. Findlay, L. Isbister, and B. Peekeekoot. "Native Health Care: An Alternative Approach." *Canadian Medical Association Journal* 136 (1987): 695-696.

Berlin, E.A., and W.C. Fowkes Jr. "A Teaching Framework for Cross-Cultural Health Care: Application in Family Practice." *Western Journal of Medicine* 139 (December 1983): 934-938.

Canadian Council on Multicultural Health. *Equity in Health: Health Planning for the Canadian Mosaic.* 1988.

Canadian Public Health Association. *Ethnicity and Aging: The Report on the National Workshop on Ethnicity and Aging.* Ottawa: 1988.

Deagle, G.L. "The Art of Cross-Cultural Care." *Canadian Family Physician* 32 (1986): 1,315-1,318.

Department of Health and Human Services. *Report of The Secretary's Task Force on Black and Minority Health.* Washington, D.C.: 1985.

Doyle, R., and L. Visano. *Access to Health and Social Services for Members of Diverse Cultural and Racial Groups.* Report prepared for the Social Planning Council of Metropolitan Toronto, 1987.

Harwood, A. *Ethnicity and Medical Care.* Cambridge: Harvard University Press, 1981.

Head, W. *An Exploratory Study of Attitudes and Perceptions of Minority and Majority Health Care Workers.* Ontario Human Rights Commission, 1985.

Health and Welfare Canada. *A New Perspective on the Health of Canadians.* Ottawa: Government of Canada, 1974.

_____. *Achieving Health for All: A Framework for Health Promotion.* Position paper produced for the Department. Ottawa, 1986.

_____. *Canadian Task Force on Mental Health Issues Affecting Immigrants and Refugees: After the Door Has Been Opened.* Government of Canada, 1988.

Henderson, G., and M. Primeaux, eds. *Transcultural Health Care.* Don Mills: Addison-Wesley Publishing, 1981.

Leininger, M. "Transcultural Nursing." *The Canadian Nurse* (December 1984): 42-45.

Lyons, A.S., and R.J. Petricelli. *Medicine: An Illustrated History.* New York: Harry N. Adams, 1978.

Masi, R., ed. *Multiculturalism and Health Care: Realities and Needs.* Canadian Council on Multicultural Health. Toronto, 1989.

Masi, R. "Multiculturalism, Medicine and Health," a six-part series. *Canadian Family Physician* (October 1988 to March 1989).

Multicultural Health Coalition. *Partnerships in Health Number 2: Meeting the Needs of a Multicultural Society.* Multicultural Health Coalition, London, Ontario, 1988.

Secretary of State, Government of Canada. *Visible Minority Canadians: Detailed Ethnicity Data: 1986 Census.* Policy and Research, Multiculturalism and Citizenship.

Waler-Morrison, N., J. Anderson, and E. Richardson. *Cross-Cultural Caring: A Handbook for Health Professionals in Western Canada.* Vancouver: University of British Columbia Press, 1990.

World Health Organization. *Targets for Health for All.* 1985.

First Nations, Race and the Idea of a Plural Community: Defining Canada in the Postmodern Age

ALLAN SMITH

Much attention is given to the role that managing linguistic and ethnic tension must play in stabilizing the world's increasingly heterogeneous national systems. The new phase of conflict and rapprochement in South Africa, growing Aboriginal consciousness in Australasia and Scandinavia, and the stresses produced by the presence of Turkish, North African and East Indian workers and immigrants in the classical nation-states of western Europe are obvious examples.

Linguistic and ethnic difficulties are no less facts of Canadian and American life than they are in the world as a whole. Continuing unease between Blacks and Whites on both sides of the border, the anxiety caused by the recent arrival of substantial numbers of Asian immigrants, and the rising militance of Aboriginal peoples suggest that matters are at least as complicated in these two societies as elsewhere.

North America's Aboriginal peoples and the immigrants who have come here from non-European societies cannot, of course, be treated as though they are the same. Important differences of history, culture, status and position distinguish these groups from each other in a number of ways, of which the possession by one and the lack by the other of a territorrial base and an ancient North American lineage are only the most evident. But there are four distinct senses in which they occupy common ground. Each has been the object of sustained, unrelenting, systematic and institutionalized discrimination on the part of the continent's European-descended majority. Each has made serious efforts in the last several decades to alter its position relative to that of other groups. Each has profited from global developments, be they centred on the struggle for self-determination of Native peoples, the breakdown of the racially homogeneous nation-state in Europe, or the events now unfolding in South Africa. And each has been affected in its efforts to re-shape its relations with the whole by the existence of a national ideology peculiar to the larger society in which it dwells.

If it is clear that essentially racist categories of thinking defined the place assigned to North America's visible minorities before the Second World War, it is equally obvious that those categories began to lose their force and legitimacy during and after the great conflict. And if it is plain that many factors of widely varying sorts acted together to produce this result, it is also evident that one—the simple need to find a *modus vivendi* for living together as transportation, technology and integrated economies drove the world's peoples closer to each other – gradually became more prominent. These realities were operating generally, and certainly on this continent. What needs to be noted is the peculiar character of the arguments used to relate them to practical action here.

The way in which "national tradition" shaped inter-group relations was not always and everywhere in evidence. When the Americans began in 1943 to modify their view of how Asians might be understood in relation to the national whole, what resulted was shaped almost entirely by the exigencies of their war-time alliance with Chiang Kai-shek's China. Ending Chinese exclusion, wrote President Roosevelt, would at once "correct an historic mistake and silence the distorted Japanese propaganda . . . [and recognize China's] great contribution to the cause of decency and freedom."[1] For its part, the immediate post-war period's decision to broaden the modification of restrictions on immigration to include Filipinos and East Indians was produced mainly by a concern to remove the ground for charges of racism. So far were proponents of this measure from talking in "traditional" American terms about admitting the oppressed and downtrodden to the land of opportunity that such advocates of it as Congresswoman Clare Booth Luce made a point of linking their support for it to the fact that, in limiting admissions from these places to 100 a year, what was being proposed would not "lower our living standards and weaken our culture."[2]

By 1952, however, the Walter-McCarran Immigration and Nationality Act allowed Asians to be brought to the republic as individuals to be judged in terms of their capacity and merit, and not just as members of a racial group; the number of Chinese admitted to the United States from

1952 to 1960 shot up from virtually nothing to 27,502.[3] The 1965 Immigration Act carried that process forward to the point where its absolute abandonment of racial criteria could be proclaimed in a presidential ceremony at the Statue of Liberty that was clearly intended to associate the new immigrants of colour not only with their predecessors from Europe but also with those predecessors' experience in fitting in, adjusting and becoming good Americans. As President Johnson put it, the Act "repairs a deep and painful flaw in the fabric of American justice; . . . those who come [now] will come because of what they are – not because of the land from which they spring."[4]

By the 1970s the thrust toward the new American ethnicity was complicating the argument that what the individual brought by way of cultural or racial baggage ought to count as nothing as that individual moved to adopt American values, profess the American faith, and distinguish himself or herself through personal effort and striving. The new thrust, however, never involved abandonment of the idea that Americans were defined essentially by their possession of those values and that faith. Asian-Americans, certainly, felt no diminution in their need to show how "American" they had become, sometimes with quite extraordinary anxiety that their efforts be seen and appreciated. "America," ran Harry H.L. Kitano's remarkable 1969 effusion, "likes success stories – the bigger the better. Therefore, America should enjoy the story of the Japanese in the United States, . . . for it is a story of success Japanese-American style, . . . [of a] hero [who] pulls himself up by the bootstraps."[5] Whether one looked at what Asian-Americans were saying or at what others were saying about them, one saw a common message: they were to be seen as a people whose American experience, like that of others before them, had brought fully into play the individualist virtues so clearly definitive of life in the great republic.

The national faith's involvement in the changing sense of blackness and its meaning was obvious from the outset. The 1954 Supreme Court decision in Brown vs. the Board of Education of Topeka secured the principle that one's position before the law was no longer to be viewed as something mediated by race. Major national publications (*Time, Newsweek, U.S. News and World Report*), encouraged sympathy for the mainstream civil-rights movement by presenting it as a force committed to "American" values, thus ensuring that those values would be seen as having a close association with that movement.[6]

This, of course, did not mean that all was smooth sailing. Not a few Whites continued to operate in terms of the "old" racist ideas. And Blacks as well still saw race as something more than a mere irrelevance. In their case, however, this complicated matters, not so much because it involved adherence to old patterns of thought and behaviour, but because it led to something quite new. They maintained their sense of themselves as members of a racially defined group, and maintained their defensive posture of seeking to ease relations with the White majority by behaving in ways consistent with that majority's image of them.[7] But at the same time, they adopted a much more aggressive stance. Taking up ideas ultimately grounded in the notions of *négritude* and identity developed by such thinkers as Frantz Fanon, they urged celebration of blackness as a badge of distinction and even superiority. And, some of them asserted, not only was blackness to be seen as "beautiful," but it might also be viewed as the foundation on which separate, self-contained, racially defined communities could stand.[8]

But, though all this was important, its significance ought not to be exaggerated. Most discussion of blackness and its meaning was informed not by the notion that status and membership in the community were to be viewed as in some way related to race, but by the idea that these things should be seen as a function of individual worth and accomplishment. Blackness was certainly not to be disregarded as an element in one's identity. It was a component of that identity in much the same sense that being Polish or Italian or Norwegian helped make up the *personae* of those Americans graced by involvement with the ethnic groups those terms designated. And, just as one's character as a member of such a group had not stood in the way of his or her incorporation into the American mainstream, so also the fact of being what was increasingly referred to as "Afro-American" need not present insurmountable obstacles to those characterized by that reality as they moved toward the same destination. As one Black American put it, "hard work, education, individual initiative, stable family life, property ownership – these have always been the means by which ethnic groups have moved ahead in America; . . . these 'laws' of advancement apply absolutely to black Americans also."[9]

This encouraging fact did not mean that Afro-Americans were exactly like other immigrant groups. As any examination of income, education and employment statistics would make clear, they stood in a different, inferior, position. But this had little to do with race. Historical experience was the critical factor. Afro-Americans were "behind" because of the debilitating effects produced by centuries of involuntary immigration and slavery. And if the problem were socio-economic, and the causes of it the same, it followed that its resolution lay in that area too. Affirmative action programs evolved that helped individual members of that group overcome the disadvantages of their background so that they might compete with others on a footing of genuine equality and fairness. On no account, so friends argued, were the programs to be seen as validating any sort of permanent or special status for a group of people defined in racial terms. Race, to be sure, was a prerequisite for assistance, but that was so only because of its link with social and economic deprivation. Once that had been eliminated, *prima facie* evidence that the United States had become a "racially neutral"[10] society would exist, individuals would be able to compete freely and equally, and colour would be no more a badge of identity – or a ground for either reverse or regular discrimination – than one's tie to the culture of Ireland, Czechoslovakia or Finland, for example.

The national ethic's intervention in the way understanding of the native Indian came to be framed was hardly less complicated than its presence in the debate about Asians and Blacks. Initially, it seemed as though there would hardly be complications at all. Post-war ideas about the importance of seeing "through" racially based stereotypes to the individual "behind" seemed clearly to be combining with long-standing notions about moving Indians into mainstream society by undermining the supports of their collective identity. The 1950s certainly saw a revival of the kind of thinking that had undergirded the Dawes Act (1887), with legislators such as Utah Senator Arthur Watkins spearheading moves to undo the work of the Roosevelt administrations' Indian Reorganization Act (1934) by returning to the notion that the Indians' relationship to the land be allowed to evolve in ways consistent with individual property ownership.

The Indian Freedom Program ran afoul of the revived Indian consciousness of the 1960s and 1970s, but the formation of the American Indian movement (1968), the getting by the Indians of favourable land settlements in Alaska, Maine and Massachusetts, as well as the uprisings of Alcatraz, Mount Rushmore, Fort Sheridan and, above all, Wounded Knee (1973) did not succeed in replacing "American" modes of thinking about the Indian "problem" with ones based on a strong and clear sense that Indians were a group – or groups – and should be dealt

237

with as such. The Nixon administration abandoned the Indian Freedom Program in 1970, schooling was sometimes altered in ways that allowed Native teachers to deal with Native culture, and in 1975 Congress committed itself to a policy of "self-determination" designed to allow those willing and able to sustain it a share in running their own affiars. An assertion that "the Indian world may really have been a genuine, influential civilization worth taking seriously in American history" could be made.[11] But a tendency to see Indians as members of an ethnic minority destined, like all the others, to accommodate itself to the mainstream was much in evidence too. One commentator's observation that "their situation is in some ways singular" was thus followed up by the observation that they "have confronted the complete range of dilemmas familiar to other American minorities" and the even more telling assertion that "modern" pan-Indianism is the crucible in which elements in the larger society combine with elements in Indian life to produce new definitions of identity within the American social order."[12] Another presented "the first Americans . . . as people who are an integral part of modern American life. . . . American Indians are vital, integral parts of American society and indeed are important currents in the American mainstream."[13] A third was careful to stress Indian concern with at least a measure of autonomy – but even he ended by emphasizing the fact that their relationship was to the whole, and that it would be worked out on the whole's terms: the Indians might want "greater control over their own lives and futures," but they were also to be seen as moving "into more active engagement with the larger society."[14] And the use of the term "first Americans" itself spoke volumes, for it made clear the existence of a deep conviction that for all that might set the Indians apart, they were to be understood as part of the national whole, different from other Americans, to be sure, but set apart from them chiefly in terms of the time of their arrival on the American shore. Even the Indians themselves might occasionally get caught up in this way of seeing things. Their advocates certainly suggested on more than one occasion that what they wanted for themselves and their associates was perfectly intelligible in terms of familiar and accepted American ways of understanding human aspirations and meeting human needs. Not hesitating, even at the height of agitation in 1969, to identify itself as "American," one group – the American Indian Task Force – made it plain that, in asking for "the right to pursue our sacred dream . . . ," it was seeking nothing more or less than movement toward an objective that was definitely American. A quest of that kind, as the Task Force put the matter, "is the American way. We claim our birthright."[15]

It is not surprising that defining the terms upon which people of colour could be brought within the framework of the American polity as fully functioning members should have been resolved in ways altogether consistent with the individualist, egalitarian and homogenizing elements of the American tradition. Once race lost its legitimacy as a tool for the hierarchical ordering of human beings, the deeply entrenched idea that Americans were individuals united to each other and to the whole by the bonds of a common faith in equality, individualism and the American way of life was bound to come to the forefront. This did not mean that all traces of a pluralistic view of the nation disappeared completely from view. President Reagan himself could pronounce his ideal to be an "orderly, compassionate, pluralistic society – an archipelago of prospering communites and divergent institutions."[16] And by 1989 sociologist David Bell classified the United States as "a modern civil society, one that is heterogeneous and often multi-racial," and one in which the problem of order and government turned on recognition of "the principle of toleration and the need for plural communities to agree on rules governing procedures within the frame of constitutionalism."[17]

For the most part, however, rhetoric of this kind yielded to description and imaging of a much more conventional American sort. Reagan's most consistently sounded note was shaped by his concern to avoid any sense that he was underwriting the balkanization of American society feared by such commentators as Kevin Philips.[18] Reagan's speeches simultaneously signalled his view that there was an overarching American faith to which Americans responded as individuals and his sense that this truth needed to be consistently, forcefully and regularly underscored. And, if the re-articulation of traditional values present in what one observer calls his "culture of national pride" was intended to reinforce the fact that all were bound together by virtue of their common participation in an overarching system of values,[19] the same was true of the extraordinary image that President Bush presented to his fellow Americans when he talked of their society as an ostensibly plural one, the components of which stood out like a "thousand points of light in a broad and peacefuly sky." Quite apart from the fact that Bush's exegesis of these words' meaning rendered race invisible by referring to many sorts of groups – church, neighbourhood, educational – without mentioning ones defined by colour, the image implied an America whose different parts

239

were to be understood as essentially the same. And not only did that image represent the nation as a thing made up of elements only distinguishable from each other in terms of their brightness and intensity; it also portrayed those elements as anchored and stabilized by their setting in the "broad and peaceful sky," causing them to move in a kind of heavenly lockstep, incapable of any independent motion and thrust.[20]

Even presidential candidate Jesse Jackson's compelling metaphor of the Rainbow Coalition yielded to the power of belief in the American way. Increasingly concerned to emphasize elements of unity rather than division, Jackson first moved away from the image of the rainbow to that of the quilt – something, as he told the Democratic National Convention in 1984, that was, in spite of its variegated pattern, "held together by a common thread."[21] As his campaign developed, it became ever clearer that, while the existence of racially defined groups might have been his place of starting, it would not be where he intended to finish. What, he began to argue, was important about groups was the way membership in them operated to keep people out of the mainstream. The way to remedy that situation was not to confirm and entrench the existence of those groups but to make them "disappear" as things "controlling" the fate of those belonging to them. Just as being of Italian or Greek descent had ceased to operate as a phenomenon denying full participation in American life to those characterized by it, so also must the same happen in regard to "blackness," "yellowness" and "redness." The need was to create an effective citizenship for visible minorities, to give "a united voice to those Blacks, browns, Native Americans, Asian Americans, Arab Americans, Jewish Americans and Caribbean Americans and the poor who lack power,"[22] something that could be done only by diminishing the importance of what set them apart in favour of what would unite them with each other and with Americans in general. For Jackson, in short, the only problem with the existing model of American society was that too many Americans were not represented in it. Those Americans lacked power and effective citizenship, and the way to resolve their difficulty lay in rendering their groupness "invisible" so that they could be dealt with, and act, as what the American creed insisted they were: citizens entitled to their share of involvement in and control over how their society at large was run.

Once again, the enduring strength of the quintessential American idea was evidenced. Americans were defined by their common orientation toward a set of values and the behaviour they enjoined. Far from having

240

developed into something to be conceived of as a community of communities, their society remained what it had always been held to be, a comity of principle, commitment and idea. The acceptance of membership in this comity united individual Americans to each other and to the whole they combined to make up. As Everett Carll Ladd argued in 1987, "the United States is a nation founded on an ideology . . . which is given force and coherence by a far-reaching commitment to the individual." It was, in consequence, to this "expression of a nation-defining consensus on political values," to the Constitution embodying it, and to the individual American acceptance of it, that one must look in order to grasp and comprehend the character of the whole.[23]

Canadians, too, viewed the problem of race in the post-war period through the lens provided for them by their own sense of society. But, where analyzing the problem had had one consequence south of the border, it produced quite a different outcome north of it. Canadians had learned to see that national whole quite differently from how Americans had. Canadians were quite incapable of dismissing the importance of linguistic and ethnic group affiliations as factors of consequence in the process by which both individual identity and one's relationship to the whole were defined. They came to terms with the new non-racist thinking not by viewing race as something to be, in principle, discounted, as the Americans did, but by granting it status as a constituent of identity and a mediator of one's relations with the whole, which was no more or less worthy of recognition than others.

This did not mean that the Canadian approach was at all times dominated by this sort of recognition of race. Citizenship and Immigration Minister Ellen Fairclough certainly defended her department's 1962 moves to end racially based quotas on immigration by focusing on the recognition that this would give to the individual. The proposed changes, she insisted, would permit "any suitably qualified person" to be considered for immigration "entirely on his [sic] own merits."[24] Similarly, the federal government's 1969 white paper proposing the abolition of Aboriginal status was, in its view of Indians as candidates for assimilation into the White mainstream, built on the notion that group characteristics associated with race and visible difference were to be treated as of virtually no consequence.[25] And even the 1988 Multiculturalism Act, in the very course of stressing the country's racial and cultural diversity, could be used as a vehicle for projecting the idea that Canada, "a family of individuals," must never lose sight of the integrity of the person.[26]

If, however, the Canadian recognition of race and colour was by no means a universal, unqualified and omnipresent phenomenon, it was enough in evidence to warrant the claim that Canadians did see these things as realities still having to be recognized. When immediate post-war supporters of enfranchising Asian Canadians assembled their case, they put it together not by treating race as something to be set aside, but by drawing new conclusions from the fact of its existence; it remained a reality, but, where its presence as such had once been viewed as the ground for an understanding of society framed in terms of hierarchy and exclusion, it must now be seen simply as an instrument for the categorization of certain groups of citizens to be accepted and accommodated. As the Vancouver *News-Herald* put it in 1946, "in a new world, drawn from all races," maintaining a policy of discrimination based on colour made no sense.[27]

Post-war proponents of rights for ethnic groups now claimed that the status and posture of the group justified the extension of rights. This was particularly evident in the part of the suffrage argument for Chinese Canadians. Thus they deserved their right to the franchise not on the grounds that proper and just treatment of the individual required it, but because the Chinese Canadian community as a collective entity had earned the right to have it. Generally loyal and patriotic during the war, that community's contribution of personnel to the armed forces was particularly noteworthy. So striking a display of civic and military virtue on the part of one of society's components clearly merited the obvious and appropriate response from society at large, and it was to ensure that it got that response that the vote had been conferred. That was why British Columbia MP George Pearkes drew explicit attention to the notions of obligation and responsibility at play in the decision. "The Government of B.C. has given the franchise not only to these young [service]men," he stated, "but to all Canadian-born Chinese."[28]

Supporters of the restoration of the right of Japanese Canadians to live and travel anywhere in Canada similarly founded their case on arguments that turned on a sense of society as an agglomeration of groups – racial as well as other kinds – though in this case the emphasis was placed on the relationship that treating each of them fairly bore to the smooth and harmonious functioning of the whole. Canada, proclaimed the *Winnipeg Free Press,* is "a nation of minorities." Maintaining any one of them in a position of inferiority was fraught with great danger, for, "if this precedent is once established for one minority, it can be applied to any minority," a situation that would lead not only to un-imaginable injustice but also complete social breakdown.[29]

The sense that racial groups existed, and that law and policy was to operate on them as such, might even extend to collectivities not yet a part of Canadian society. Fairclough herself, for all her emphasis on using immigration reform to open the way for the triumph of individual merit, made it clear that the 1962 changes would profit groups of people defined in racial terms: "The chief beneficiaries," as she told the House of Commons, "will be the Asians, Africans, and nationals of Middle Eastern countries."[30]

As time passed, the emerging Canadian sense that race was a reality to be accommodated became particularly evident in arguments about its relevance to the nation's character as a political society. The tendency in the United States was to move away from the notion that race was a factor of consequence. One sees, as a result, a clear shift away from the idea that politicians identifiable in terms of their membership in visible minorities should be seen as nothing other than representatives of their groups to the notion that they were to be viewed as the agents of racially mixed constituencies to whose voters they could relate as if race had ceased to be a factor. The first stage was classically manifested in the case of Harlem Congressman Adam Clayton Powell, that if one was Black one's voters would be too. This gave way to the idea that this need not at all be the case, as epitomized by the new Black mayors of the 1960s. The "disappearance" of race was even more clearly evident in the election of S.I. Hayakawa to the United States Senate in 1976. Attributed almost entirely to his defence of "American" values while president of San Franciso State College, his victory perfectly embodied the idea that voter and candidate should deal with each other in terms of their interests as citizens and Americans. It was, as one commentator put it, Hayakawa's "defiance of radicals at [that institution that] propelled him into the United States' Senate."[31] Racial awareness and identification did not as a practical matter vanish altogether, and Black members of the Congress, for example, caucused as a group. But the principle was clear. Members of racial minorities in politics were to be seen, not as represen-tatives of their communities, but as proof of the fact that racism was ceasing to impede the citizen as he or she sought status and advancement within a polity very much to be understood as a collection of free, autonomous and equal individuals. Even, then, as Jesse Jackson's emergence as a national political figure was held to signal the decline –

perhaps the end – of racism, it could also be seen as exemplifying the kind of mobility and achievement long thought to be at the heart of the American idea. As *Time* magazine put it in 1988, Jackson had not only "taught white America that a black person is . . . somebody," he has also taught it that "he can be anybody. Even President of the United States."[32]

In Canada the sense that the political process had in some formal way to recognize and allow for the existence of the racially defined groups that helped make up the society over whose affairs it was presiding became steadily stronger. This did not completely define the understanding of things held by all members of visible minorities who occupied elective office. New Democrats Rosemary Brown and Howard McCurdy have been as concerned with cleavages of class and gender as with those of race, while even Lincoln Alexander's sojourn in the House of Commons as a member of so non-ideological a party as the Conservatives saw him function and identify himself as more than simply a Black MP. But, if these elected politicians have not especially wanted to see themselves – or to be seen – as giving a kind of virtual representation to the racial group of which they are members, others have quite willingly conformed to the view of society that understands it as composed of various sorts of groups to which reality their presence in public life offers testimony. Douglas Jung certainly did not hide what he felt to be the relationship between his election as the first Chinese Canadian MP and what, in his view, this meant for the way Canadian society as a whole was to be understood. Moe Sihota's maintenance of his close ties with the Indo-Canadian community following his 1986 election to the British Columbia Legislature was altogether consistent with the early identification of him as in some sense a representative of one of the many groups of which the country consisted. And the fact that Manitoba Legislature member Elijah Harper moved to dispatch the Meech Lake Accord in the name of the nation's Aboriginal peoples makes plain the way he viewed himself and his responsibilites.

That members of racially definable groups who hold public office have come increasingly to play a part in validating and giving expresssion to the idea that Canada is a society of racially based as well as other sorts of particularism is at its plainest in relation to appointments to public office. The appointees, almost without exception, have received what they got not just as a recognition of their individual ability and distinction but also as a sign that the groups to which they belong have status as component parts of the Canadian community. Certainly the Diefenbaker

Conservatives' strong orientation toward an understanding of Canada as a class-, race-, and even gender-differentiated society led it to use the Senate in the course of its efforts to encourage that view of matters. And if the 1960 appointment of James Gladstone as the first Native Indian Senator was the earliest outcome of this determination, the Trudeau government's 1984 selection of Anne Cools as the first Black member of that body showed its vitality. By 1990 the use of appointees to signal the fact that Canada was a nation of many sorts of particularism was established enough to ensure that the Citizens' Forum on National Unity, organized to provide a vehicle for the expression of public opinion on national unity and constitutional reform, would include a Black and a Native Indian as well as French speakers, representatives of the regions, ethnics and women.

At the provincial level, too, the same point was made, and in exactly the same way. When British Columbia Premier W.A.C. Bennett included Kamloops Mayor Peter Wing in his delegation to the 1968 constitutional conference, his action did not simply underscore the fact that Canada was a nation of particularisms, or even the reality that those particularisms varied from region to region. It also drove home the point that some of them were racially based. Ontario Premier David Peterson's choices of a Black and a Chinese for his cabinet were intended to underscore the racially heterogeneous character of his province. Lincoln Alexander's 1986 appointment as the first Black lieutenant-governor of Ontario was, as federal cabinet minister David Crombie put it, meant to be "a symbol to this province, that in this province there is a place in the Ontario sun for everybody."[33] And, when in 1988 David Lam became British Columbia's first lieutenant-governor of Chinese origin, the message was equally clear. Given the fact that his "role through life has been that of a bridge builder, offering help to those of different cultures," it was altogether appropriate that he should be the Crown's representative in a jurisdiction where racial diversity was especially evident.[34]

Perhaps the clearest indication of the fact that the Canadian sense of nation conditioned a response to the problem of race and community quite different from that of the Americans is to be seen in the realm of ritual and symbolism. Ceremony, sign and rite, of course, function in both societies in broadly the same way, as does their Durkheimian role in enforcing social solidarity. But the manner in which they fulfill that function has turned out to be not at all similar. In the United States, the fixed and homogeneous character of the nation that symbols represent,

245

and membership in which public ritual affirms, assures that those symbols and rituals will be stable and unchanging. Embodiments of a nation and a national faith are always and everywhere the same; they must themselves not vary or alter. When the moment came to show that, like the nation itself, these symbols and rituals could have as much meaning for persons of colour as they did for White Americans, this was done, not by changing them, but by demonstrating that they could accommodate and embrace those different sorts of persons. So strongly did this imperative operate that when the organizers of the great civil-rights march of 1963 decided to focus on the nation's capital, they were moved to make the very monuments of the country's commitment to democracy and freedom their focus. Concentrating particularly on associating themselves with the Washington Monument and the Lincoln Memorial, their occupancy of the space between and around those grand edifices showed that what they were seeking simply had to be seen as entirely consistent with the spirit of nation with which those fixed, stable and constant structures had always resonated. And when, on its side, official America reached out to show that race was now not to be perceived as an obstacle to involvement in the public life, it too moved to use symbol and ceremony to make the point, by bringing Blacks publicly and clearly into context with them very much as they stood. The fact that race was now held at the highest levels not to matter could, as a result, be indicated by a widely circulated photograph showing Martin Luther King in the Oval Office with President Johnson.[35]

By the 1980s the thrust to show that existing symbol and ritual were capacious enough to epitomize the involvement of all sorts of people in the national life had broadened considerably. King was given a national holiday, "an honour granted to only one other U.S. citizen, George Washington."[36] Others besides Blacks were being explicitly linked to the sacred mysteries, rites and texts of the republic. The cover of *Time* magazine's special issue marking the two-hundredth anniversary of the Constitution thus featured the celebrated opening words of the document superimposed on a background of white, yellow, black, brown and red faces.[37] A striking colour photograph of two elderly Chinese American women against the backdrop provided by a wall painting of the American flag[38] made clear that proximity to Old Glory itself could be used to suggest full and complete participation in the life of the nation.

Nowhere was the concern to associate minorities with the stable and unchanging symbols of American life clearer than in the way those minorities were brought into contact with military dress. Sometimes, of course, that dress did vary. General MacArthur wore non-regulation clothing during the early period of America's involvement in the Second World War, and "in Vietnam uniforms were drastically modified by love beads and peace slogans." Departures from the norm in physical appearance, too, were tolerated, as, for example, was demonstrated by Black soldiers' winning the right to wear Afros. All this, however, was done on an *ad hoc* basis. There remained, in principle, "a standardized uniform to symbolize the nation," which counted as "a symbolic declaration that an individual will adhere to group norms and standardized roles." The garment simply could not be allowed to lose its character as a thing always and everywhere the same. The American armed forces therefore issued no clerical collars for Christian chaplains, no yarmulkes for Jews, and "efforts by military personnel to use turbans have also met with failure."[39] Subgroup affiliation suggested a diminution of the loyalty to the army and to the state it served. These adornments thus made way for a style of dress that, like so much else in the life of the republic, reinforced the sense that the whole – whether army or society – was made up of essentially undifferentiated individuals linked directly to it. So deeply entrenched is the idea that in putting on a uniform of a recognized sort one was, as it were, taking on the outward and visible sign of an inward and common identity that that idea might even affect the significance of non-military dress. When the South African Black leader Nelson Mandela appeared on the streets of New York in June 1990 wearing a New York Yankees jacket and cap, the message was clearly conveyed.[40] He could quite appropriately be costumed in clothing whose long-standing association with a central element in American civilization made it the perfect way to symbolize that identification; he was worthy of identification with the fundamental values and assumptions of American society.

In Canada, the relation between national symbol and the new view of race was rather different. Far from signalling their recognition of the racial minorities' altered status by associating the members of those minorities with the fixed and unchanging things of the nation, Canadians set out to accomplish that all-important goal by modifying the configuration, set and design of those things themselves. In this, as in other areas, they were acting in conformity with national tradition, for the early emergence of strong particularisms had made it nothing short of mandatory that symbol, song and ritual be framed in terms reflective

247

of diversity and pattern. Even in the days of Canada's strong British orientation, the devices used to represent the nation stressed the variegated character of its people – as the *Maple Leaf Forever*'s (1871) reference to the "Lily, Thistle, Shamrock, [and] Rose" makes clear.[41] The national anthem itself defined the country's unity in terms of its inhabitants' occupancy of a shared geographical space ["the true north"] rather than in those of unifying creed or common ethnicity. The lyrics of the piece were written in two languages, and the meanings conveyed in each of these were so dissimilar as to have virtually nothing in common.[42]

In time, as awareness of ethnic pluralism as well as linguistic duality deepened, symbols changed to reflect it. By the 1960s, the "old" national flag was retired from service and a new one designed – one that was more fully capable of embodying what was now perceived to be the country's character. Just how far the move to change symbol to accord with "reality" might go was indicated by Prime Minister Pearson's preferred design. Displaying three maple leaves – one for Canadians of English-speaking background, one for those of French and one for all the others – it manifested an obvious and complete acceptance of the idea that tradition and continuity were acceptable only insofar as they might be compatible with the ever-greater variety that the passage of time seemed to be bringing. Even the flag finally adopted sent the same sort of message. And when the new flag was flown in public, the circumstances of its appearance almost always reflected the fact of diversity too. It was generally raised – save at purely federal functions – in company with those the provinces had selected to express and embody their several senses of identity.

It is hardly surprising, then, that, once race presented itself in its post-war guise, it, too, became a reality to be accommodated by change and alteration. Various sorts of symbolic form accordingly found themselves caught up in a kind of flux and movement. The thrust in that direction certainy became evident in public architecture. The formidably consistent neo-classicism of Washington's public buildings stood in its uniform "republican" character at the opposite pole from the mixing of styles evident in Ottawa. In marked contrast to Washington's buildings, Ottawa's Gothic Parliament and its chateauesque Supreme Court tended literally to build an acknowledgement to heterogeneity into the nation's physical representation. By the 1980s the extraordinary Museum of Civilization was designed by Métis architect Douglas Cardinal. Not only did that building's long, low, curved and flowing lines root it firmly in the Métis tradition of involvement with the Canadian prairie landscape (Cardinal had wanted a structure "inspired by the land and people here"),[43] but, seen in association with all that lay around it, it also perfectly embodied the point that Canada had to be understood in terms of the presence in it of several different types of groups, racial as well as cultural and linguistic.

Willingness to adapt and modify symbolic displays in order that racially based heterogeneity be "seen" is particularly evident in relation to the vexing question of military and para-military dress. Linked to a tradition that since the eighteenth-century acceptance of the kilt has not viewed uniforms as in some way needing to acknowledge the cultural and racial specificity of their wearers, Canadian authorities in both the armed and police forces have been moving to alter dress codes in ways consistent with the new awareness of racial heterogeneity. The Canadian armed forces now permit the wearing of turbans, and various city police forces allow Native officers to wear braids.

Even the Canadian Constitution has in its symbolic dimension as well as its legal import evolved in ways consistent with the general pattern. Once by virtue of its language provisions a "sign" that Canada was to be viewed as linguistically dual, it has gradually come to "stand for" (as well as institutionalize) the fact that the country has also to be seen as a collection of groups differentiated by gender, ethnicity and race. The changes made in its character by the 1960 Bill of Rights were certainly seen as conveying this message. They indicated that the position of racial as well as other minorities was now recognized, a fact that, had it been a reality 20 years earlier, would have had a decisive relevance for "the relocated Japanese of World War II."[44] More clearly still, the 1982 Charter of Rights was taken as a quite unambiguous sign of the country's character as (among other things) a society of groups, each of which had rights and some of which were racial in nature. The kind of "segmental accommodation" evident in the new document's recognition of Aboriginal peoples clearly indicated, thought one observer, that the country was very much to be seen in this way.[45] What had been done to provide for gender, race and the disabled, observed another, made it at least as obvious that the nation should be understood in terms of "concepts of community based on shared characteristics such as race, sex or handicap, that transcend provincial boundaries.[46] And, said a third, the fact that "the Charter . . . hand[s] out particular constitutional niches to particular categories of Canadians, such as women, aboriginals, etc."[47]

very clearly reinforced a view of the country as something to be understood as a congeries of groups, some of which were racially defined.

There are important differences in the manner in which the Canadian and American understandings of nation and society has led inhabitants of the two countries to respond to the issue of race. Thanks to quite dissimilar views concerning whether, to what extent, and in what ways the individual's identity and relation to the whole is mediated by subgroup affiliations, the two societies have, in fact, followed paths that could hardly be more separate.

Neither of these routes is in some clear way superior to the other. The American effort to end discrimination by insisting that the citizen be seen and judged as an individual has been, at best, a qualified success. The Canadian approach to the matter also leaves much to be desired. But if honours are not to be awarded on the basis of the relationship that these approaches bear to what has so far happened, perhaps they can be conferred on the ground of their consistency – or lack of it – with what appears likely to come. In this respect, the Canadian approach has a clear and definable edge. Altogether in harmony with the emerging sense that society is to be seen in more complex ways than the liberal, homogenizing, conformitarian model allows, its utility as a guide to action and understanding in the future seems, in fact, all but guaranteed.

It is certainly hard to deny this approach's congruence with the developing notion – articulated by William H. McNeill and others – that homogeneous societies inhabited by essentially undifferentiated individuals are, in the sweep of history, anything but "normal." McNeill's case for the way the world should be seen – in it, he asserts, "marginality and pluralism were and are the norm of civilized existence" – offers, in fact, nothing short of a rendering on the global scale of the sense of things in terms of which Canadians have for some time been tending to think. His argument rests on the view that this sense of things emerged only in the quite special conditions obtaining in western Europe during the eighteenth century, and turns even more centrally on the claim that whatever realities may once have validated it are now disappearing.[48]

Equally difficult to dispute is the harmony between the Canadian idea and what theorists are beginning to posit concerning the relationship among race, identity and culture. Following the anti-racist revolution of the 1940s to its logical conclusion, they have developed the view that it makes no more sense to dismiss all awareness of race as involving "socially imagined"[49] categories that are inevitably racist than it does to reject the idea that feelings of identity may in varying degrees be based on a sense of things shared with persons perceived to be members of the same racial group. They have asserted that one can notice that awareness, those feelings, and the culture they help produce without being obliged to view them hierarchically in relation to others. In doing so, they have done much to show just how consistent with the Canadian sense of things the emerging understanding of the relationship is. J.G. Herder himself, they point out, insisted that race as well as language and ethnicity helped define the different cultures whose variety and equality he wished to celebrate. He rebukes Kant for his belief in the inferiority of Blacks to Europeans.[50] Herder put this essential conviction even more clearly in his observation that "the shapeless rocks with which the Chinese ornaments his garden" were no less evidence of "the plan of reflective understanding [that] is everywhere observable" than was "the ideal beauty of Greece."[51] The thrust to establish the claim that the culture that emerges from the activity of a racially definable group is to be treated as a cultural "fact," no more or less worthy of note, study and appreciation than any other such reality, is even more obvious in what contemporary theorists have been saying on their own behalf. John Rex has insisted on the importance of examining what emerges from the circumstance that "individuals may value physical characteristics similar to their own, identify with them, and pursue actions with them so that they come to share not merely physical but cultural characteristics."[52] M. Michael Rosenberg has similarly stressed the legitimacy of looking at the consequences of race's functioning "as a symbolic marker used by individuals to characterize themselves and others."[53] And Janet Helms's concern to bring under review what is produced by the "sense of group or collective identity based on one's perception" that he or she shares a common racial heritage with a particular racial group" is no less clearly evident.[54]

Hardest of all to put in question is whether the Canadian approach is consistent with what has been establishing itself as the conventional, postmodern wisdom of the age. Many-dimensioned, but based essentially on the notion that the nature of the relationship between language and the reality it purports to describe precludes any grappling with "essences," "absolutes" or the "real," that wisdom invites us to deal with the world in terms of the tentative, indeterminate, contingent and provisional, valuing all that we come into contact with in terms of its potential, not to bring us to a sense of what is "right," "authoritative" or "final," but

251

to enrich our understanding of the problem, or situation, or reality we confront. And if, in the words of Jean-François Lyotard, it is clear that "postmodern knowledge . . . refines our sensitivity to differences and reinforces our ability to tolerate the incommensurable,"[55] it is no less obvious that the Canadian sense of society, resting as it does and must do on the idea that there *is* no idea, no orthodoxy, no universalizing discourse in terms of which an *imperium* of language, ethnicity, culture or race can be imposed, is characterized by just the sort of demanding but liberating thrust toward the open, accommodative and essentially indefinable that is at the heart of that way of seeing the world.

There is, then, much of a general and wide-ranging nature to be said in support of the proposition that the things Canadians have been doing in the domain of multi-racial management mesh perfectly with what the contemporary sense of society and the world suggests ought to be done. Perhaps, however, the most dramatic indication of these actions' consistency with what is developing is something much more focused, specific and surprising – Americans themselves are showing signs of movement in this direction. Finally forced by the sheer intractability of race and racial consciousness to confront the realities those phenomena represent and help shape, not a few citizens of the republic have in the very recent past been turning away from the liberal-individualist idea of society and moving toward one framed in terms that concede a much larger role in the community's making to various sorts of groups – not the least important of which are those racial formations themselves. Going, in consequence, far beyond the quite limited pluralism they adopted in the 1960s and 1970s, they have been starting to think and act in terms of a sense of the sort of real and substantial diversity that simultaneously allows a link between race, culture and identity and demonstrates acceptance of the idea that the individual's involvement in the whole may after all be mediated by more enduring and substantial factors than those associated with simple ethnicity.

NOTES

1 "Message from the President of the United States Favoring Repeal of the Chinese Exclusion Laws," House Document 333, 78th cong. 1st sess. (Washington, D.C., 1943), serial 10,793, pp. 1-2. Cited in Shih-Shan Henry Tsai, *The Chinese Experience in America* (Bloomington: Indiana University Press, 1985), 115. See also Jack Chen, *The Chinese of America* (San Francisco: Harper and Row, 1980), 206; and, for an early detailed study, Fred W. Riggs, *Pressures on Congress: A Study of the Repeal of Chinese Exclusion* (New York: King's Crown Press, 1950).

2 *Congressional Record,* 10 October 1945, pp. 9,529-30. Cited in David Reimers, *Still the Golden Door: The Third World Comes to America* (New York: Columbia University Press, 1985), 15.

3 Tsai, *Chinese Experience,* 139.

4 *New York Times,* 4 October 1965. Cited in Reimers, *Still the Golden Door,* 86.

5 Harry H.L. Kitano, *Japanese-Americans: The Evolution of a Subculture* (Englewood Cliffs: Prentice-Hall, 1969), xi.

6 Richard Lentz, *Symbols, the News Magazines and Martin Luther King* (Baton Rouge: Louisiana State University Press, 1990).

7 In order," notes Daniel C. Thompson, "to facilitate their own survival under various conditions and degrees of servitude, discrimination and individual and institutionalized hostility, [blacks] have invented, refined, and borrowed intact a variety of survival techniques and strategies" (Daniel C. Thompson, *Sociology of the Black Experience* [Westport: Greenwood Press, 1974], 39).

8 Raymond L. Hall, *Black Separatism in the United States* (Hanover: University Press of New England, 1978).

9 Shelby Steel, "On Being Black and Middle Class," *Commentary* 85, 1 (January 1988):47. The classic Black statement of this position is Thomas Sowell, *Ethnic America: A History* (New York: Basic Books, 1981).

10 George Bundy, "The Issue before the Court: Who Gets ahead in America?" in *A History of Our Time,* 2nd ed., edited by William H. Chaffe and Harvard Sitkoff (New York: Oxford University Press, 1987), 409. For a slightly different statement of this position, see Bundy's "Beyond Bakke: What Future for Affirmative Action?" *Atlantic Monthly* 242, 5 (November 1978):69-73.

11 William Brandon, *The Last Americans: The Indian in American Culture* (New York: McGraw-Hill, 1974), 22.

12 Hazel W. Hertzberg, *The Search for an American Identity: Modern Pan-Indian Movements* (Syracuse: Syracuse University Press, 1972), vii, viii.

13 William Hodge, *The First Americans: Then and Now* (New York: Holt, Rinehart and Winston, 1981), vii, 504.

14 Stephen Cornell, "American Indians: Asserting Their Rights," *Dialogue* 74, 4 (1986):39.

15 "Press Statement to Congress Made by American Indian Task Force, 12 November 1969" (cited in Alvin M. Josephy, ed., *Red Power: The American Indians Fight for Freedom* (Lincoln: University of Nebraska Press, 1971), 141.

16 William A. Schambra, "Progressive Liberalism and American 'Community,'" *The Public Interest* 80 (Summer 1985):47.

17 Daniel Bell, "'American Exceptionalism' Revisited: The Role of Civil Society," *The Public Interest* 95 (Spring 1989):56.

18 Kevin Philips, "The Balkanization of America," *Harper's* 256 (May 1978):37-47.

19 William H. Chaffe, *The Unfinished Journey: America since World War II* (New York: Oxford University Press, 1986), 483.

20 "President Bush's Address to Congress, February 9, 1989," in *President Bush: The Challenge Ahead* (Washington: Congressional Quarterly, Inc., 1989), 122-123.

21 Quoted in Roger D. Hatch and Frank E. Watkins, eds., *Reverend Jesse L. Jackson: Straight from the Heart* (Philadelphia: Fortress Press, 1987), xvii.

22 *Ibid.,* xiii.

23 Everett Carll Ladd, "The Constitution as Ideology," *Dialogue* 79, 1 (1988):31.

24 Canada. House of Commons. *Debates,* 19 January 1962, 9.

25 Statement of the Government of Canada on Indian Policy, 1969 [the White Paper] (Ottawa 1969).

26 Hon. Gerry Weiner, Minister of State (Multiculturalism), in Canada. House of Commons. *Debates,* 11 July 1988, 17,428.

27 19 July 1946 (cited in Carol F. Lee, "The Road to Enfranchisement: Chinese and Japanese in British Columbia," *B.C. Studies* 30 (Summer 1976):61.

28 Canada. House of Commons. *Debates,* 2 May 1947, 2,715.

29 Quoted by Angus MacInnis in *ibid,* 15 March 1948, 2,227.

30 *Ibid.,* 19 January 1962, 10.

31 Robert Lekachman, *Visions and Nightmares: America after Reagan* (New York: Macmillan, 1987), 7.

32 "Taking Jesse Seriously," *Time,* 11 April 1988, 22.

33 Quoted in Darcy Henton, "Lt.-Gov. 'Line' Pledges He'll Work for All Ontarians," *Toronto Star,* 21 September 1985.

34 Quoted in Keith Baldrey, "B.C.'s 25th Lt.-Gov. Calls Post Milestone," *Vancouver Sun,* 10 September 1988.

35 *Time,* 3 January 1964, 13.

36 Jacob V. Lamar, Jr., "Honoring Justice's Drum Major," *ibid.,* 27 January 1986, 16.

37 "The Constitution at 200," *ibid.,* 6 July 1987, special issue, cover.

38 *Ibid.,* 9 April 1990, 32.

39 Nathan Joseph, *Uniforms and Nonuniforms: Communication through Clothing* (New York: Greenwood Press, 1986), 36, 67, 88.

40 "Morning Stroll," *Globe and Mail,* 27 June 1990, front-page photograph.

41 Alexander Muir, "The Maple Leaf Forever," in *A Canadian Song Book,* edited by Sir Ernest Macmillan (Toronto: Dent, 1938), 6.

42 Adolphe-Basile Routhier's original version, written in 1880, had a distinctly militant, even martial, tone, referring at one point to the country's "bras [qui] sait porter l'épee . . . [et] la croix." Robert S. Weir's 1908 English rendering focused more consistently on the landscape, representing the country as the "true north . . . where pines and maples grow." For both, see Macmillan, *Canadian Song Book,* 3-4.

43 Quoted in "Showcasing Canada," *Maclean's,* 10 July 1989, 39.

44 J.R. Taylor (Vancouver Burrard). Canada. House of Commons. *Debates,* 4 July 1960, 5,699

45 Michael Asch, *Home and Native Land: Aboriginal Rights and the Canadian Constitution* (Toronto: Methuen, 1984), 86.

46 Katherine Swinton, "Competing Visions of Constitutionalism: Of Federalism and Rights," in *Competing Constitutional Visions: The Meech Lake Accord,* edited by K.E. Swinton and C.J. Rogerson (Toronto: Carswell, 1988), 283.

47 Alan C. Cairns, "Ritual, Taboo and Bias in Constitutional Controversies in Canada," The Timlin Lecture, 13 November 1989, University of Saskatchewan, 7.

48 William H. McNeill, *Polyethnicity and National Unity in World History* (Toronto: University of Toronto Press, 1986), 6.

49 Robert Miles, *Racism* (London: Routledge, 1989), 71.

50 Perry Anderson, "England's Isaiah," *London Review of Books* 12, 24 (20 December 1990):7.

51 J.G. Herder, *Reflections on the Philosophy of the History of Mankind* [1784-1791], transl. and intro. F.E. Manuel (London: 1968), 98 (cited in Brian J. Whitton, "Herder's Critique of the Enlightenment: Cultural Community versus Cosmopolitan Rationalism," *History and Theory* 27, 2 (1988):153.

52 John Rex, *Race and Ethnicity* (Milton Keynes: Open University Press, 1986), 15.

53 M. Michael Rosenberg, et al., eds., *An Introduction to Sociology,* 2nd ed. (Toronto: Methuen, 1987), 544.

54 Janet Helms, *Black and White Racial Identity: Theory, Research and Practice* (New York: Greenwood Press, 1990), 3.

55 Jean-François Lyotard, *The Postmodern Condition: A Report on Knowledge,* transl. G. Bennington and B. Massumi (Minneapolis: University of Minnesota Press, 1984), xxv.

Contributors

JOHN BERRY Department of Psychology, Queen's University

PER BRASK Department of English, University of Winnipeg

CAROLE CARPENTER Division of Humanities, York University

MAREK DEBICKI Department of Political Studies, University of Manitoba

LEO DRIEDGER Department of Sociology, University of Manitoba

GREG GAULD Multiculturalism and Citizenship Canada

RAYMOND HEBERT Département des sciences politiques, Collège Universitaire de St. Boniface

STELLA HRYNIUK Department of History, University of Manitoba

MYRNA KOSTASH Edmonton, Alberta

GISELE LALANDE Radio Canada, Montreal

RALPH MASI Canadian Council on Multicultural Health, Toronto

Contributors

KAS MAZUREK Faculty of Education, University of Lethbridge

RICHARD OGMUNDSON Department of Sociology, University of Victoria

PAUL MATTHEW ST. PIERRE Department of English, Simon Fraser University

ALLAN SMITH Department of History, University of British Columbia

GERHARD STILZ Department of English Philology, University of Tübingen, Germany

CECYLE TREPANIER Département de géographie, Université Laval

FRED WAH Department of English, University of Calgary

PAMELA WHITE Statistics Canada, Ottawa